Benziger

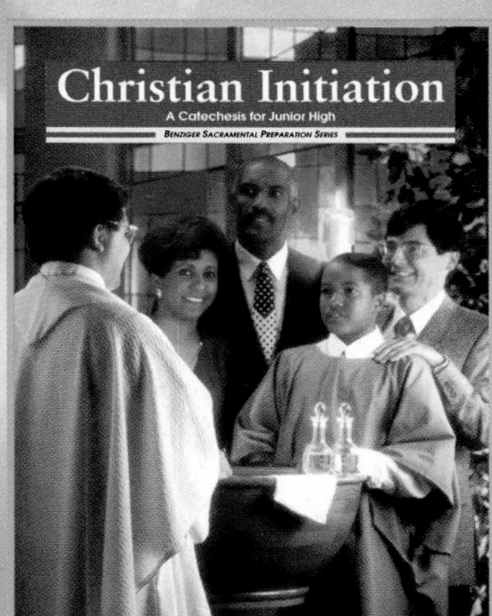

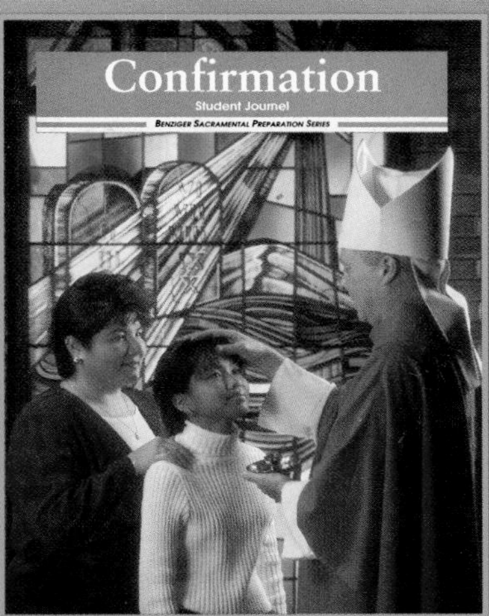

- CATECHISM
- FAMILY
- LITURGY
- STORY

All come together in Benziger's New Sacramental Preparation Program

With Benziger, young people learn that Sacraments are for life!

Benziger's New Sacramental Preparation Series

FIRST MAJOR SERIES published after the release of the *Catechism of the Catholic Church*

ONLY SACRAMENTAL SERIES to involve the family at all levels in simple and effective ways suited to today's busy schedules

MOST COMPLETE LITURGICAL CATECHESIS for the sacraments available anywhere

MOST EFFECTIVE USE OF STORIES—from Scripture and daily life—to develop a thorough understanding of the Sacraments

Benzige

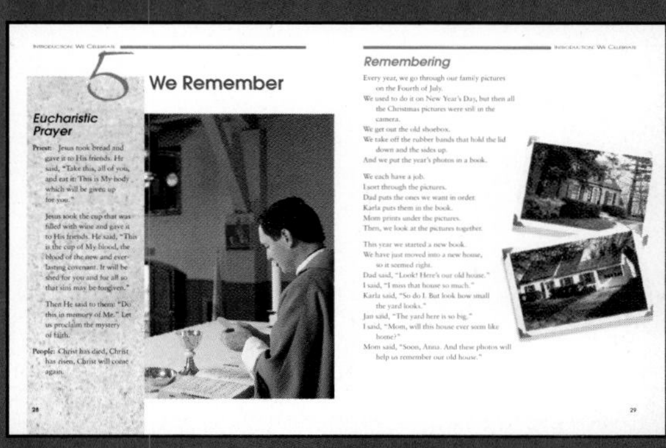

Benziger's New Sacramental Preparation Series provides a happy and informative experience for children preparing to receive the sacraments.

Benziger provides creative and dynamic lessons in perfect harmony with the sacramental catechesis found in the *Catechism of the Catholic Church*.

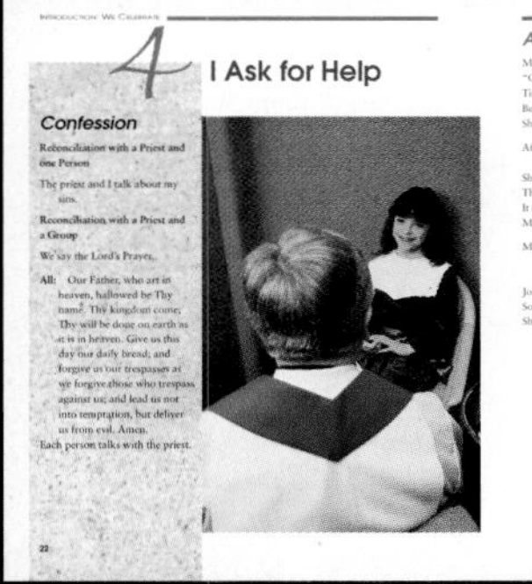

Student texts shown here:

First Eucharist:
The Communion program for primary grades

Eucharist:
The Communion program for middle grades

First Reconciliation:
The Penance program for primary grades

Reconciliation:
The Penance program for middle grades

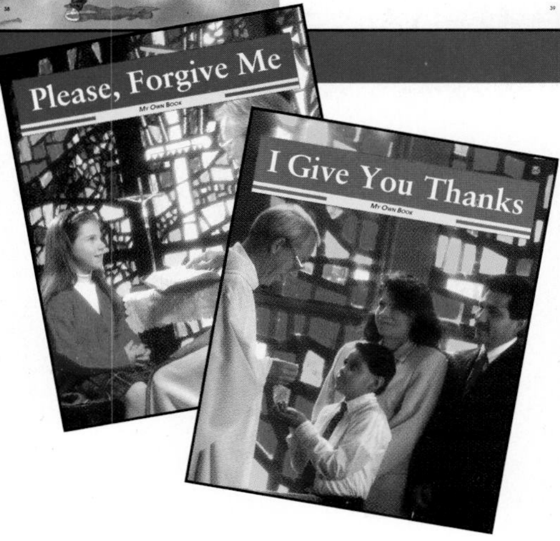

My Own Book

Young students personalize their learning experience by filling-in, drawing, cutting, and pasting their own special First Communion and First Reconciliation booklets.
Shown here:
I Give You Thanks
Please, Forgive Me

Catechists and families will find everything they need in ALL-IN-ONE teaching editions

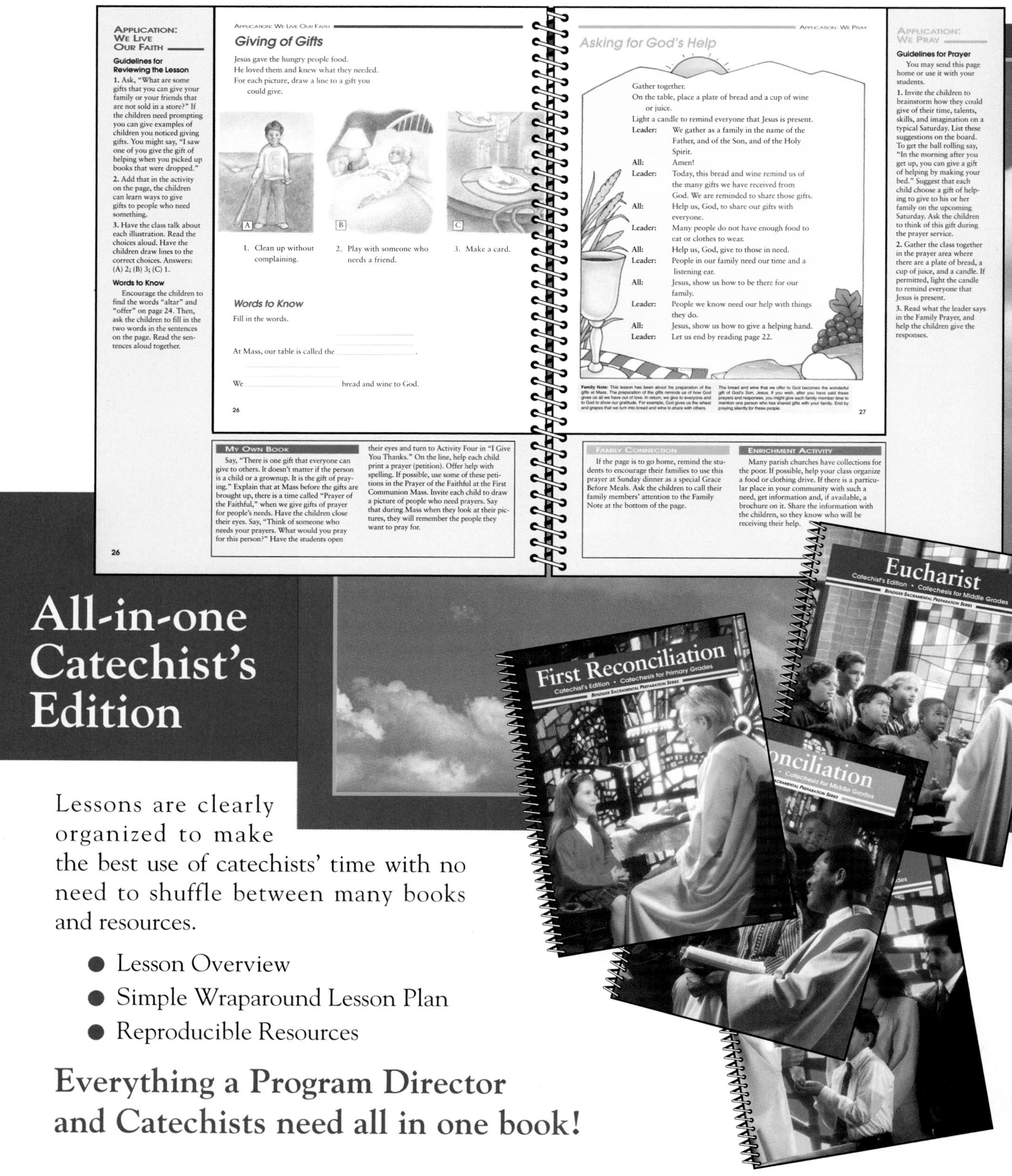

All-in-one Catechist's Edition

Lessons are clearly organized to make the best use of catechists' time with no need to shuffle between many books and resources.

- Lesson Overview
- Simple Wraparound Lesson Plan
- Reproducible Resources

Everything a Program Director and Catechists need all in one book!

Family Edition also available in Spanish.

APPLICATION: WE CELEBRATE

Guidelines for Reviewing the Lesson

1. In this activity, your child will be decorating a room at Cana for the wedding feast at which Jesus was present.
2. Read the page aloud up to the Words to Know section.
3. Say, "Here's an activity where you can celebrate with Jesus. Let's be there with Jesus and show how happy everyone is. Decorate the room for a party."
4. Encourage your child to use available drawing materials to decorate the room.
5. Ask, "What did the people drink at this party? In this picture, let's put some cups of wine on the table."

Words to Know

Encourage your child to find the words "Mass" and "Eucharist" on page 6. Then, ask your child to print the words "Mass" and "Eucharist" in the sentences on this page. Read each sentence aloud, and have your child repeat it back to you.

INTRODUCTION: WE CELEBRATE

Loving

Moses and Aaron were able to do what God had called them to do. They led the Israelites safely away from Egypt. They freed the people from their slavery.

At first, the Israelites were happy. But soon, they did not know what to do with their new freedom. They began to fight and argue among themselves. They stole one another's food and clothing, and they lied and cheated. Children disobeyed their parents. Old people were left to die. It seemed that no one loved anyone else any more.

"Our lives are miserable," the people complained to Moses. "You should have left us in Egypt."

Moses didn't know what to say. But he knew that God would have an answer. After all, God had promised to be with them.

Rules of Love

So Moses climbed Mount Sinai to pray. "The people need to know You love them," Moses said to God. "Please give them some sign that You care."

Moses prayed for three days. On the third day, there was a clap of thunder. Lightning flashed across the sky, and the whole mountain shook. Finally, God spoke.

"I am the Lord, your God, who brought you out of Egypt. You shall have no gods but Me.

You shall not use My name in vain.

Remember the Sabbath and keep it holy.

Honor your father and mother.

You shall not kill.

You shall not commit adultery.

You shall not steal.

You shall not lie.

You shall not desire your neighbor's wife.

You shall not desire anything that belongs to your neighbor."

14

INTRODUCTION: WE CELEBRATE

Then, Moses was told that these Ten Commandments were a sign of His love. "Tell the people how much I love them," God said. "Let them know that I want the best for them. If they truly love Me, they will follow My commandments."

Moses brought the Ten Commandments back to the people. And wherever the people traveled, they carried God's rules with them. They knew they had been chosen to be loved by God, and to show their love in return.

(*based on Exodus 16, 20*)

Thinking about Scripture

- What problems did the Israelites have in dealing with their freedom?
- How can rules be a sign of love?

15

APPLICATION: WE CELEBRATE

Guidelines for Prayer

1. Say, "You know a lot about the Mass because you've been going to Mass. Now, you can learn the real names of the things in church."
2. Read the text aloud. Then, describe the pictured objects and people, and ask your child to find and name them. Here is an example: It's a cup that the priest puts the wine in (chalice).
3. With your child, collect kitchen objects that are like those used in the Mass. Suggestions: cup (chalice), plate (paten), bread (host), wine, table (altar), tablecloth (altar cloth).
4. After you have finished naming the objects and talking about them, pray the little prayer to Jesus together.

FUN WITH NEW WORDS

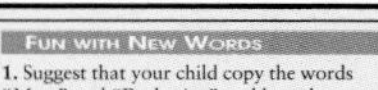

1. Suggest that your child copy the words "Mass" and "Eucharist," and learn how to spell them.
2. Mix up the order of the letters of the words and ask your child to rearrange the letters so that the words are spelled correctly.

FAMILY CONNECTION

The Eucharist helps us to grow in love. Plan with your child a way to say thank you to someone who has shown love to your family. Or you can say thanks to mom who drove everyone to school that week or to dad who made dinner. To stay with the party theme of the story of Cana, consider giving a very informal family party for this person. You might just serve snacks, but help your child experience the "specialness" of gathering with the family to honor someone.

14

FAMILY CONNECTION

Plan on going to Mass early one day to let your child name as many objects and people in the Church as he or she can. Other family members can help, too.

STORY BANK

If you'd like, read the first Story Bank story, "Visiting," on page 76, to your child. Then ask, "How did Angelo get to know Bob? How do you get to know more about something?" Emphasize the importance of gathering and celebrating to show you care.

15

All-in-one Family Edition

Material is clearly organized and presented in simple language that makes sacramental preparation an event for the entire family.

- Lesson at a Glance
- Simple Wraparound Lesson Plan
- Special Helps for the Family

The Benziger Series can be taught entirely in the home.

Primera Comunión

Edición de familia

BENZIGER SACRAMENTAL PREPARATION SERIES

EDICIONES DE FAMILIA

Primera Comunión and *Primera Reconciliación ediciónes de familia* are available for Hispanic families or the parish with first-language Hispanic children. (Winter 1995-96)

Family Magazines help the whole family strengthen its sacramental life together.

Three magazines are available, each with

- multigenerational activities
- conversation starters
- informative articles
- television viewing guide
- bibliography
- guides for family prayer

The Eucharistic Family covers Part Two of the new Catechism. Helps make the Mass more a part of daily life in the home. Accompanies both Eucharistic programs.

The Reconciling Family covers Part Three of the new Catechism. Helps the family establish moral guidelines and focuses on the importance of forgiveness. Accompanies both Reconciliation programs.

Family of Faith covers Parts One and Four of the new Catechism. Offers practical help for fostering faith in the home. Accompanies the *Confirmation* and *Christian Initiation* programs.

PLUG INTO **Positive** *feelings*

What are your child's feelings as the day of First Eucharist approaches? Is he or she
proud, nervous, scared, joyful, full of expectation, neutral? I don't like neutral or scared.
But joyful expectation–that's great. After all, Eucharist is much more than information and
knowledge; it is about feelings–about a loving relationship with Jesus.
By the time your child receives Christ in Eucharist, his or her feelings about it have been
under construction a long time. Ideally, he or she has already met Christ in the goodness he
or she sees in you. If you are loving and kind, he or she will see Jesus in the same way. Your
words and actions are important, and they come from the feelings you carry in your heart.
It is from the heart that you communicate to your child. How you feel about Christ, the
Church, and this sacrament will lead your child closer to Christ or put distance into the
equation.
I'm sure you want to make First Eucharist a positive experience in your child's life. That
often means new clothes, a cake, and a family celebration. But if your attention is tied up
more in the practical arrangements than in preparing the heart of your son or daughter, you
may miss a huge opportunity to grow together in Christ. Your child is likely to feel that
the peripherals are what's important, and that the rest of it–the Eucharist itself–is
only marginal. Because you have a post-event party to plan, classes and
requirements that need to be fulfilled, and questions of your own about
faith, you most likely have a mixed set of feelings about your son or
daughter's First Eucharist. You'll need to sit down and address these
feelings individually until your mind is eased and your sights focused.

Feelings Are Always Charged

Feelings about Eucharist are something like electricity. They come in
positive and negative, and they are always charged. It's a rare person
who has no negative feelings about life, but if those feelings are
aimed at God or the Church, they are like a force field standing
between Eucharist and the human heart. Most people deal with
feelings that impact their faith–from alcoholism to a painful
divorce, or family conflicts. Do these feelings affect their
children? Of course. However, the result need not be
negative.
Negative feelings can open a circuit rather than
blow a fuse. Coming to God in need with
trust rather than resentment makes your
faith that much stronger. Such trust is
rewarded in Eucharist. Through
the offering of His Body and

...arts, wipes away tears, and offers a peace that darkness
... with real life! This feeling-level discovery makes a big
...ecognizes the good feelings in your heart about
difference in life. ...
Eucharist, he or she will see it as something good for his or her own life too.

Passing on Positive Feelings

If Eucharist is already a positive experience in your life, you may still have some difficulty
presenting its concept to your child. So you may be looking for some new ways to think
about the sacrament that are age-appropriate. The following are some dynamic
presentations of Eucharist that can be shared with and understood by your child:
• Eucharist is more than just a ritual. It is an action that grasps the saving hand of God
and prepares a room within your heart for the love of Christ to dwell. In Exodus, one of the
most passionate cliff-hanger accounts you'll ever find in Scripture, God freed the Hebrews
from slavery. He led them by the hand, out of captivity, across the Red Sea–an impassable
barrier. He gave them a mysterious bread to eat as they wandered in the desert on the way
to the Promised Land. The Eucharist parallels the story of Exodus. Jesus came to free all
people from struggles with every kind of slavery. He parts seas of addiction, hatred, and
other seemingly impossible barriers. He feeds Christians today with a mysterious bread–
His Body and Blood–as they wander through deserts of frustration seeking a land of
refreshment and peace.
• Of course, you don't always have to think of the Eucharist in such gripping terms.
It can also be useful to compare the Eucharist to a dinner at home with close friends.
Imagine you're preparing the meal, while laughing and talking about big and little
things with your friends who stand nearby. Then you serve dinner. Everyone lingers
at the table–glasses are refilled, plates are handed back for seconds. The chatting
continues on afterward until no one can stay awake any longer. In the end, it's not
so much the meal that brought you together but the friendship that the evening
celebrates.
• Beyond this personal relationship with Jesus that you experience in
Eucharist you can recognize your union with others–people who also belong
to Christ. The Eucharist is God's saving grace for all that calls those who
receive it to a mindful generosity. To share in the Body of Christ, you
minister to the parts of His Body that are in need–the poor, the excluded, the
hungry. "If you love me, care for my lambs," Jesus told Peter.

Feelings Under Construction

As you share your feelings about Eucharist with your child, be sincere and
honest, but don't set up unreasonable expectations. For instance, don't tell
your child that receiving the Eucharist is going to be the happiest day of his
or her life. It's unrealistic and way too much to lay on a child. Maybe it
should be the best of all days, but if anything goes wrong–he or she gets in
the wrong pew after communion, the cousins get into a royal spat at the
party–it could just as easily be a bad day. At the end of such a day, a young
person may come away with the feeling that if this was the climax, then
the rest of his or her life is going to be very dismal indeed. Instead, begin
making connections to help your child experience a "positive" day–the
gateway to good feelings about a relationship with Jesus.

Catholic Parenting

The three magazines together provide an effective course in Catholic parenting based on the *Catechism of the Catholic Church*.

A fresh, thorough, and complete catechesis on Christian Initiation for junior-high students.

ALL NEW

WHO ARE YOU, ANYWAY?

Here is a chance for you to identify yourself in just the way you want to be identified. Below is your personal file. Within that file, put as much information as you can cram into the space. (You won't be marked for neatness, so draw, color, or use abbreviations.)

List your name (the way you like it), the music you like, the foods that make you drool, what you hate, your favorite color—just cram your folder full of you!

Believe

PERSONAL STORIES

Be honest! You have watched those television shows where people tell *everything*, haven't you? Most people love to listen to stories about the troubles and joys other people have. If you have ever kept a diary, spent time journaling, or swapped stories about yourself with your friends, you are one of those who love personal stories.

Everybody has a story to tell. Personal stories show values, hopes, and dreams. Personal stories reveal who people really are. The next story is a bit of fantasy, but it will help you get the idea. (You might also uncover some things about the life of Jesus you will want to ask about later.)

Whose Story?

Once upon a time (or so a legend has it), the Lord God—Holy and Blest!—wanted to make sure that the story of Jesus got written and got written right. So the Lord God—Powerful and Abiding!—sent an angel to a scribe to guide him through the story.

The angel told the scribe what the Lord God—Wise and Wonderful!—had in mind and asked if he wanted the job. The scribe jumped at it. And why not? After all, it's not every day that you get the Lord God—Marvelous and Fabulous!—as a client.

So the scribe took his pens, his ink pots, and his paper under his arm. The angel took the scribe under its wing. And off they both went to find and follow Jesus, and to record all that He said and did.

Joy and Favor

The angel whisked the scribe to a stable in Bethlehem, then to a sheep-dotted hillside that lay under an angel-crowded sky. The scribe paid attention, met with great joy, and scribbled down what he met.

In an instant, the angel transported the scribe into the desert, where he witnessed Jesus in a devilish duel. The scribe paid attention, met with great courage, and scribbled down what he met.

Wisdom and Power

Scarcely before the scribe could work up a thirst, the angel sailed him to the banks of a river. Jesus rose dripping from its waters, glistening like the sun. The scribe paid attention, met with great favor, and scribbled down what he met.

Next, the scribe found himself sitting on the angel's shoulders. All around was a great crowd of people. They were all listening intently as Jesus spoke of new creation, new heavens, new earth.

9

Christian Initiation

A Catechesis for Junior High

Benziger Sacramental Preparation Series

The most requested sacramental catechesis of all. This program for grades six to eight provides an overview of the sacraments of Christian Initiation for young people who have not been baptized, for those who have been baptized but have not received the other sacraments, or for those young people who need a thorough review of the Church's sacramental life.

Every young Catholic will benefit from this exciting overview of what it means to be a follower of Jesus.

The book includes:

- Baptism
- Confirmation
- Eucharist
- A special catechesis for Reconciliation
- A Little Catechism of basic teachings

Spirit-filled catechesis New *Confirmation* for junior-high.

Confirmation prepares junior high students to receive the Gift of the Holy Spirit and to make their life-long commitment to the Catholic Church.

Each student keeps a journal to record personal experiences as a growing and active Christian (for grades six to eight).

Catechetical outline

1. Created in God's image - Wisdom
2. The Jesus story - Knowledge
3. Eucharist - Reverence
4. Loving service - Courage
5. Community - Understanding
6. Covenant - Right Judgement
7. Faith journey - Wonder and Awe

National Catholic Sales Office	***Benziger Publishing Company*** 25 Crescent Street, 1st Floor Stamford, CT 06906 Telephone: 203-964-9109 / 800-551-87(
For Orders from Other Countries	***McGraw-Hill International Serv*** 220 East Danieldale Road DeSoto, TX 75115, U.S.A. Telephone: 214-224-111, Ext. 247 Fax: 214-224-5444
Canadian Orders	***McGraw-Hill Ryerson Ltd.*** 300 Water Street Whitby, Ontario L1N 9B6, Canada Telephone: 905-430-5000 Fax: 905-430-5020 Telex: 065-25169

RE91148-6

Reconciliation

Catechist's Edition for Middle Grades

General Editor
Gerard P. Weber, S.T.L.

Contributing Editors
Irene H. Murphy
Helen P. Whitaker

Benziger Publishing Company
Mission Hills, California

Illustrations:
Kevin Davidson, Rosanne Litzinger, Norm Merritt, Mike Muir, Linda Sullivan, Susan Staroba, Maryann Thomas

Photography:
Stephen McBrady

Nihil Obstat:
Msgr. Joseph Pollard, S.T.D., V.F.
Censor Deputatus

Imprimatur:
†Roger M. Mahony
Cardinal of Los Angeles
December 6, 1994

The nihil obstat and imprimatur are official declarations that a book or pamphlet is free of doctrinal or moral error. No implication is contained therein that those who have granted the nihil obstat and imprimatur agree with the contents, opinions, or statements expressed.

Send all inquiries to:
BENZIGER PUBLISHING COMPANY
15319 Chatsworth Street
Mission Hills, California 91345

Printed in the United States of America.

ISBN 0-02-655931-5 (Student Edition)
ISBN 0-02-655932-3 (Catechist's Edition)

1 2 3 4 5 WEB 99 98 97 96 95

Contents

1	Welcome!	5
2	Rules of Love	13
3	Right and Wrong	21
4	I Confess	29
5	Being Sorry	37
6	Changing Your Life	45
7	I Am Forgiven	53
8	Forgiving Others	61
	Glossary	69
	Things to Know about Reconciliation	72
	How to Go to Confession	73
	An Examination of Conscience	75
	Music	76
	Prayers	78
	Lists Catholics Remember	80

A Look at *Reconciliation* Catechist's Edition

Here is a quick rundown of the features of the book. Each lesson follows the same plan.

Lesson Plans

Directions for presenting the eight lessons appear in margin columns alongside the corresponding student text pages. Along the bottom of the page are these features:

- *Enrichment Activity* Suggestions to help the students deepen their understanding of the lesson.
- *Fun with New Words* Ideas for introducing vocabulary.
- *My Own Book* A Reconciliation book, "I Celebrate Reconciliation," that the students will make themselves.
- *Music Note* Songs to sing that are provided in the program.
- *What Is the Lesson?* Concepts the students need to understand.
- *Family Connection* Ideas for sending home the We Pray page.

Lesson Background Pages

Before each of the eight student lessons, you will find two tinted insert pages. To help you prepare the lesson, these pages contain the following features:

- *Lesson Number* and *Title*
- *Focus*
- *Catechetical Objectives* Several key points within the lesson.
- *Lesson Overview* A brief quotation directly from the *Catechism of the Catholic Church*, and simple explanations of each of the four lesson sections.
- *The Church's Wisdom* The theology supporting the lesson.
- *Catechist Resources* Useful videos and books for personal enrichment.
- *Classroom Resources* Videos, books, and music cassettes to use with your students.
- *Before Beginning the Lesson* Suggestions to help you prepare for the lesson, including a list of necessary materials.
- *New Words* A listing of terms introduced in the lesson, with their definitions.
- *Catechist Prayer* A prayer to help you prepare yourself spiritually to teach the lesson.

1 Welcome!

Focus

The sacrament of Reconciliation welcomes us back in love and in friendship by God and the community.

Catechetical Objectives

- To remind the students of their baptismal membership in God's Family.
- To teach the students that God's love is a forgiving love.
- To engender in the students a positive attitude toward the sacrament of Reconciliation.

Lesson Overview

Lesson 1 addresses the reality of sin and the responsibility people have to be in a continual process of conversion:

"The new life received in Christian initiation has not abolished the frailty and weakness of human nature, nor the inclination to sin that tradition calls concupiscence, which remains in the baptized such that with the help of the grace of Christ they may prove themselves in the struggle of Christian life. This is the struggle of conversion, directed toward holiness and eternal life to which the Lord never ceases to call us" *(Catechism of the Catholic Church, #1426).*

INTRODUCTION: WE CELEBRATE

- In Reconciliation, the Greeting assures us that Jesus welcomes us and calls us to Him. A story of Moses helps the students see that God reaches out to those people that others shun.

DEVELOPMENT: WE BELIEVE

- The students learn that God offers a loving welcome in the sacrament of Baptism and loving forgiveness and welcoming back in the sacrament of Reconciliation. The Scripture story of the call of Matthew shows what it is to follow Jesus.

APPLICATION: WE LIVE OUR FAITH

- The students will draw a picture-story that exemplifies forgiveness.

APPLICATION: WE PRAY

- The students write, draw, and pray about the signs of God's presence in their lives.

The Church's Wisdom

Here is the theology supporting Lesson 1.

"No human being, however, is perfect. We are all sinners" *(National Catechetical Directory, #125).*

Baptism is the first sacrament of reconciliation, as well as the first of the three sacraments of initiation. Baptism celebrates our membership in the Family of God, the Church. God invites us, and we accept the invitation. This sacrament confers a permanent character, and the sacrament of Baptism is never repeated. Once we are baptized, we can never become "unbaptized."

We are always on the journey toward God, and in need of ongoing conversion. This conversion is assisted or directed through the power of the Holy Spirit in the sacrament of Reconciliation. In this sacrament, people have the opportunity to celebrate forgiveness.

Catechist Resources

AUDIOVISUAL:

- "Baptismal Theology of the Second Vatican Council" (V/Adults/Two 25 min. segments/Our Baptismal Covenant with Christ #4/St. Anthony Messenger Press and Franciscan Communications) Part one examines the theology of Baptism in light of Vatican II. Part two looks at the Rite of Christian Initiation of Adults.

BOOK:

- Dallen, James. *The Reconciling Community: The Rite of Penance* (Pueblo Publishing Company) This book presents the complex development of ecclesial repentance from the Church's first centuries to the present time.

Classroom Resources

AUDIOVISUAL:

- "Baptism, the Sacrament of Belonging" (V/Intermediate/ 8 mins./St. Anthony Messenger Press and Franciscan Communications) Scarred by fire and loneliness, Alfredo is drawn by the warmth and love he sees among the other orphan children in a community home. This parable depicts both the beginning and the culmination of the journey of faith.

BOOK:

- Fox, Paula. *Monkey Island.* (Orchard) This is a story about eleven-year-old Clay who fends for himself on New York streets after his mother leaves their welfare hotel.

Before Beginning the Lesson

TO DO:

- Be prepared and enthusiastic.
- Learn the students' names and at least one special thing about each one (siblings, pets, sports, and the like) as quickly as you can.
- If possible, take a snapshot of each student to help you to memorize the name and face, and to include in the My Own Book "I Celebrate Reconciliation" as a memento.
- Follow the procedures of the catechetical office.
- Reproduce the Family Letter on pages 113–114, one for each family.
- Relax and enjoy this privileged experience!

TO HAVE ON HAND:

- Student texts
- Writing and drawing materials
- Bible
- Chalk

FOR OPTIONAL ENRICHMENT ACTIVITIES:

- Booklet or folder materials (page 5)
- Poster board or shelf paper (page 7)
- Benziger *Come, Follow Me* Grade 4 music cassette and cassette player (page 8)
- Blank 3 x 5 cards, crayons (page 8)
- Slip of paper, envelope (page 9)
- Strips of paper, fine tip markers, clear contact paper (page 9)
- The video "Baptism, the Sacrament of Belonging," TV/VCR (page 11)

New Words

Look at the wrap on page 9 for a suggestion to introduce the new vocabulary words to the students. The vocabulary words are italicized or boldfaced in the student's text. The boldfaced words are further discussed in the We Catholics Believe box. All vocabulary words are also defined in the Glossary on pages 69–71.

- **Baptism:** This sacrament of initiation washes away sin, gives new life, and joins us to God's Family.
- **Blessed Trinity:** Our name for one God who is Father, Son, and Holy Spirit.
- **Catholic:** The baptized who follow the authority of the pope and the bishops.
- **disciple:** Someone who believes in and follows Jesus.
- **Israelites:** Another name for the Jewish people.
- **Jesus:** The Son of God and our Savior.
- **penitent:** A person who is sorry for sinning.
- **Reconciliation:** The sacrament of healing that celebrates God's loving forgiveness of sin.
- **sacrament:** One of the special signs and celebrations of God's love.

Catechist Prayer

A moment of quiet reflection just for you.

"I have not come to call the righteous to repentance but sinners" *(Luke 5:32).*

Jesus, Redeemer, in You I hear Creator God's invitation to love. Help me answer that invitation with a powerful trust. Send Your Spirit to help the children hear this invitation and answer it with joy. Amen.

If you wish, extend God's invitation to love to the catechist in the next room. You may wish the catechist well and offer to share your chalk, if you have enough to spare.

1 Welcome

The Greeting

Priest: In the name of the Father, and of the Son, and of the Holy Spirit.

Penitent: Amen.

Priest: May the Lord Jesus welcome you. He came to call sinners, not the just. Have confidence in Him.

Penitent: Amen.

Lesson Plan

INTRODUCTION: WE CELEBRATE

Guidelines for Using the Text

1. Read the title of the lesson to the students. Ask volunteers to share what their families do to make them feel welcome after they come home from school or from playing.
2. Tell the students that welcoming is an important part of celebrating the sacrament of Reconciliation, too. The text on this page is one form of prayerful greeting used in the sacrament. Write the word "penitent" on the chalkboard, and tell the students that a penitent is a person who is sorry for sinning. The word penitent is used to describe the person participating in the sacrament of Reconciliation.
3. Read the priest's part of the Greeting aloud, and have the students read the penitent's responses. Ask the students to identify the prayer (the Sign of the Cross) that opens the Greeting. Point out that the Mass begins with a similar greeting.
4. Explain to the students that throughout this class they will be studying the Rite (or official prayers and actions) of Reconciliation.

MY OWN BOOK

As an ongoing activity, you may wish to have the students make their own Reconciliation booklets or folders, entitled "I Celebrate Reconciliation." The students may copy the heading and text from page 5 onto a nice sheet of paper. Suggest that the students draw a picture of themselves in a scene of welcoming. The student may be the one being welcomed, or may be the welcoming person. Suggest that the students keep this project in a folder, or collect the pages each week, to keep the pages from wear and tear. Be sure the students write their names on the page if the pages will be collected each week.

INTRODUCTION: WE CELEBRATE

Guidelines for Using the Scripture Story

1. Before beginning the reading, ask the students if they have ever been chosen to do something (to be part of a team, to represent the school, or the like). Allow volunteers to provide examples. Then, tell the students that they will be hearing a story about a famous person who was chosen.

2. Read aloud the story on these two pages (from Exodus 2, 3, 4).

3. After the reading, ask if the students recognize the names of any of the characters in the story. If you wish, you may provide more background on Moses, the great leader and prophet of the Israelites. Use a Bible to point out that this story comes from the Old Testament, or Hebrew Scriptures.

4. Ask volunteers to respond to the two questions listed under Thinking about Scripture. You may continue discussing the story, using the questions on page 7 as a model.

The Chosen One

Moses grew up in the royal palace of the Egyptian Pharaoh, but he never quite fit in. The rest of Pharaoh's grandsons teased and taunted him. "You're adopted!" they told him. "Your mother was an **Israelite** slave!" They even imitated his stutter.

"I'm not adopted!" Moses shouted. "I hate the Israelites!" And to prove so, he beat up one of the Israelite boys who was a palace slave.

Word of the teasing came to Pharaoh's daughter. She called Moses aside. "It's time I told you the truth," she said. "You really are adopted. Your Israelite mother placed you in a basket and put you in the river. She did not want you to be killed or to become a slave. I found you and named you 'Moses,' which means 'drawn out of water.' I took you home and raised you as my own."

From then on, Moses became aware of how cruelly the Egyptians treated the Israelites.

One day, Moses saw an Egyptian whipping an Israelite worker. In anger, Moses killed the Egyptian and buried his body where no one would find him. The next day, Moses saw two Israelite slaves fighting. He decided to run away from Egypt and all of the violence and hatred found there.

Moses went to Midian where he lived safely as a shepherd. He grew up and got married. No one, not even his new bride, knew that he was a murderer.

God Speaks

One day, while Moses was tending sheep, he saw a burning bush. The fire burned and burned, but the leaves of the bush stayed green. Curious, Moses stepped closer. Suddenly, a voice spoke to him from the bush.

"Do not come any closer," the voice said, "for I am God."

Moses thought for sure God would punish him for being a murderer. But instead, God said, "I have seen the suffering of My people in Egypt. I have decided to send you to Pharaoh, so that you can free the Israelites from their slavery."

ENRICHMENT ACTIVITY

Ask the students to respond briefly, in writing, to this question:

What is God calling me to do right now? What is my answer?

"But I am a murderer," Moses confessed.

"I know," God replied, "but I want you anyway."

"If I go back to Egypt, Pharaoh will kill me," Moses said.

"I shall be with you," God promised. "No one will harm you."

"I can't do it," Moses argued. "I stutter, and my speech is slow."

"Your brother Aaron speaks well. He can speak for you."

Moses stopped arguing. It was clear that God had chosen him, and not someone else. Although Moses was afraid to return to Egypt, he also felt proud. He was an Israelite, after all, and his people needed him. He knew God loved him in spite of his sin. Maybe he could learn to return that love.

(based on Exodus 2,3,4)

Thinking about Scripture

- Why do you think God chose Moses to lead the Israelites to freedom?
- Why didn't Moses immediately say yes to God?

INTRODUCTION: WE CELEBRATE

Talking about Scripture

About the Story:

1. What did the Pharaoh's grandchildren tease Moses about?

2. How did Moses react to the teasing?

3. How did Moses change after he learned he was adopted?

4. How did Moses know he was chosen by God?

About You:

1. Have you ever been teased, laughed at, or left out?

2. What did you do about it?

3. Have you ever felt special?

4. Has anyone ever helped you believe you could do more than you thought you could?

WHAT IS THE LESSON?

Be sure the students understand these key ideas:

- Being teased or laughed at can help us know how others feel when they are teased or laughed at.
- Even if we do wrong things, we can change.
- God will always love us and forgive us.

ENRICHMENT ACTIVITY

Have the students form small groups. Distribute art materials to each group. Direct the groups to brainstorm about the idea of being chosen, focusing on the good feelings that can come from such things as being chosen to live in a family through adoption, to be part of a group, or to play on a team. Then direct the groups to make a decorated poster that lists all the advantages of being chosen. Allow time for groups to share their work, and display the finished posters in the classroom.

Development: We Believe

Guidelines for Using the Text

1. Read aloud the first three paragraphs of God's Love. If time allows, ask volunteers to respond to the idea that God loves us and chooses us all the time.

2. Read the text section The Call to Love aloud. If the students are unfamiliar with Scripture stories give more background into the imperfect people mentioned in the text. Ask for additional examples of people who were chosen by God. Write the term "disciple" on the chalkboard, and make sure the students are familiar with its meaning. In Jesus' time, people often attributed illness or rowdy behavior to the work of demons or devils.

3. Read Welcome Home aloud, making sure the students understand the meaning of the terms introduced in the text. If time allows, encourage students to share what they know about their baptisms. Ask the students if they are familiar with other names for the sacrament of Reconciliation (Forgiveness, Penance, confession).

God's Love

Just about everyone, sooner or later, knows how Moses felt. Perhaps you have felt left out. Maybe you didn't receive an invitation to a friend's party. Maybe you were not chosen to be on a team. Perhaps others have teased you and called you names. Or you might have done something that you felt would keep someone from liking you again.

Being rejected or left out or teased hurts. Jesus knew that because people criticized Him and laughed at Him. They talked about Him and the way He lived and the things He said.

There is Someone who will never reject you or stop loving you. There is Someone who will always make you feel wanted and at home. That Someone is God.

The Call to Love

You don't have to be perfect for God to love you. God loves you right now, the way you are. God's love is so strong that it is bigger than any wrong you might do. No matter what, God keeps on loving you and calling you to become the best person you can be.

This kind of love is hard to believe. And yet there are many stories in the Bible which show how God has loved imperfect people. Moses, who spoke directly to God, was a murderer. Jonah, whom God sent to speak His word, was a coward.

Jesus, too, chose imperfect people to be His friends. The Apostle Peter had a quick temper. James and John often fought with one another. Judas sometimes loved money and power more than he loved people. And Mary Magdalene was so wild that people said she had "seven demons" inside her.

Welcome Home

Just as God welcomed all these people into His Family, so God welcomes you. When your life began, you became the newest member of God's Family. When you received the **sacrament of Baptism,** you became a member of a

Music Note

You may wish to teach the song "We Are a Kingdom People," student text page 76. Words and music notation can be found on page 135 in the Catechist's Edition. Use Benziger *Come, Follow Me* Grade 4 music cassette to help the students learn the song.

Enrichment Activity

Distribute small cards and crayons to the students. Suggest that they read the last paragraph and decide which sentence about God's forgiving love they like best. Next, have them print the idea on a card and then decorate their cards.

special part of God's Family—the Catholic Church. The word catholic means "for everyone." Everyone is welcome in the **Catholic Church**. Everyone can belong.

At your baptism, the priest or deacon poured water on you. The water is a sign of new life and new beginnings. As the priest or deacon poured the water, he said, "I baptize you in the name of the Father, and of the Son, and of the Holy Spirit."

These same words are used at the beginning of the sacrament of **Reconciliation**. These words remind you of your baptism. By these words, you say you believe in the **Blessed Trinity**. You want to live as a follower of Jesus.

These words also remind you that God's love is a forgiving love. When you do wrong and feel sorry, God will take you back. God will help you start over. You are called to respond to God's love through the sacrament of Reconciliation. In this sacrament, God says, "Welcome back!"

We Catholics Believe

The Jewish people are called **Israelites** because they are the children of Jacob, whose name was also Israel.

The seven **sacraments** are signs and celebrations of God's power and love. The sacrament of **Baptism** gives new life, washes away sin, and joins us to God's Family.

The members of the **Catholic Church** are baptized and follow the authority of the pope and bishops.

In **Reconciliation,** a person confesses his or her sins to a priest, expresses sorrow for these sins, and promises to do better. The priest forgives the person, in the name of God and the members of God's Family.

Blessed Trinity is our name for the one God who is Father, Son, and Holy Spirit.

Jesus is the Son of God and our Savior.

DEVELOPMENT: WE BELIEVE

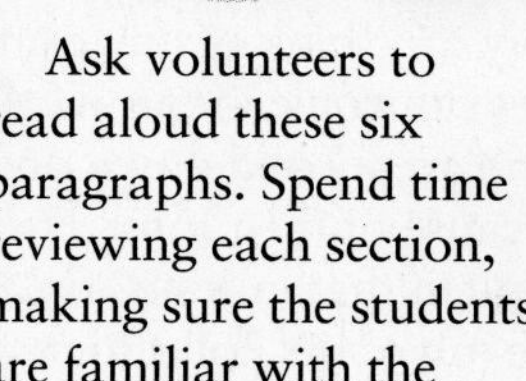

Ask volunteers to read aloud these six paragraphs. Spend time reviewing each section, making sure the students are familiar with the religious vocabulary introduced. You may ask the students to use these terms in original sentences to test their understanding.

FUN WITH NEW WORDS

Play a round of "Say the Secret Word" for a fun way to learn the new vocabulary words. Write one of the words from the vocabulary list and seal it in an envelope. It is the "secret word." Have each student recite a vocabulary word and definition of personal choice from the lesson. If the student can "Say the Secret Word," the game ends with a grand flourish of accolades for all the students.

ENRICHMENT ACTIVITY

Have the students design I.D. cards for themselves as members of the Catholic Church. You might want to have the students include a cross and the words of the Sign of the Cross in their design. If you wish, protect the I.D. cards with clear contact paper.

The Call of Matthew

Matthew went to work each day at the customs post. It was his job to collect taxes from the people and to pay the Roman government. Many people did not trust Matthew, and they disliked him because of his job.

One day, **Jesus** came by the customs post. He saw Matthew sitting there. "Follow Me," Jesus told him.

Matthew didn't know why Jesus was calling him. He only knew that suddenly he felt happy and loved. Leaving everything behind, he got up and followed Jesus.

That night, Matthew gave a big dinner for Jesus at his house. He invited many people, including other tax collectors he knew.

Some people complained about this to Jesus. "Why do you eat and drink with tax collectors and sinners?" they asked Him.

Jesus answered, "Those who are healthy do not need a doctor. Only the sick do. I have not come to call those who are perfect. I have come to call sinners."

From that day, Matthew was one of Jesus' *disciples,* one who believes and follows Jesus. This man that no one had trusted was very glad that Jesus had needed him.

(*based on Matthew 9: 9–13*)

Thinking about Scripture

- What made Matthew want to follow Jesus?
- What is one way you are needed by Jesus?

10

Development: We Believe

Guidelines for Using the Scripture Story

1. Before beginning the reading, ask the students if they can think of any examples of people in our world who are looked down on because of their jobs. Then, explain that in Jesus' time, the job of tax collector was especially hated because these people collected money for the Roman government, which ruled the country of Palestine.

2. Read aloud or retell in your own words the story of the Call of Matthew, based on Matthew 9:9–13.

3. After the reading, ask volunteers to respond to the two questions listed under Thinking about Scripture. You may continue discussing the story, using the questions below as a model.

Talking about Scripture

About the Story:

1. What did Matthew do when Jesus said, "Follow Me"?

2. Why do you think Matthew gave a dinner party?

About You:

1. Is there anyone who could make you leave your life behind by saying "Follow me"?

2. Would your neighbors be surprised if Jesus chose to eat dinner with you? Why or why not?

3. How do you feel about the idea that no one is perfect?

What Is the Lesson?

Be sure the students understand these key ideas:

- Jesus calls each of us to join Him.
- Even if we sin, Jesus always loves us.

Enrichment Activity

Distribute drawing materials to the students. Direct them to make a drawing of Matthew and the other tax collectors at the dinner table with Jesus. Let the students share their pictures.

A Forgiveness Story

The followers of Jesus had faults, yet Jesus forgave them and challenged them to live the way He did.

You can do the same. Use the boxes to draw a picture-story about a time someone hurt you or made you angry. Let the final drawing show you forgiving the person in words or actions.

Vocabulary

Write your own definitions for the following words:

Catholic ______________________________

Reconciliation ______________________________

Application: We Live Our Faith

Guidelines for Reviewing the Lesson

Invite the students to complete "A Forgiveness Story," a picture-story on this page.

Vocabulary

Direct the students to write their vocabulary definitions. After the writing has been completed, ask volunteers to share their definitions. If there is time, ask a number of students to take turns using each of the vocabulary words in a sentence.

Enrichment Activity

If time permits, view the video "Baptism, the Sacrament of Belonging." See page 4B.

Guidelines for Prayer

1. If the students will not be taking their texts home, you may assign the art activity as a classroom exercise. Let the students meet, in small groups first, to brainstorm signs of God's love in their lives.

2. Then, distribute art materials and have the students work independently on filling the frame with words or drawings.

3. Allow time for students to share their work.

4. Sing or play "We Are a Kingdom People." Ask the students to join you in praying the prayer on the page. Close the prayer with the Sign of the Cross, prayed slowly and reverently.

Signs of God's Love

God shows His love for you and for your family in many ways. God has created a wonderful world for you to live in. God has given you life and people who care about you. God has given you many gifts and talents.

Find a time when the members of your family can meet. Then, work together to fill the frame below with words or pictures that are signs of God's love for your family.

Finally, say this prayer together:

Heavenly Father, we see Your love in our home and in the ways we show we care. You are present when we smile at one another and when we take the time to listen. We feel Your presence when we forgive and when we show that our love will never end. Help us make this love grow. Amen.

Family Note: Lesson 1 opens with the Greeting that begins the sacrament of Reconciliation. The purpose of the lesson is to explain that God always loves us, inspite of our faults, and shows us love in many ways.

FAMILY CONNECTION

If possible, the students may take their texts home to work with their families on the art activity. Point out the Family Note on this page, and ask the students to bring this note to their parents' attention. Send the Family Letter home if the letter was not distributed at registration time.

2 Rules of Love

Focus

The knowledge of the Ten Commandments as a sign of God's faithfulness and eternal love is very important.

Catechetical Objectives

- To help the students view the Ten Commandments as a sign of God's faithfulness and eternal love.
- To explain the meaning of covenant.
- To show the students that they have a covenant relationship with God by virtue of their membership in God's Family.

Lesson Overview

Lesson 2 is about God's Covenant with people and how people are to live in peace and justice:

"The Ten Commandments state what is required in the love of God and love of neighbor. The first three concern love of God, and the other seven love of neighbor" *(Catechism of the Catholic Church, #2067).*

INTRODUCTION: WE CELEBRATE

- God's rules are rules of love. The Ten Commandments are the rules that God gave Moses as signs of love.

DEVELOPMENT: WE BELIEVE

- God made a covenant with the Israelites and gave them the Ten Commandments so that they could grow in love. That covenant is our covenant, too. The Great Commandment helps us understand the importance of loving one another.

APPLICATION: WE LIVE OUR FAITH

- The students interpret the Commandments.

APPLICATION: WE PRAY

- The students gather to pray to the Holy Family.

The Church's Wisdom

Here is the theology supporting Lesson 2.

"The commandments determine the essential bases of behavior, decide the moral value of human acts and remain in organic relationship with humanity's vocation to eternal life, with the establishment of God's kingdom in people and among people" *(Youth of the World, #6).*

Many people find themselves trying to balance two basic philosophies of life. The first, "Rugged Individualism," is the philosophy that suggests people create their own rules. The second, "The Rules," is the philosophy that suggests rules must be followed with no deviation.

God's covenant with us has a different spin. The Ten Commandments and the Greatest Commandment are God's Word for all of us, with which we are to measure our behavior. The covenant invites us to love—first God, and then others, as well as self. That's the rule. Simple, and to the point. Whatever we do, whatever decision we make, however we order our lives, love must be the criteria.

Catechist Resources

AUDIOVISUAL:

- "Moses, Exodus and the Covenant" (V/Adult/Two 25 min. segments/The Story of the Old Testament Covenant #3/St. Anthony Messenger Press and Franciscan Communications) Part one speaks of the Exodus experience. Part two examines the concept of tradition as well as life, love, and law.

BOOK:

- Sloyan, Gerard S. *Catholic Morality Revisited.* (Twenty-Third Publications) With wit and insight, the author underlines the Catholic tradition of social morality. He cites the personal implications in the use of possessions, the use and abuse of our bodies, and today's collective understanding of success and failure in a for-profit culture.

Classroom Resources

AUDIOVISUAL:

- "It's So Nice to Have a Wolf around the House" (V/Intermediate/11 mins./Learning Corporation of America) This video is about a wolf named Cuthbert Q. Devine, who has been bad in the past. Cuthbert tries to reform his ways by bringing happiness to the household of an old man and his pets.

BOOK:

- Biffi, Inos. *The Ten Commandments.* (Eerdmans Publishers) Each commandment is treated individually to fully explain how a Christian, young or old, is to live. The Beatitudes are also included in this book.

Before Beginning the Lesson

TO DO:

- Be prepared and hospitable.
- Have all necessary materials at hand.
- It is week two, and you already belong to these students!

TO HAVE ON HAND:

- Student texts
- Bible
- Writing and drawing materials
- Chalk

FOR OPTIONAL ENRICHMENT ACTIVITIES:

- Booklet or folder materials, preselected magazine pictures, paste or glue (page 13)
- Cardboard medallions, fine tip markers, single hole punch, ribbon or yarn (page 14)
- Benziger *Come, Follow Me* Grade 4 music cassette and cassette player (page 16)
- Set of ten slips of paper with one commandment written on each (page 19)
- Video "It's So Nice to Have a Wolf around the House," TV/VCR (page 20)

New Words

Look at the wrap on page 17 for a suggestion to introduce new vocabulary words to the students. The vocabulary words are italicized or boldfaced in the student's text. All vocabulary words are also defined in the Glossary pages 69–71.

- **covenant:** A solemn agreement.
- **Great Commandment:** "You shall love the Lord, your God, with all your heart, with all your being, with all your strength, and with all your mind. And, you must love your neighbor as yourself" *(based on Matthew 22:34–40).*
- **Ten Commandments:** The laws God gave Moses on Mount Sinai.

Catechist Prayer

A moment of quiet reflection just for you.

"Whoever loves Me will keep My word" *(John 14:23).*

Jesus, You call each of us to wholeness in Your healing love. Help me show the students that Your law of love is not a restriction, but the only way to true freedom. Let us always answer yes to God's love. Amen.

If possible, bring a healthy snack to share with the other catechists following the lesson. The shared snack will serve to nourish the body and build community.

2 Rules of Love

The Word of God

Priest: Come to Me, all you that labor and are heavily burdened, and I will give you rest.

Penitent: Glory and praise to You, Lord Jesus Christ.

Priest: The Lord be with you.

Penitent: And also with you.

Priest: A reading from the holy Gospel according to Matthew (or Mark, or Luke, or John).

Penitent: Glory to You, Lord.

Lesson Plan

Introduction: We Celebrate

Guidelines for Using the Text

1. Read the title of the lesson aloud, and ask volunteers to suggest what this phrase might mean. What do rules have to do with love? Where can we find the rules that will help us love one another?

2. Explain to the students that the text on this page refers to the part of the sacrament of Reconciliation in which the priest and the penitent share a reading from the Bible, which is the Word of God.

3. Read the priest's part of this text aloud. Let the students read the penitent's responses.

4. Remind the students that this part of the rite of Reconciliation is similar to the Liturgy of the Word at Mass. In both cases, we turn to the Word of God in Scripture for a message of hope.

5. Ask volunteers to suggest what kind of rest Jesus is offering in the sacrament of Reconciliation. Help the students understand that life would be much more difficult if we had no rules or guidelines to follow.

My Own Book

If the students are working on "I Celebrate Reconciliation" as an ongoing project, you may have them design a page for the sharing of the Word of God at this time. The students may copy the Gospel verse "Come to Me, all you that labor" *(Matthew 11:28)* at the top of the booklet page. Provide a selection of magazine pictures which depict scenes of workers (factory or office workers, teachers or hospital staff, musicians or farmers).

The students select a picture and paste the picture on the page beneath the Gospel verse.

Guidelines for Using the Scripture Story

1. Before beginning the reading, ask if any of the students know what happened to Moses after God sent him back to Egypt. Let volunteers tell what they know of the story of the Passover, providing correction or clarification where necessary. If the students are unfamiliar with this event, you may summarize it briefly, telling the students that the story you will now read picks up where Lesson 1 left off.

2. Read (or retell in your own words) the story of the giving of the Ten Commandments, based on Exodus 16, 20. You may wish to ask a number of volunteers to read the Ten Commandments aloud.

3. Distribute writing materials, and ask the students to respond briefly in writing to Thinking about Scripture.

4. Discuss the story, using the questions on page 15 as a model.

Loving

Moses and Aaron were able to do what God had called them to do. They led the Israelites safely away from Egypt. They freed the people from their slavery.

At first, the Israelites were happy. But soon, they did not know what to do with their new freedom. They began to fight and argue among themselves. They stole one another's food and clothing, and they lied and cheated. Children disobeyed their parents. Old people were left to die. It seemed that no one loved anyone else any more.

"Our lives are miserable," the people complained to Moses. "You should have left us in Egypt."

Moses didn't know what to say. But he knew that God would have an answer. After all, God had promised to be with them.

Rules of Love

So Moses climbed Mount Sinai to pray. "The people need to know You love them," Moses said to God. "Please give them some sign that You care."

Moses prayed for three days. On the third day, there was a clap of thunder. Lightning flashed across the sky, and the whole mountain shook. Finally, God spoke.

"I am the Lord, your God, who brought you out of Egypt. You shall have no gods but Me.

You shall not use My name in vain.

Remember the Sabbath and keep it holy.

Honor your father and mother.

You shall not kill.

You shall not commit adultery.

You shall not steal.

You shall not lie.

You shall not desire your neighbor's wife.

You shall not desire anything that belongs to your neighbor."

ENRICHMENT ACTIVITY

Distribute cardboard medallions in the shape of double stone tablets (the traditional symbol for the commandments) to the students. Print the Roman numerals I, II, and III on the chalkboard, and have the students copy these onto the left portion of their medallions. Then, print the Roman numerals IV, V, VI, VII, VIII, IX, and X on the chalkboard, and have the students copy these onto the right portion of their medallions. (Explain the significance of these numerals, traditionally used to represent the Ten Commandments, to the students, who may be unfamiliar with the Roman numeral system.) Have the students color or decorate their medallions. Punch a hole in the top center of each medallion, and tie a loop of ribbon or yarn through the holes so that the students may wear their medallions.

Then, Moses was told that these **Ten Commandments** were a sign of His love. "Tell the people how much I love them," God said. "Let them know that I want the best for them. If they truly love Me, they will follow My commandments."

Moses brought the Ten Commandments back to the people. And wherever the people traveled, they carried God's rules with them. They knew they had been chosen to be loved by God, and to show their love in return.

(*based on Exodus 16, 20*)

Thinking about Scripture

- What problems did the Israelites have in dealing with their freedom?
- How can rules be a sign of love?

Introduction: We Celebrate

Talking about Scripture

About the Story:

1. What happened to the Israelites after they were freed from their slavery?

2. Why did Moses go to Mount Sinai?

3. When did Moses receive a sign from God?

4. What was the sign?

5. What did God say the Ten Commandments were a sign of?

About You:

1. Have you ever tried to play a game, cook something, or do an activity without rules? What happened?

2. What are some of the family rules you follow?

3. In what way can you see that love is being shown in the rules your family makes for you?

What Is the Lesson?

Be sure the students understand these key ideas:

- Without rules, the world could not function.
- Most of the rules at home and in school are ways to keep people safe.
- The Ten Commandments are God's rules, given as a sign of God's love and forgiveness.

Enrichment Activity

Have the students form small groups. Direct the students to talk about what rules they need to follow during an average day. Then, have the groups make up lists of these rules, with an explanation of each that tells why the rule is necessary. Allow time for the groups to share their lists.

Development: We Believe

Guidelines for Using the Text

1. Read the first three paragraphs of the text to the students. After the reading, stress that these paragraphs tell what the Ten Commandments meant to the Israelites.

2. Read Growing in Love to the students, stressing that the meaning and the purpose of the Ten Commandments to the members of God's Family today is very important.

3. Next, go through the chart on page 17 with the students. You may want to read each of the commandments aloud and have the students respond by reading its meaning. Pause to clarify where necessary.

The Ten Commandments

On Mount Sinai, God made a **covenant** with the Israelites. God's part of the covenant was to show saving love at all times. The people's part of the agreement was to respond in love to God and to one another.

When people love you very much, they see the good in you. They see what is possible for you. And when you know you are loved, you want to be the best you can be. This is how it was to be between God and the Israelites.

The Ten Commandments showed the Israelites what God expected of them. The commandments also were a sign of God's presence with them. When Moses brought the Law down from the mountain, the Israelites looked upon it as their most precious possession.

Growing in Love

The covenant God made with the Israelites is our covenant, too. We show responsibility and gratitude for God's promise of saving love when we follow the commandments.

We grow in our love for God and for others whenever we follow the Ten Commandments. The first three commandments tell what is expected of us in our relationship with God. The last seven commandments tell what is expected of us in our relationship with ourselves and with others.

Throughout our lives, we grow in our understanding of the Ten Commandments. Read through the commmandments. Think about what they say to you at the age you are now and what they'll mean to you as you grow older.

Music Note

You may wish to review the song "We Are a Kingdom People," student text page 76. Words and music notation can be found on page 135 in the Catechist's Edition. Use Benziger *Come, Follow Me* Grade 4 music cassette to help the students review the song. If you wish, play the song during one of the activities as background music.

Enrichment Activity

The Scriptures remind God's People to keep the words of the covenant alive in their minds and hearts. Orthodox Jewish men follow this instruction literally, wearing special headbands and medallions that carry the words of God's promise in Hebrew. Write the words of God's promise—"You will be My People, and I will be your God"—on the chalkboard. Have the students copy these words onto the backs of their Ten Commandments medallions.

Commandment	What It Means
I am the Lord, your God. You shall have no other gods besides me.	Think about God and talk to God often. Tell others about your faith.
You shall not take God's name in vain.	Use God's name and Jesus' name with respect. Do not use God's name in anger or make fun of any holy person, place, or thing.
Keep holy the Sabbath.	Celebrate Sunday with the Eucharist, joy, thanksgiving, and rest.
Honor your father and mother.	Obey and respect your parents. Be kind to all older people.
You shall not kill.	Respect and care for all living things.
You shall not commit adultery.	Respect your body and the bodies of others. Be modest in the way you dress and act.
You shall not steal.	Do not take things from others. Do not cheat.
You shall not lie.	Tell the truth. Do not gossip about others.
You shall not desire your neighbor's wife.	Remember that marriage is holy. Show respect for family life.
You shall not desire anything that belongs to your neighbor.	Do not be jealous of what others have. Be a good sport and a good loser. Do not waste money on things you do not need.

We Catholics Believe

A **covenant** is a solemn agreement between two people or nations. God's covenant with the Israelites was a sacred and loving agreement. God promised to be with them always; the Israelites promised to follow the Ten Commandments. God's covenant is different from ordinary covenants, because it is based on complete love and respect. It also lasts forever.

The **Great Commandment** is the name given to the words of Jesus that tell us to love God and our neighbor.

DEVELOPMENT: WE BELIEVE

We Catholics Believe

Read these two paragraphs to the students, pausing after each to make sure the students understand the terms introduced.

FUN WITH NEW WORDS

A game of "Moses and the People" is a challenge to help memorize the vocabulary for this lesson. Direct the students to write the definitions to the new vocabulary words. After the writing is completed, ask volunteers to take turns at being Moses. Moses will read one of the definitions and let the other students, the people, tell what word is being defined. If the students seem to enjoy this activity, include the commandments with a positive definition. (Example: I respect what belongs to others.)

Development: We Believe

Guidelines for Using the Scripture Story

1. Before beginning the reading, ask the students for examples of times when they may have argued with someone. Help the students understand the difference between reasonable argument and fighting or quarreling.

2. Read aloud (or tell in your own words) the story of Jesus' teaching of the Two Great Commandments, drawn from Mark 12:28–34 and John 15:9–17.

3. Ask volunteers to respond to Thinking about Scripture. You may continue discussing the story, using the questions below as a model.

Talking about Scripture

About the Story:

1. Why did the people argue about God's Word and God's Law?

2. What answer did Jesus give about the commandments?

3. What did Jesus tell His disciples later?

About You:

1. What are some of the ways that you show you are Jesus' disciple?

2. Who are some of the people in your life to whom you show love?

The Command to Love

In the days of Jesus, there were many teachers who spent all their time studying God's Word and God's Law. People took their covenant with God very seriously.

One day, some people decided to ask Jesus to settle a question for them. They wanted to test Jesus' knowledge of the Scriptures. We call His answer the **Great Commandment** because it sums up all of God's rules of love.

"Teacher," they asked Him, "which commandment is the greatest?"

Jesus answered, "You know the commandment your ancestors taught you: 'You shall love the Lord, your God with all your heart, with all your soul, with all your strength, and with all your mind.'" Jesus added another line. "You shall love your neighbor as yourself."

The people were amazed. Not only had Jesus answered correctly, He had also given them an answer no one could argue with!

Later, on the night before He died, Jesus talked to His disciples in private. He explained more about what God expected of them. "I give you a new commandment," Jesus told them. "Love one another as I have loved you. This is how people will know that you are My disciples, if you have love for one another."

(*based on Mark 12:28–34 and John 15:9–17*)

Thinking about Scripture

- Say the Great Commandment in your own words.
- Why do you think love is such an important part of God's Law?

What Is the Lesson?

Be sure the students understand these key ideas:

- Jesus taught that love of God, self, and neighbor is at the heart of God's Law.
- We may use Jesus' example to learn how to love others.

Enrichment Activity

Distribute writing materials to the students. Direct them to print Jesus' new commandment at the top of their papers, and then write some actual ways to follow Jesus' example of love in their own daily lives with their families.

Keeping the Rules

Each commandment tells a good way to live. Draw a line that connects the commandment to the action it tells to do.

Commandment	**What to Do**
I am the Lord your God . . .	Admit to the wrong you did.
Honor your father and mother.	Pay for what you want in a store.
You shall not steal.	Do your chores without being told.
You shall not kill.	Pray and love God.
You shall not lie.	Eat healthy foods.

Each commandment also tells what *not* to do. Draw a line that connects the commandment and the action it says to avoid.

Commandment	**What Not to Do**
Keep holy the Sabbath.	Fight with your brothers and sisters.
Honor your father and mother.	Be jealous of something your friend has.
You shall not want your neighbor's goods.	Pretend not to hear your mom when she needs you.
You shall not take God's name in vain.	Miss Mass on Sunday because you feel lazy.
You shall not kill.	Use Jesus' name when you are angry.

Vocabulary

Write your own definitions for the following words:

Covenant ________________________________

Word of God ________________________________

Application: We Live Our Faith

Guidelines for Reviewing the Lesson

1. Direct the students to work independently on the two sections of the matching activity. Remind them to read the directions carefully and then to complete the activity using a pencil to draw the lines.

2. After the students have finished working, discuss their answers. Refer the students to the chart on page 17. Have the students erase and correct any incorrect matches.

Enrichment Activity

In advance of this activity, prepare several sets of ten slips of paper, with a commandment written on each slip. To carry out a review of the Ten Commandments, have the students form small groups. Give each group one set of slips containing the Ten Commandments. Let the students in each group take turns choosing a slip, reading the commandment written on it, and explaining the meaning of the commandment in their own words. Move from group to group, listening in on the explanations and encouraging the students' efforts.

Guidelines for Prayer

1. If the room you are using has a prayer space, gather the students into this space. If possible, have a picture or statue that represents the Holy Family placed on the prayer table, if one is available, or on the desk or shelf.

2. Lead the prayer and sing or listen to "We Are a Kingdom People," as suggested in the Music Note found on page 16.

3. If you wish, show the video "It's So Nice to Have a Wolf around the House" after the prayer service.

We Pray to the Holy Family

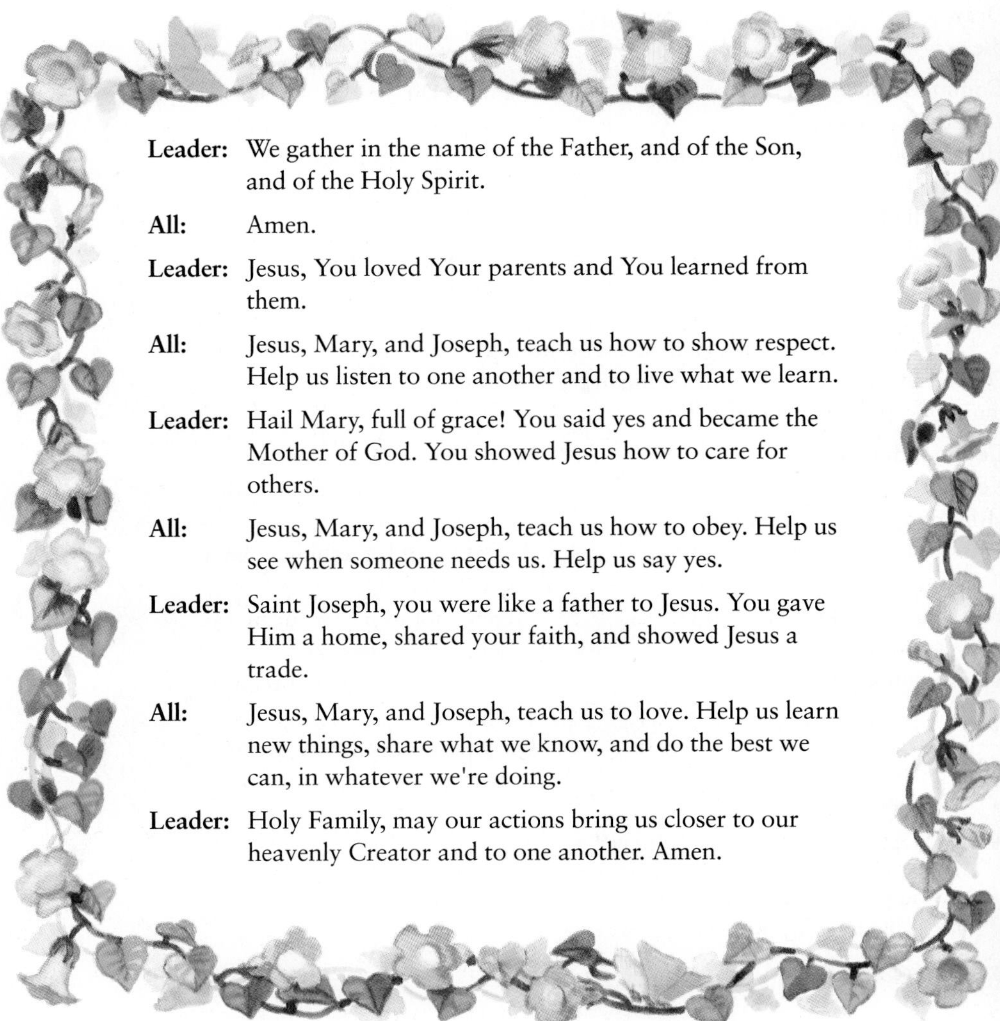

Leader: We gather in the name of the Father, and of the Son, and of the Holy Spirit.

All: Amen.

Leader: Jesus, You loved Your parents and You learned from them.

All: Jesus, Mary, and Joseph, teach us how to show respect. Help us listen to one another and to live what we learn.

Leader: Hail Mary, full of grace! You said yes and became the Mother of God. You showed Jesus how to care for others.

All: Jesus, Mary, and Joseph, teach us how to obey. Help us see when someone needs us. Help us say yes.

Leader: Saint Joseph, you were like a father to Jesus. You gave Him a home, shared your faith, and showed Jesus a trade.

All: Jesus, Mary, and Joseph, teach us to love. Help us learn new things, share what we know, and do the best we can, in whatever we're doing.

Leader: Holy Family, may our actions bring us closer to our heavenly Creator and to one another. Amen.

Family Note: Lesson 2 opened with the second step in the sacrament of Reconciliation: listening to Scripture. It continued into an explanation of the Ten Commandments as signs of God's faithfulness and love. Jesus gave us a new commandment that we call the Great Commandment. Talk about all of these commandments with your child and how they relate to everyday living.

FAMILY CONNECTION

If the students take their texts home, suggest that "We Pray to the Holy Family" be prayed together with the family. Before the prayer, invite the family to select a favorite family television program that all family members will enjoy. Before the program begins, prepare a snack, pray the litany together, and enjoy the program. Point out the Family Note on this page, and ask the students to bring this note and the Family Letter to their parents' attention.

3 Right and Wrong

FOCUS

Examining one's conscience is necessary in order to celebrate the sacrament of Reconciliation.

CATECHETICAL OBJECTIVES

- To help the students understand the difference between right and wrong action.
- To explain that an informed conscience can help the students choose between right and wrong.
- To encourage the students to respond faithfully to God's Law in their daily lives.

LESSON OVERVIEW

Lesson 3 is about each person's responsibility to form a proper conscience:

"Conscience must be informed and moral judgment enlightened. A well-formed conscience is upright and truthful. It formulates its judgments according to reason, in conformity with the true good willed by the wisdom of the Creator. The education of conscience is indispensable for human beings who are subjected to negative influences and tempted by sin to prefer their own judgment and to reject authoritative teachings" *(Catechism of the Catholic Church, #1783).*

INTRODUCTION: WE CELEBRATE

- The Examination of Conscience is part of the communal penance service; it is also a gift that helps us keep track of our moral choices. The story of Adam and Eve shows that people can choose to obey or disobey God's Law.

DEVELOPMENT: WE BELIEVE

- The gift of free will lets us choose to obey or disobey God's Commandments. The gift of conscience lets us know the difference between right and wrong. The parable of the Two Sons shows obedience and disobedience in action.

APPLICATION: WE LIVE OUR FAITH

- The students review basic Catholic beliefs.

APPLICATION: WE PRAY

- The students experience reflective prayer, a way for all the students to focus on who they are now, what they wish for the future, and primarily, to think about the goodness inside each of them.

THE CHURCH'S WISDOM

Here is the theology supporting Lesson 3.

"Catechesis seeks to help people form right consciences, choose what is morally right, avoid sin and its occasions, and live in this world according to the Spirit of Christ, in love of God and neighbor" *(National Catechetical Directory, #105).*

Life is a most precious gift and blessing from God. The most daring gift and blessing from God may very well be free will. The human capacity to choose God, good, peace, harmony and the like is ours. The human capacity to choose against God and the ways of God is also ours. It is the responsibility of all the baptized to be ever in the process of maturing in the ways of God. It is also the responsibility of all the baptized to guide and encourage others, especially the children, in the ways of God.

God indeed loves all people totally to have created humankind with the capacity to choose or not to choose the good that is intended for all. God, being all-knowing, trusts that the basic good that is in all people, created in the image of God, is ever coming to be. Today is a great day to reflect on the good decisions we have made so far and to make revisions, if necessary.

Catechist Resources

AUDIOVISUAL:

- "Forming a Healthy Christian Conscience" (V/Adults/ Two 25 min. segments/Christian Morality and Forgiveness #4/St. Anthony Messenger Press and Franciscan Communications) Part one of this video reflects on our notion and image of God and offers insight into the nature of God. Part two challenges the viewer to consider what implications our image of God has for our daily life.

BOOK:

- McCormick, Patrick. *Sin as an Addiction.* (Paulist Press) The traditional understanding of sin is presented with the approach of describing the addictive nature of sin.

Classroom Resources

AUDIOVISUAL:

- "Up is Down" (16mm film/Intermediate/6 mins./Pyramid Films) This classic animated tale about a boy who walks on his hands illustrates the conflict between conformity and creativity. His upside-down perspective is different from the view of most people. Experts "cure" him and he finally walks upright. But he remarks, "If you want me to stay on my feet, you'll have to change things first."

BOOK:

- Bruchac, Joseph. *The First Strawberries, A Cherokee Story Retold.* (Dial Books) This delightful legend tells of the first man and woman who lived together in love and respect. One day they argue and part company. The man wants to apologize, and the Sun helps by sending fresh strawberries.

Before Beginning the Lesson

TO DO:

- Be prepared and have all the materials necessary to present Lesson 3.
- Welcome each student as he or she enters the room.
- If possible, meet as many of the families as you can. Call if possible, and make an appointment to visit the families at home.
- Reproduce the Family Letter on pages 115–116, and send one to each family.
- Check with the catechetical office to be sure of scheduled meetings or schedule changes.

TO HAVE ON HAND:

- Student texts
- Bible
- Writing and drawing materials
- Chalk

FOR OPTIONAL ENRICHMENT ACTIVITIES:

- Booklet or folder materials, fine tip markers (page 21)
- Mural materials, rolled paper (such as butcher, newsprint, or shelf paper), markers or crayons (page 22)
- Benziger *Come, Follow Me* Grade 4 music cassette and cassette player (page 24)
- Colored construction paper, masking tape (page 25)
- Writing materials, index cards, fine tip markers (page 25)
- Slide and slide projector or poster of the night sky, candle, if permitted (page 28)

New Words

Look at the wrap on page 25 for a suggestion to introduce new vocabulary words to the students. The vocabulary words are italicized or boldfaced in the student's text. All vocabulary words are also defined in the Glossary pages 69–71.

- **conscience:** God's gift that helps us know right from wrong.
- **examination of conscience:** A step in reconciliation that involves taking an honest look at choices we have made.
- **free will:** God's gift that allows us to choose to talk with Jesus or away from God.
- **grace:** A share in God's life and love.
- **original sin:** The first sin.
- **parable:** A special story used by Jesus to teach His Way.
- **sin:** Choosing to do wrong.

Catechist Prayer

A moment of quiet reflection just for you.

"But when He comes, the Spirit of truth, He will guide you to all truth" *(John 16:13).*

Holy Spirit, show me the way to walk in Your light. Be with the students as they choose; help them choose rightly. Keep us all from temptation, and lead us always to the truth. Amen.

If you wish, listen to classical music on the way to the class. If the students come to your home for the lesson, play a tape, find a station, or play the stereo at home. Listen for the whisper of the Spirit in the music.

3 Right and Wrong

Examination of Conscience

Leader: God, our Father, sometimes we have not behaved as Your children should.

Penitents: But You love us and come to us.

Leader: We have given trouble to our parents and teachers.

Penitents: But You love us and come to us.

Leader: We have quarreled and called each other names.

Penitents: But You love us and come to us.

Leader: We have been lazy at home and in school, and have not been helpful to our parents (brothers, sisters, friends).

Penitents: But You love us and come to us.

Leader: We have thought too much of ourselves and have told lies.

Penitents: But You love us and come to us.

Leader: We have not done good to others when we had the chance.

Penitents: But You love us and come to us.

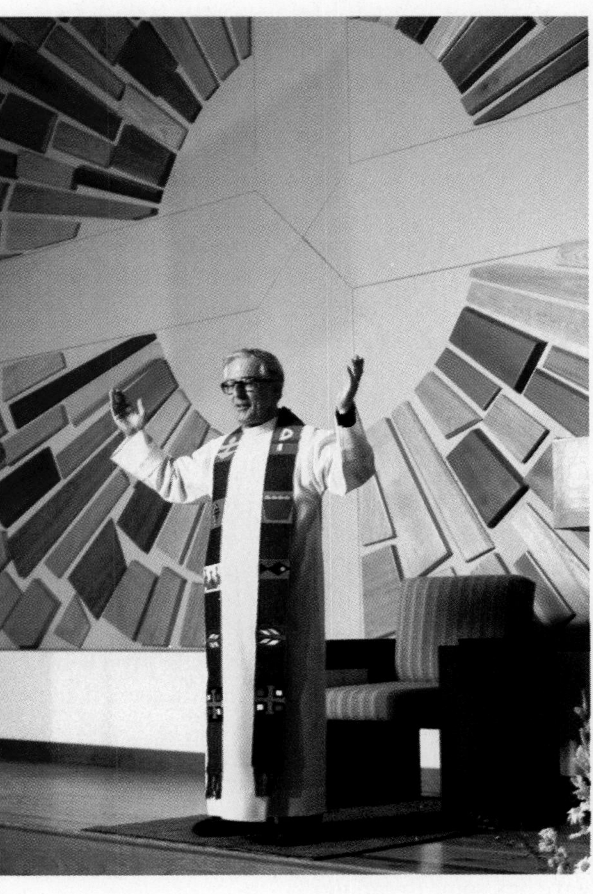

Lesson Plan

Introduction: We Celebrate

Guidelines for Using the Text

1. Before beginning the reading, write the word "conscience" on the chalkboard, and ask volunteers for definitions. At this point, it is enough for the students to understand that the conscience is a gift from God to help us make right choices.

2. Introduce this text by reminding the students of the part of the Mass (the Penitential Rite) when we pause to think about those things we have done wrong. Explain that we do much the same thing in preparing for Reconciliation. We ask ourselves whether we have truly followed God's rules and the example of Jesus. This is called an examination of conscience. Then, explain to the students that the sacrament of Reconciliation can be celebrated in two different ways. We can prepare to confess our sins individually, or we can listen to God's Word and examine our consciences as a group before confessing individually. The words on this page come from the communal celebration of the sacrament.

3. Read the leader's part of the Examination of Conscience aloud, and let the students read the penitents' responses. After the reading, ask if there are any questions before moving on.

My Own Book

If the students are working on "I Celebrate Reconciliation" as an ongoing project, you may have them design a page for the Examination of Conscience at this time. Suggest that the students print "The Penitential Rite" at the top of the page. Then, they may select one or two of the leader's prayers and draw a picture that depicts the chosen prayer. At the bottom of the page, they print "But You love us and come to us."

Guidelines for Using the Scripture Story

1. If you wish, spend a few moments providing some background on this story, which is based on the accounts of Creation and the Fall found in the Book of Genesis. Explain that from the beginning of time, people have wondered about the beginning of the world and about the origin of evil and temptation. The biblical story of Adam and Eve, with which many of the students may already be familiar, is the way that the Jewish people and the Christians, who accepted the Hebrew Scriptures, have traditionally explored answers to these questions.

2. Read aloud the story on these two pages. This retelling uses the word Tempter instead of devil or Satan. Young students, influenced by popular movies or television shows, may show some fascination for the traditional personification of evil. It is important to stress that even though the temptation to sin may be very strong, "the Devil made me do it" is not a valid excuse to sin. Students who are excessively influenced by media portrayals of possession or Satanic powers may need reassurance from you or from a parish priest.

3. After the reading, allow time for students to respond to Thinking about Scripture on page 23. If you wish, discuss the story using the questions on page 23.

Obeying

In the beginning, God created the heavens and the earth and all that live within them. Then, God created Adam, the first man, and Eve, the first woman. They were created with an understanding heart, wisdom, and knowledge. God loved Adam and Eve very much and gave them a beautiful garden in which to live.

The garden was lush with all kinds of trees and herbs and bushes and flowers. And in the middle of the garden, God planted a special tree. It was a tall, beautiful tree. God called it the Tree of Knowledge.

"You can eat as much as you want from every tree in this garden," God told Adam and Eve. "But you may not touch the Tree of Knowledge. If you eat from that tree, you will know about good and evil. You will know suffering and pain. One day, you will die."

Adam and Eve did as God told them and lived in peace.

The First Sin

Now the Tempter was jealous of Adam and Eve's happiness. So the Tempter came to Eve in the form of a serpent.

"Aren't you hungry?" the serpent asked her. "Why don't you try some of this fruit? It looks sweet and juicy."

"No," said Eve. "If I eat that fruit, God said I will die."

The serpent laughed. "You won't die. You'll just get smart. Once you eat the fruit of this tree, you'll know as much as God."

Eve was hungry. The serpent's words seemed to make sense. She knew she was breaking her promise to God, but she took some fruit from the tree and ate it. It was delicious! Eve thought Adam would like it, and so she gave him some to eat, too.

Just then, God called out to Adam and Eve.

Suddenly, they felt cold and afraid. They knew they had done wrong. From then on, Adam and Eve would no longer be so understanding and wise. They would

ENRICHMENT ACTIVITY

Distribute drawing materials and suggest that the students work on a mural of the Garden of Creation. Encourage the students to be fanciful in the animals and plants they include. Title the mural: "In The Beginning . . ."

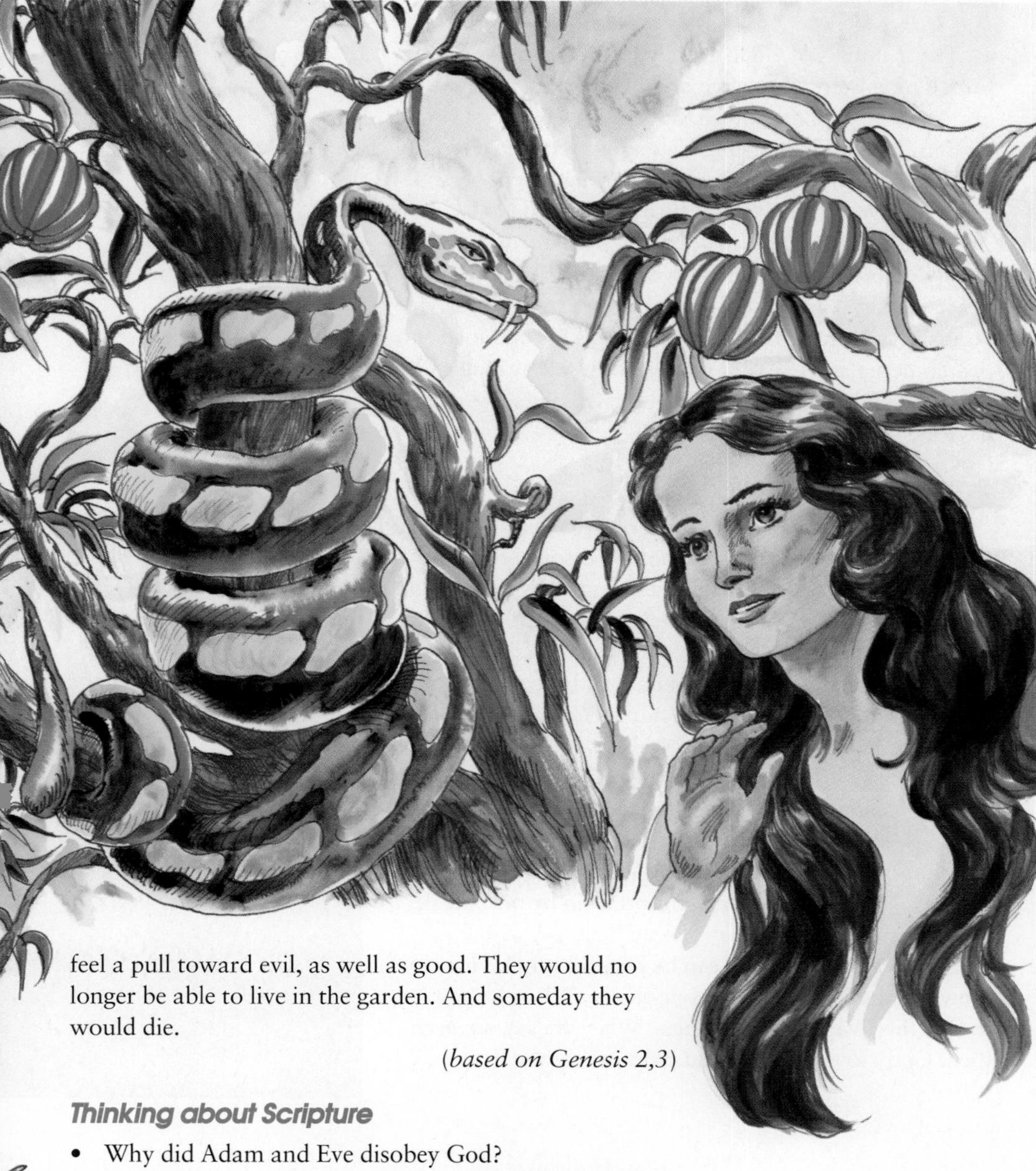

feel a pull toward evil, as well as good. They would no longer be able to live in the garden. And someday they would die.

(*based on Genesis 2,3*)

Thinking about Scripture

- Why did Adam and Eve disobey God?
- What does the story about Adam and Eve tell about the way sin entered the world?

Introduction: We Celebrate

Talking about Scripture

About the Story:

1. What did God call the special tree planted in the garden?

2. What did God tell Adam and Eve about the tree?

3. Whom did Eve talk to about the tree?

4. What happened after Adam and Eve ate the fruit?

About You:

1. Has anyone ever told you to do something that you knew was wrong?

2. What did you do? What were the results of your action?

What Is the Lesson?

Be sure the students understand these key ideas:

- The world God created was good.
- Evil came into the world because of a wrong choice made by human beings with free will.
- Help your students to understand the purpose of storytelling in Scripture. The Genesis accounts of Creation and the Fall are poetic descriptions of real truths.

Try to avoid a too-literal approach that focuses on the number of days the Creation took, where Adam and Eve lived, and so on. Conversely, do not allow your students to dismiss this powerful story as a fairy tale.

Development: We Believe

Guidelines for Using the Text

1. Read the first two paragraphs of the text on this page to the class. Write the terms "original sin" and "grace" on the chalkboard, making sure the students understand the meanings of these terms as they are defined in the text.

2. Next, read the text section Sin and Forgiveness aloud. Pause frequently for questions or reactions. To make sure that the students understand the meaning and types of sin, you may provide examples of mortal sin and venial sin. The students may also volunteer to offer examples.

3. Ask a student to summarize the three conditions for mortal sin, writing these on the chalkboard.

4. Read Pulling Us to Good aloud. This text section elaborates on the definition of conscience which you introduced at the beginning of the lesson. Help the students understand that their conscience is not some outside voice they will hear literally, but a part of their own minds and hearts which must be educated, or informed, in order to assist in making choices.

Right and Wrong Choices

The members of God's Family have a special reason for telling the story of Adam and Eve. We are all children of those first parents, and so the results of that first sin are with us. Every human being feels a pull between choosing what is right and choosing what is wrong. Every person can make wrong choices and turn away from God.

We call the choice of the first people to turn away from God **original sin.** Jesus saved us from original sin but its effects—sin, misery, and evil—are still with us. In Baptism, we receive God's **grace**—God's life and love—to overcome sin and evil. But it does not work by magic. We have the gift of **free will.** Throughout our lives, we always have a choice.

Sin and Forgiveness

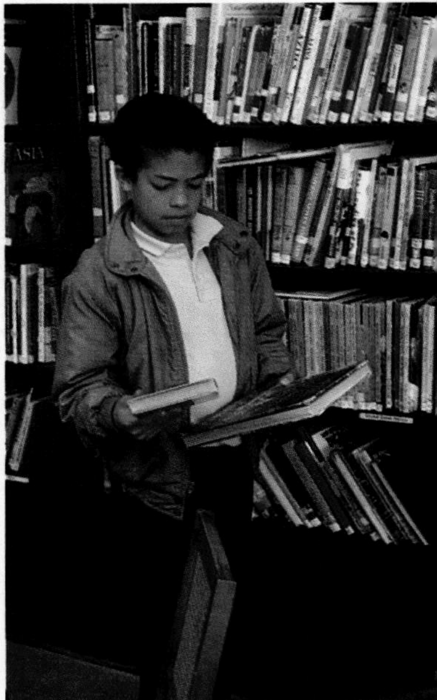

Like Adam and Eve, we can choose to obey God's Commandments, or we can choose to disobey them. Sin is choosing to do wrong. It means turning away from God. **Sin** hurts the sinner and sin hurts others, too.

Nothing can hurt God, but sin hurts our friendship with God. *Venial sin* weakens our friendship. *Mortal sin* is very serious, because it ruins our friendship with God. Mortal sin is sometimes called "deadly sin," because it separates us from grace, our share in God's life.

Every sin involves a choice. A sin is mortal when the action is seriously wrong, the person knows the action is seriously wrong, and chooses to commit the action anyway. No one can commit a mortal sin by mistake or by accident.

Nothing, not even sin, can make God stop loving us. How we answer that love is our choice. When we say yes to that love, we grow in holiness. When we say no, even then, God's love is strong and pulls us to good.

Enrichment Activity

Have the students turn to page 75 of their texts. Read through the Examination of Conscience slowly and prayerfully with the students, asking them to reflect quietly on those areas of their lives in which they have the most difficulty responding to God and to others with love. This is a good practice for preparing for sacramental confession.

Music Note

You may wish to teach the song "Choices," student text page 76. Words and music notation can be found on page 136 in this Catechist's Edition. Use Benziger *Come, Follow Me* Grade 4 music cassette to help make the learning a pleasant experience.

Pulling Us to Good

God gives us a special gift to help us know how to use the freedom to choose. It's called **conscience.** Conscience is the ability we have to say, "This is a good choice," or "That is a sin." It's not something that goes off automatically, like an alarm clock. We need to work with our conscience and to practice using it wisely. Prayer, study, and the sacraments are ways to form our conscience and keep it on the right track.

Jesus gave us the sacrament of Reconciliation to help us make peace with God and with God's Family. One step in the sacrament of Reconciliation is an *examination of conscience.* This involves taking a close and honest look at the choices made and the actions taken. We ask ourselves: Which were good choices? Which were against God's Law? What are some reasons I made the choices I did? How did these choices affect me? affect others? How can I make better choices in the future?

We Catholics Believe

Original sin is the first sin. Only Jesus and His Mother, Mary, were born without original sin. Baptism frees us from original sin, but its effects are still with us.

In Baptism, we receive **grace,** a share in God's life and love, to overcome sin and evil.

God's gift of **free will** allows us to choose to walk with Jesus or to walk away from God.

Sin is forgiven in the sacrament of Reconciliation.

The **conscience** is the ability to know right from wrong. This gift is developed by listening to the teachings of the Church, and by praying, studying, and participating in the sacraments.

DEVELOPMENT: WE BELIEVE

We Catholics Believe

Ask volunteers to take turns reading these paragraphs aloud. As a review of the material, you may ask the students to close their books and respond orally as you quiz them on the meanings of the highlighted terms.

ENRICHMENT ACTIVITY

Distribute writing materials, and have the students compose brief prayers asking God's help in making right choices. You may wish to have the students copy their prayers onto small index cards and decorate the borders. Ask the students to keep their prayers for use during We Pray at the close of the lesson.

FUN WITH NEW WORDS

Prepare colorful construction paper signs with the vocabulary word on one paper and the definition on another. Use the vocabulary words from Lesson 3. If you wish, add words from the previous lessons, also. Have one sign per student. Tape vocabulary words on the backs of some of the students. Tape the corresponding definitions to the fronts of the others. Allow the students to mill about in an open space and look for their matches. When a match is made, the pair says the word and definition together.

Development: We Believe

Guidelines for Using the Scripture Story

1. Read aloud or retell in your own words the story of the Two Sons, based on Matthew 21:28–31. Be sure the students are clear on the meaning of "parable."

2. After the reading, allow time for students to respond briefly in writing to Thinking about Scripture. Let the students share their answers in small groups.

3. You may continue discussing the story using the questions below as a model.

Talking about Scripture

About the Story:

1. What is a parable?

2. What did each of the two sons say they would do?

3. What did each of the two sons actually do for the father?

About You:

1. What does it mean to obey?

2. When is it hard for you to obey?

The Two Sons

Jesus told many special stories, or *parables,* as a way of teaching. One day, He told His friends this story.

There was a vineyard owner who had two sons. Since it was harvest time, the man needed extra help in his vineyard. So he went to his first son. "I really need your help today," he said. "Please come with me to the vineyard."

The first son shook his head. "I can't work for you today," he answered. "I already made plans with my friends."

Disappointed, the man went to his second son. "I need your help with the grapes today," he said.

"I'll be right there," the boy answered.

The man went to the field, expecting his second son to follow. But the second son changed his mind. "I know I told my father I would help him," he thought. "But it's hot today, and I'd much rather go swimming." So he went swimming, and never went to the field.

Meanwhile, the first son was on his way to meet his friends. He thought to himself, "My father is always very good to me. I made him sad today when I said I wouldn't help him. I can always play with my friends another day." So the boy hurried to the vineyard to help his father.

Jesus looked at His friends. "Which one of these boys obeyed his father?"

(*based on Matthew 21:28–31*)

Thinking about Scripture

- How would you answer Jesus' question?

What Is the Lesson?

Be sure the students understand these key ideas:

- We show obedience through action, not just words.
- Obedience is a way to show love.

Enrichment Activity

Distribute drawing materials and ask the students to illustrate a scene from this parable. Encourage the students to bring their artwork home and to retell the parable to family members.

Obeying God's Law

We can live our faith by knowing our beliefs. Fill in the blanks to make the sentences complete.

1. Sin is choosing to do ________________.
2. We suffer from sin, pain, and misery, which are the results of the first sin, called ________________ sin.
3. ________________ sin is sometimes called deadly sin.
4. God gave you a ________________________ to help you know right from wrong.
5. For a sin to be mortal, it is necessary that:
   a. The action is ________________ wrong.
   b. The person ________________ it is ________________ wrong.
   c. The person freely ________________ to do the wrong.
6. ________________, which is God's life and love within us, helps us overcome sin and evil.
7. Sin is forgiven in the sacrament of ________________________________.
8. An ________________________ of ________________________ helps us look at the choices we made.

Vocabulary

Give an example of each:

Venial sin ____

Mortal sin ____

Parable ____

APPLICATION: WE LIVE OUR FAITH

Guidelines for Reviewing the Lesson

1. Have the students read the directions for completing the sentences in Obeying God's Law. Then, have the students work independently on the sentence completion.

2. Have the students exchange books with a partner to check the exercise. Answers: (1) wrong; (2) original; (3) Mortal; (4) free will; (5) (a) seriously, (b) knows, seriously, (c) chooses; (6) Grace; (7) Reconciliation; (8) examination, conscience.

3. Then, have the students work independently on their vocabulary definitions. As a vocabulary review, you may ask volunteers to read their definitions while the class supplies the word being defined.

ENRICHMENT ACTIVITY

Distribute writing materials, and ask the students to create their own contemporary version of the Parable of the Two Sons. (Students may work in groups if it is more convenient.) Allow time for volunteers to share what they have written.

Application: We Pray

Guidelines for Prayer

1. Gather the students around the prayer table if one is available in the room, or in an open space. Darken the room and light a candle, if permitted. Have a slide of the night sky projected on the screen or wall. You may also use a poster of a night sky. Lead the students in "Grace-Filled Lives."

2. If students have written prayers as an enrichment activity for this lesson, close the lesson by inviting volunteers to pray their prayers aloud. Or, pray together the Examination of Conscience from student text page 21. Close your prayer time by playing or singing together "Choices."

Grace-Filled Lives

One way to pray is to ask yourself questions. Then, give yourself time to think about the answers. Try that with this prayer:

Leader: People have always asked, "Who am I?" King David asked this question in this way:

All: A reading from Psalm 8:

O Lord, I behold Your heavens, and the work of Your fingers, the moon and stars which You set in place. Who am I that You should care for me?

Leader: Let us be quiet and reflect. Think about who you are right now. (Pause briefly after each question.) What makes you happy? What are some of your worries? What is important to you? Think about the future. What would you like to be doing ten or fifteen years from now? You have been made in God's image. That means you are good. Spend a little time thinking about the goodness inside of you. (Pause).

All: God, our Creator, thank You for your gift of grace. May this sharing of Your life help us as we try to follow Jesus to Your kingdom. Amen.

Family Note: Lesson 3 focuses on the examination of conscience. Your child talked about sin—original, venial, and mortal—and the fact that an informed conscience helps a person know right from wrong. The prayer service on this page is an example of reflective prayer.

Family Connection

If the students take their texts home, suggest that the family pray "Grace-Filled Lives" at bedtime. Also remind the students to point out the Family Note on the bottom of page 28. The Family Letter should also be brought to the families' attention.

4 I Confess

Focus

Confession of sin is an essential part of the sacrament of Reconciliation.

Catechetical Objectives

- To teach the importance of taking responsibility for one's choices and actions.
- To point out that responsible people consider the consequences of their decision before they act.
- To help the students distinguish between sins and accidents or mistakes.

Lesson Overview

Lesson 4 explores confession, or admitting responsibility for wrongful behavior, as necessary for reconciliation with God and others:

"The confession (or disclosure) of sins, even from a simply human point of view, frees us and facilitates our reconciliation with others" *(Catechism of the Catholic Church, #1455)*.

INTRODUCTION: WE CELEBRATE

- The prayer "Confession" clearly states the elements of telling our sins. A story about a little girl and her friend introduces the concept of accidents, mistakes, and sin, and the need for someone to tell our sins to.

DEVELOPMENT: WE BELIEVE

- The sacrament of Reconciliation is Jesus' loving gift to help us grow in responsibility. The Scripture story of the Good Thief shows how deeply Jesus loves those who turn to Him in sorrow for their sins.

APPLICATION: WE LIVE OUR FAITH

- The students will practice determining whether an action is a sin, an accident, or a mistake.

APPLICATION: WE PRAY

- The students will gather to pray for God's guidance in knowing the difference between right and wrong and in taking responsibility for their actions.

The Church's Wisdom

Here is the theology supporting Lesson 4.

"Catechesis for the sacrament of Reconciliation: An understanding of sin, of oneself as a sinner, and of the conditions requisite for a serious sin are necessary preliminaries in catechesis for this sacrament" *(National Catechetical Directory, #125)*.

All persons are created in the image and likeness of God. Most believers are able to make this statement and accept this truth. Living as if it is true is not as simple.

It takes a certain amount of intelligence and skill to sin. One must understand free will, intentionality, choices, and decision-making.

The sacrament of Reconciliation affords people the opportunity to keep spiritually focused on following Gospel values. The sacrament of Reconciliation, the counsel of Scripture and of the faithful, the ongoing revelation of God through the teachings of the Church, and the Holy Spirit all provide a foundation to support our faith.

All persons are created in the image and likeness of God. All persons have a fundamental nature of holiness. All that is necessary is to work out the details. Take courage, God is in our midst.

Catechist Resources

AUDIOVISUAL:

- "The Divine Self: A Foundation for Moral Relationships" (V/Adults/Two 25 min. segments/Christian Morality and Forgiveness #4/St. Anthony Messenger Press and Franciscan Communications) This video presents a reflection on being created in the image and likeness of God. Part one is about who God looks like, or what your image of God is. Part two examines how we choose to live as temples of the Holy Spirit.

BOOK:

- Vanderhaar, Gerard. *Why Good People Do Bad Things.* (Twenty-Third Publications) The author challenges readers to examine their lives and the effect of their actions or in-actions on the social environment. He offers positive and constructive means to change moral and political consciousness and to act for the greater good of humankind.

Classroom Resources

AUDIOVISUAL:

- "There's Nobody like You" (V/Intermediate/Four 7 min. stories/The Christophers) This video presents four stories celebrating the uniqueness of each individual. They illustrate that each one of us is special and has special gifts which make us valuable and lovable.

BOOK:

- MacDonald, George. *The Lost Princess: A Double Story.* (Eerdmans Publishing) This is a fairy tale about two spoiled girls, a princess and a shepherdess, whose encounters with a mysterious Wise Woman deep in the forest help them grow in character and self-control.

Before Beginning the Lesson

TO DO:

- Have all necessary materials at hand to present Lesson 4.
- If possible, invite the pastor or parish priest to visit the class.
- You are a marvelous, wonderful, worthwhile person—just because you are. Be at peace.

TO HAVE ON HAND:

- Student texts
- Writing and drawing materials
- Bible
- Chalk

FOR OPTIONAL ENRICHMENT ACTIVITIES:

- Booklet or folder materials, fine tip markers (page 29)
- Drawing materials, blank note cards and envelopes, writing materials (page 31)
- Benziger *Come, Follow Me* Grade 4 music cassette and cassette player (page 32)
- Paper and pencils, invited clergy (page 33)
- Transparency, overhead projector (page 33)
- Construction paper or light-weight cardboard, drawing materials, fine tip markers, clear contact paper, single hole punch, yarn or ribbon (page 35)

New Words

Look at the wrap on page 33 for a suggestion to introduce new vocabulary words to the students. The vocabulary words are italicized or boldfaced in the student's text. All vocabulary words are also defined in the Glossary pages 69–71.

- **confession:** The act of telling your sins to a priest in the sacrament of Reconciliation.
- **consequences:** The effects of your choices or actions.
- **hell:** Total and lasting separation from God's love.
- **Messiah:** The Savior; the person picked by God to help the people of Israel live the way God wanted them to live.
- **responsible:** Answerable for choices that are made.

Catechist Prayer

A moment of quiet reflection just for you.

"O God, be merciful to me, a sinner" *(Luke 18:13).*

Creator God, you know what is in my heart. Help me choose wisely in my own life and give good example to the students. Teach us all to respond to one another in love and to take responsibility for our choices. Amen.

If you wish, select one issue from the newspaper, read it aloud even if you are alone, reflect on what it means in light of the Gospel, and pray for all the people involved.

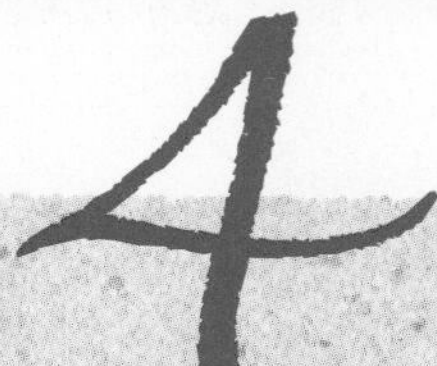

I Confess

Confession

Penitent: I confess to almighty God, and to you, my brothers and sisters, that I have sinned through my own fault in my thoughts and in my words, in what I have done, and in what I have failed to do; I ask blessed Mary, ever virgin, all the angels and saints, and you, my brothers and sisters, to pray for me to the Lord our God.

Lesson Plan

Introduction: We Celebrate

Guidelines for Using the Text

1. Before using the text, ask the students to share some of their thoughts and ideas about confessing their sins in the sacrament of Reconciliation. Ask what they know about confession and what they think their experience of confession will be. This initial discussion can be a good way to handle any misconceptions or fears your students may have about the sacrament. Another way to introduce these topics is to ask the students to write down their questions about confession and to give them to you unsigned. You can address general questions now and throughout the lesson.

2. Then, read together the prayer "I confess. . . ."

3. Ask the students if they have heard or prayed this prayer before. Remind them that this prayer is often used in the Penitential Rite of the Mass. It is used, too, in the sacrament of Reconciliation and in parish penitential services.

My Own Book

If the students are working on "I Celebrate Reconciliation" as an ongoing project, you may have them design a page for the Confession at this time. Suggest that the students title the page "Confession." Then, the students may select one phrase of the prayer and draw a picture that speaks of the phrase in his or her life. The students may then write the selected phrase beneath the picture, at the bottom of the page.

Guidelines for Using the Story

1. Ask several good readers to take turns reading aloud the story on these two pages.

2. After the reading, have the students choose partners to discuss Thinking about the Story.

3. You may continue discussing the story, using the questions on page 31 as a model.

Confessing

Tom was Patty's next-door neighbor and good friend. One day, Tom saw Patty sitting on the step of her porch. She looked very sad.

"What's the matter?" Tom asked as he sat next to Patty.

Patty sighed. "I'm in trouble with everyone," she confessed.

"Like who?" Tom asked.

"My mom and dad for one thing," Patty answered. "I lied to them last night. I said my grades in school were good. I told them I didn't need to study. So my mom and dad let me watch television. Today, they saw my report card. It's really bad. Now I can't watch television for two weeks."

"I can see why you're sad," said Tom.

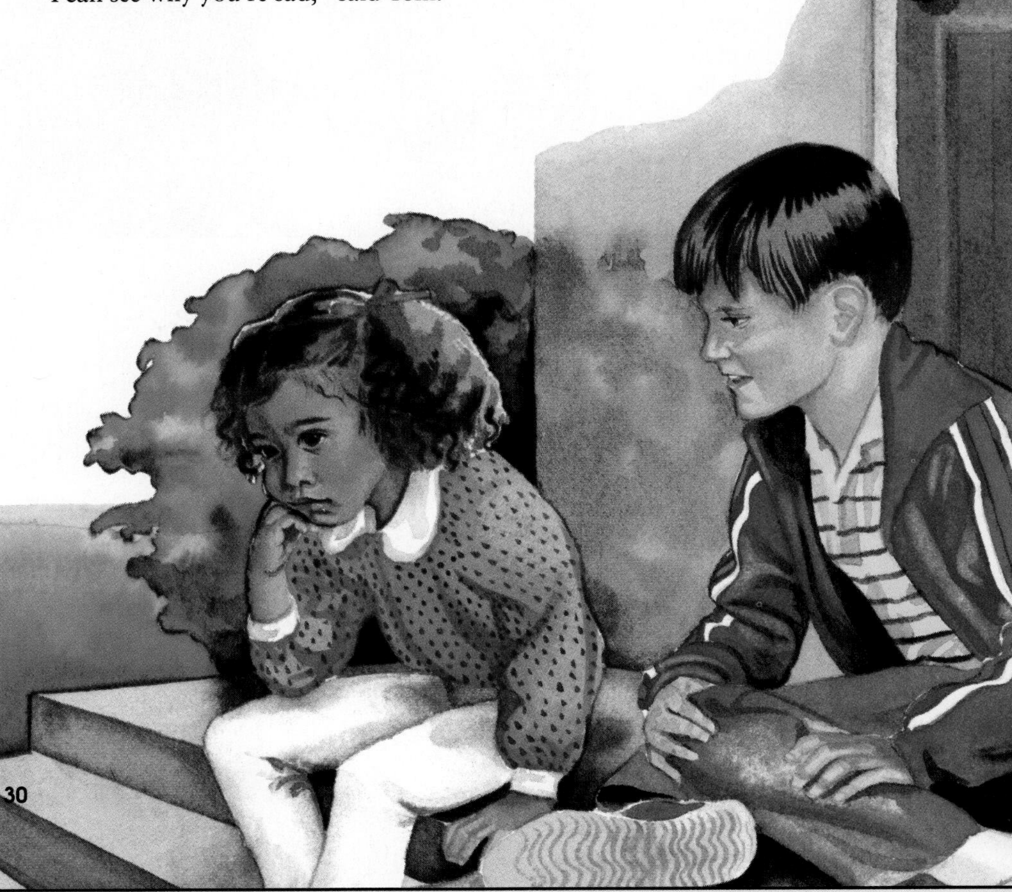

What Is the Lesson?

Be sure the students understand these key ideas:

- It helps to talk over our problems with someone else.
- It is important to take responsibility for our wrong choices.
- We do not need to blame ourselves for things which are truly accidental.

Enrichment Activity

Let the students form small groups to plan short skits depicting what might happen when Patty tells her parents about her day. Encourage the students to include Patty's parents' responses in their skits. Allow as many groups as possible to present their skits to the class.

"Yeah," said Patty, "but that's not the end of it. This morning, I was playing with my mom's hair dryer. I dropped it and cracked the handle. Now the dryer won't work."

When's It Going to End?

"Does your mom know?" asked Tom.

Patty shook her head. "I've been afraid to tell her. She's already mad at me about my grades. Besides, just now, when I went to get something to drink, I spilled a whole gallon of punch all over the inside of the refrigerator. Mom's still trying to clean the sticky mess."

Tom frowned. "You're sure having a bad day!"

Patty nodded in agreement. "I found Chrissy fooling around with my stamp collection. I yelled at her, and I pulled her hair. She cried and ran to dad. And he blamed me for being mean. Now I feel just rotten."

Tom and Patty were quiet for a moment.

Then Tom said, "Patty, I think you should look back over what happened today. Some of the trouble was your fault. You should work that out with your folks. But some of the stuff was an accident. You can forget about that."

Patty started to smile. "You're right!" She headed back in the house. "Thanks," she said. "It sure helps to talk."

Thinking about the Story

- Which actions were Patty's fault? Which were accidents?
- How did Tom help Patty?

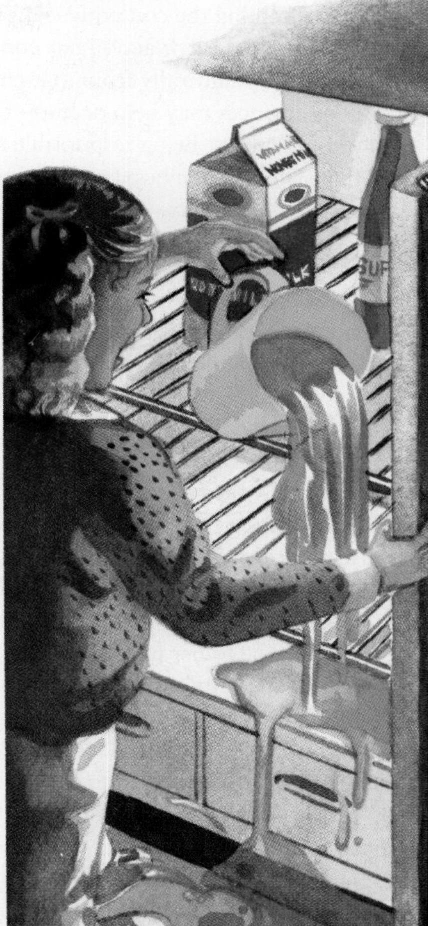

Introduction: We Celebrate

Talking about the Story

About the Story:

1. Did Tom make Patty feel bad about what she had done? Why not?

2. Why did Tom want Patty to think about what she told him?

3. What do you think Patty should do about the trouble she is in with her parents?

About You:

1. Have you ever had an experience like Patty's?

2. Does it help you to talk to someone when you are in trouble?

3. Why is it important to know the difference between accidents or mistakes and sins?

Enrichment Activity

Distribute drawing materials, and let the students make thank you cards or notes for the people who listen to them and help them with their problems, as Tom helped Patty. Encourage the students to deliver their cards.

Development: We Believe

Guidelines for Using the Text

1. Have the students read the first two paragraphs of the text. Ask volunteers for examples of acting responsibly. You might also name several kinds of choices and ask volunteers to list possible consequences.

2. Read the text section entitled Accident, Mistake, or Sin? to the students. After the reading you may ask:

- What are the differences between sinning and making a mistake?
- What are some ways that the Ten Commandments can help you make responsible choices?
- What can you do in your daily life to grow in personal responsibility?

The students are beginning to form their consciences and recognize moral responsibility. Too much emphasis on sin can lead to overly scrupulous attitudes or morbid guilt over mistakes or accidents. However, students must be helped to see that they are responsible for their choices and that they cannot try to shift the blame to others or to outside circumstances. Balance is important here, and the students may tend to shift back and forth between the two extremes at first.

3. Read the text section Confession to the students. Emphasize that it is through Jesus (and His minister, the priest) that we are reconciled to God and the community.

Responsibility

The word **responsible** comes from the same root as "respond." It means "to answer." Being responsible means knowing that there is a difference between right and wrong. It means being answerable for your choices and accepting the consequences.

Every choice or action has **consequences**—things that follow naturally from that choice or action. These consequences may help or hurt you, and they may help or hurt others. Being responsible means choosing actions that will have the best possible consequences, not only for you but for others.

Accident, Mistake, or Sin?

Sometimes, people confuse accidents or mistakes with sin. An *accident* is something that happens without your control. You do not choose to have an accident. Patty did not think: "Gee, I'd like to spill this punch all over the refrigerator."

A *mistake* involves an incorrect choice. You may think you know the right answers to your history test, but you may be incorrect. Mistakes are choices that you make without the right information.

Sin is a choice that you know is wrong, but you make anyway. Patty knew that her grades were bad, but she chose to lie to her parents so that she could watch television. Patty's lie was a sin.

Knowing the difference among accidents, mistakes, and sin is something we all need to know. But that's just the first step. Next comes figuring out how to take responsibility for our actions. Patty realized that she would need to take responsibility in different ways for lying and for hurting her sister, than for the spilling of the punch and the dropping of the hair dryer.

Confession

Jesus wants us to grow in personal responsibility. That is why He has gave us a special gift, to help everyone show sorrow for wrong choices and to learn to make better choices. This gift is the sacrament of Reconciliation.

32

Music Note

You may wish to review the song "Choices," student text page 76. Words and music notation can be found on page 136 in the Catechist's Edition. Use Benziger *Come, Follow Me* Grade 4 music cassette to help make the review enjoyable. You may also play the song during one of the quiet Enrichment Activities as background music.

Enrichment Activity

Have the class meet with the priest in the parish church, to view the Reconciliation room and the confessional. You may wish to have the students prepare questions about Reconciliation in writing ahead of time. As a resource, have the students read the questions on page 72 of their text.

In the sacrament of Reconciliation, you confess your sins to the priest. You admit that you have made wrong choices. This **confession** is usually a conversation. The priest may ask you questions. The priest may help you decide which actions were really sins and which ones were accidents or mistakes. Then the priest may suggest ways for you make better choices in the future.

This part of the sacrament is a lot like Patty's conversation with Tom. The priest is not there to yell at you or to make you feel sad. He is doing for you what Jesus did for His friends—listening, asking questions, and helping you make peace with God. You do not have to be afraid to talk to the priest about anything that is bothering you. Your conversation is private.

In the sacrament of Reconciliation, you accept the blame for your wrong actions. You say that you are sorry and that you are going to do better. These are very important steps in developing a sense of responsibility.

We Catholics Believe

Being **responsible** means to be answerable for the choices you make.

A **consequence** is something that results from a choice or action. The consequences of sin include separation from God and from God's Family. In the case of mortal sin, a person may not receive Jesus in Holy Communion until the sin has been confessed and forgiven in the sacrament of Reconciliation. We believe that a person who dies refusing to ask forgiveness for mortal sin will be separated from God's love forever. The name for this separation is **hell.**

Confession is the act of telling your sins to the priest in the sacrament of Reconciliation.

Messiah is a name for the Savior promised by God. Jesus is the Messiah.

33

DEVELOPMENT: WE BELIEVE

We Catholics Believe

Read through this section with the students, making sure they understand the meaning of the boldfaced terms. If your students have had little formal catechetical background, you may need to provide additional background on the term "hell." Help the students understand that as Christians who believe in God's promise of eternal life, we know that our actions have consequences not only in this world but in the next. Ask the students if they are familiar with the corresponding term for the state of perfect happiness with God: heaven, or the reign of God. What is most important about conveying these sophisticated theological concepts to young children is to avoid giving them the notion that heaven and hell are physical places that can be described. They are, instead, spiritual states, although realizing that has never stopped artists and poets from speculating!

FUN WITH NEW WORDS

Play a game of "Let's Build the Church." Using the chalkboard, or transparency and overhead projector, list the vocabulary words, one at a time, using dashes to stand for each letter in the word. In turn, each student may guess a letter. Write the chosen letter on the appropriate dash. When the letter appears in the word, draw a part of the church building. (Example: the square building, the steeple, the cross.) Once the word is spelled out, encourage the students to provide the definition.

Development: We Believe

Guidelines for Using the Scripture Story

1. Read aloud or retell in your own words the story of the Good Thief, based on Luke 23:33–43. Make sure the students are familiar with the use of the term "Messiah."

2. Ask volunteers to respond to Thinking about Scripture.

3. You may continue discussing the story, using the questions below as a model.

Talking about Scripture

About the Story:

1. Why was Jesus brought to "the Skull"?

2. Who was with Him?

3. How did Jesus know that the first thief was not sorry for his crimes? How did Jesus know that the second thief was sorry for his crimes?

4. What did Jesus promise the second thief?

5. Why do you think Jesus made this promise?

About You:

1. Have you ever asked for forgiveness? How did you feel?

2. What does Jesus' promise mean to you?

The Good Thief

After Jesus was sentenced to die, the soldiers took Him to a place that was nicknamed "the Skull." They crucified Him there, along with two other criminals. One of these criminals was on His right, and the other was on His left.

One of the criminals hanging there was mean to Jesus. "I thought You were the **Messiah,** the One chosen by God to save us," he said. "If so, why don't You save Yourself and us, too?"

The other criminal, however, said to the first criminal, "You have no right to speak to Jesus like that. You and I deserve this punishment. We committed bad crimes. But Jesus does not deserve this. He has done nothing wrong."

Then this criminal said to Jesus, "Remember me, Lord, when You come into Your kingdom."

Jesus knew that the criminal was sorry for his sins. So Jesus said to him, "Amen, I say to you, today you will be with Me in heaven."

(*based on Luke 23:33–43*)

Thinking about Scripture

- Why do you think Jesus forgave the second thief?

What Is the Lesson?

Be sure the students understand these key ideas:

- Jesus forgives all sinners if they are sorry for what they have done and ask forgiveness.
- Confession (admitting that one has done wrong) is an important part of asking forgiveness.

Making Choices

Decide whether each example below is an accident, a mistake, or a sin. On the lines, write an **A** if it is an accident, an **M** if it is a mistake, or an **S** if it is a sin.

_____ **1.** Your marker slips out of your fingers when you are drawing, and you make a mark on the table.
_____ **2.** You hit your brother because he is playing in your room.
_____ **3.** You set your alarm clock for 8:30 instead of 7:30, forgetting that you have an early soccer game.
_____ **4.** Your Mom asks you to take out the trash, but you pretend you didn't hear her.
_____ **5.** While wrestling in fun with a friend, you both fall, and he breaks an arm.
_____ **6.** You want money for ice cream. You take some from your sister's wallet without asking her.
_____ **7.** You take the wrong bus, and you are late for your dentist appointment.
_____ **8.** You lean over, and your glasses fall off and break.

Vocabulary

Write your own definitions for the following words:

Confess ____________________

Consequence ____________________

Responsibility ____________________

35

ENRICHMENT ACTIVITY

Distribute drawing materials and let the students make badges or pendants in the shape of a cross, the sign that Jesus was crucified and that He offers us forgiveness for our sins. The students can write their names on the crosses and decorate them.

APPLICATION: WE LIVE OUR FAITH

Guidelines for Reviewing the Lesson

1. Before assigning the review exercise, go over the definitions of "mistake," "accident," and "sin" with the students, making sure they understand the distinctions.

2. Ask the students to read the directions for the activity and to work independently on marking the statements. Remind them to think carefully before choosing each answer.

3. Discuss the answers in class. There may still be confusion in the students' minds between mistakes and accidents. Remind them that a mistake involves a choice that is not sinful, though it may have unfortunate circumstances. An accident is something which is beyond one's choice or control. Answers: (1) A; (2) S; (3) M; (4) S; (5) A; (6) S; (7) M; (8) A.

4. If you wish, extend this activity by asking volunteers to offer examples of factors that might change each of these situations. For example, Number 4 might be an accident, rather than the sin of disobedience, if a loud noise kept you from hearing your mother.

5. Direct the students to write their definitions for the vocabulary terms. After the students have written their definitions, ask them to use each of these words in a spoken or written sentence.

Application: We Pray

Guidelines for Prayer

1. Gather the students around the prayer space in the room. Invite volunteers to read the leader's part, as well as each of the reader's parts.

2. Sing or play "We Are a Kingdom People." Dismiss the students with the blessing "Go in the peace of Jesus."

Making Choices

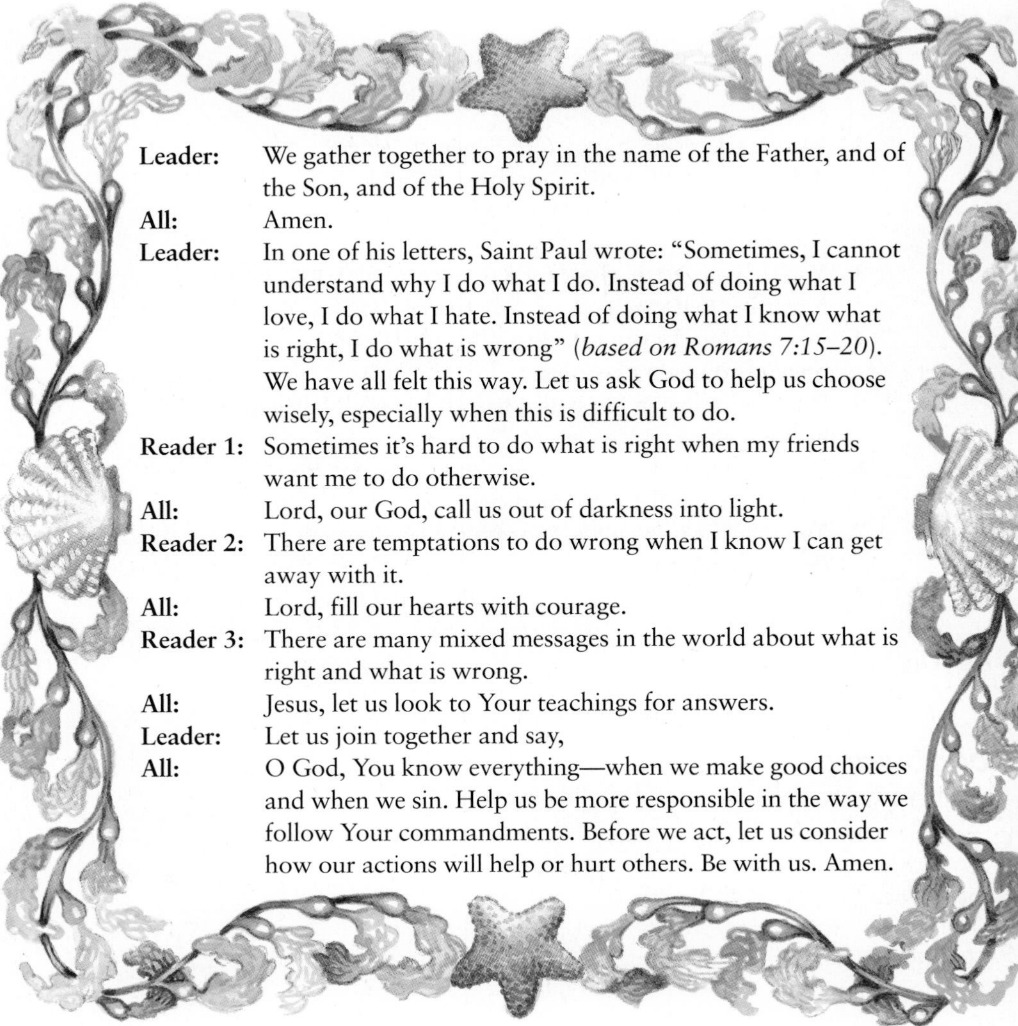

Leader: We gather together to pray in the name of the Father, and of the Son, and of the Holy Spirit.

All: Amen.

Leader: In one of his letters, Saint Paul wrote: "Sometimes, I cannot understand why I do what I do. Instead of doing what I love, I do what I hate. Instead of doing what I know what is right, I do what is wrong" (*based on Romans 7:15–20*). We have all felt this way. Let us ask God to help us choose wisely, especially when this is difficult to do.

Reader 1: Sometimes it's hard to do what is right when my friends want me to do otherwise.

All: Lord, our God, call us out of darkness into light.

Reader 2: There are temptations to do wrong when I know I can get away with it.

All: Lord, fill our hearts with courage.

Reader 3: There are many mixed messages in the world about what is right and what is wrong.

All: Jesus, let us look to Your teachings for answers.

Leader: Let us join together and say,

All: O God, You know everything—when we make good choices and when we sin. Help us be more responsible in the way we follow Your commandments. Before we act, let us consider how our actions will help or hurt others. Be with us. Amen.

Family Note: Lesson 4 focuses on the importance of confession, in everyday life and in the sacrament of Reconciliation. In our daily living, we are expected to take responsibility for our choices, and to consider the consequences of our actions before we make a choice. In the sacrament, we confess our sinful choices and offer to take responsibility to be better.

Family Connection

If the students take the text home, encourage them to pray "Making Choices" together. Point out the Family Note on this page, and ask the students to bring this note to their parents' attention.

5 Being Sorry

Focus

Contrition is an essential ingredient of the sacrament of Reconciliation.

Catechetical Objectives

- To increase the students' awareness of how sin hurts the other members of God's Family.
- To help the students realize that being sorry for sin is a prerequisite to receiving forgiveness.
- To show the students how the Golden Rule can help them be more thoughtful of others.

Lesson Overview

Lesson 5 presents the dynamics of sorrow as the most important attitude necessary for forgiveness:

"Among the penitent's acts contrition occupies first place. Contrition is sorrow of the soul and detestation for the sin committed, together with the resolution not to sin again" *(Catechism of the Catholic Church, #1451).*

INTRODUCTION: WE CELEBRATE

- Contrition is an essential part of the sacrament of Reconciliation. The opening prayer and the story of a boy who needs to say "I'm sorry" introduce this idea.

DEVELOPMENT: WE BELIEVE

- Sin hurts, and God's forgiveness heals. The Scripture story of Peter's denial that he knew Jesus and his subsequent sorrow helps us understand the pain of sin to the sinner.

APPLICATION: WE LIVE OUR FAITH

- A word puzzle brings the students a message of repentance and peace when the puzzle is solved.

APPLICATION: WE PRAY

- The students will answer some questions about broken peace in the family and then write and pray a Family Act of Contrition.

The Church's Wisdom

Here is the theology supporting Lesson 5.

"Every sin in some way affects others. There is no sin, not even the most intimate and secret one, the most strictly individual one, that exclusively concerns the person committing it" *(Reconciliation and Penance, #16).*

Many of us have been part of the following dialogue. "Finish eating your vegetables! There are children starving to death in other parts of the world!" "Send those children my zucchini!" As we continue to mature in our faith, we come to realize that it is not our plate of vegetables that will help the hungry children, but an attitude of sharing. The decisions that we make affect us, and all others. Positive decisions that are helpful, and negative decisions that are hurtful, travel the same route.

God's desire is that we become people for others. God's challenge for us is that we bring forth the reign of God which is a time of peace, justice and love for all. The path toward the reign of God is the Body of Christ, which is the baptized. The way we have to keep growing is Reconciliation, which necessitates humble contrition for all wrong that we commit with intention. We have Creator God, Jesus, and the Holy Spirit—and we have one another.

Catechist Resources

AUDIOVISUAL:

- "The Joyful Struggle to Build a Christian Society" (V/Adult/Two 25 min. segments/Christian Morality and Forgiveness #7/St. Anthony Messenger Press and Franciscan Communications) Part one of this video discusses how to build a more Christian society based on Gospel values. Part two shows our world at the crossroads, and discusses money, justice, and suggestions to become proactive.

BOOK:

- Ferder, Fran. *Words Made Flesh.* (Ave Maria Press) This is a book on human communication that successfully integrates solid scriptural research and reflection with contemporary psychological insights.

Classroom Resources

AUDIOVISUAL:

- "Names of Sin" (V/Intermediate/20 mins./St. Anthony Messenger Press and Franciscan Communications) A young girl is pressured into a deliberately mean act against her elderly, ill neighbor. Overcome by remorse and guilt, the girl needs her mother's help to understand what she has done and what she must do to show she is sorry. This video is also available in Spanish, titled "Los Nombres del Pecado."

BOOK:

- Whelan, Gloria. *That Wild Berries Should Grow: The Story of a Summer.* (Eerdmans Publishers) This uplifting story of a precocious fifth-grade city girl describes the inner transformation that takes place when she spends the summer at her grandparents' country cottage. Elsa manages to overcome her distaste for the peace and quiet of the outdoors and soon finds a wonderful appreciation for the simple life of her relatives, their friends, and the ways of nature.

Before Beginning the Lesson

TO DO:

- Have all the materials necessary for presenting Lesson 5 at hand.
- Check with the catechetical office to be sure that no meetings are scheduled or changed.
- Reproduce the Family Letter, pages 117–118, and send one home to each family.
- Be enthusiastic, and bring your smile along!

TO HAVE ON HAND:

- Student texts
- Writing and drawing materials
- Bible
- Chalk

FOR OPTIONAL ENRICHMENT ACTIVITIES:

- Booklet or folder materials (page 37)
- Benziger *Come, Follow Me* Grade 4 music cassette and cassette player (page 38)
- Index cards or bookmark forms, writing materials, drawing materials, clear contact paper (page 40)
- "Vocabulary Jeopardy" chart, index cards pre-printed with vocabulary words (page 41)

New Words

Look at the wrap on page 41 for a suggestion to introduce new vocabulary words to the students. The vocabulary words are italicized or boldfaced in the student's text. All vocabulary words are also defined in the Glossary pages 69–71.

- **Act of Contrition:** A prayer that expresses sorrow for sin.
- **community:** A group of people who share something in common.
- **contrition:** A feeling of sorrow for sin and the promise to do better.
- **forgiveness:** The act of pardoning someone who hurt you.
- **Golden Rule:** "Do to others whatever you would have them do to you" *(Matthew 7:14)*.
- **humility:** The ability to be honest about oneself.

Catechist Prayer

A moment of quiet reflection just for you.

"Lord, I am not worthy to have You enter under my roof . . . But only say the word, and [my soul] will be healed" *(Luke 7:6–7)*.

God, grant me the gifts of humility and selflessness. Help me teach the children that true strength lies in seeking justice for the sake of peace.

If possible, visit a resident at the convalescent home or hospital, or someone in your neighborhood or parish who is housebound. If you wish, take several of the students with you. Elderly citizens may appreciate visiting with the students. Be sure to get any necessary permission from the parents. Keep in mind that you will receive as much as you bring to the experience or more.

5 Being Sorry

Act of Contrition

Priest: Now, with Jesus, our Brother, we come before our Father in heaven and ask Him to forgive our sins.

Penitent: My God, I am sorry for my sins with all my heart. In choosing to do wrong and failing to do good, I have sinned against You, whom I should love above all things. I firmly intend, with Your help, to do penance, to sin no more, and to avoid whatever leads me to sin. Our Savior Jesus Christ suffered and died for us. In His name, my God, have mercy.

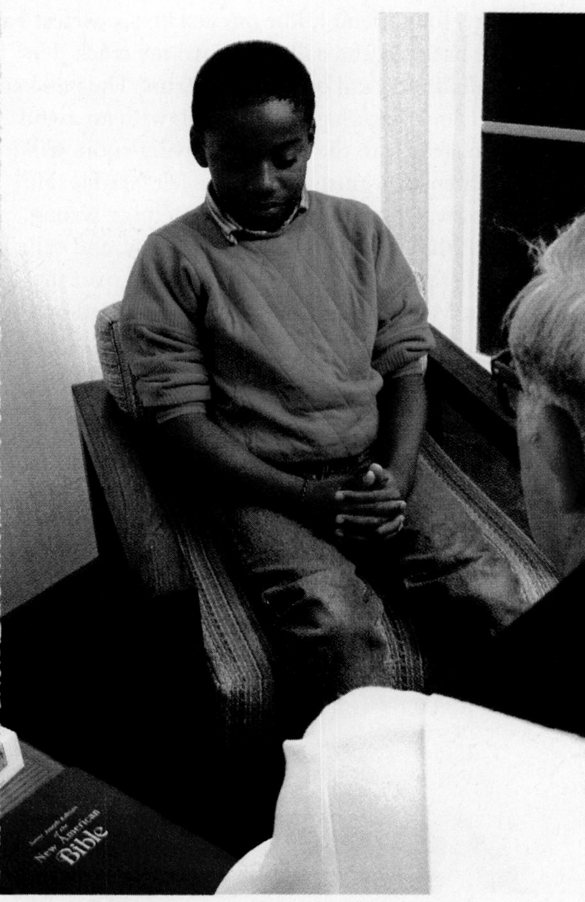

Lesson Plan

INTRODUCTION: WE CELEBRATE

Guidelines for Using the Text

1. Before beginning the reading, ask volunteers to suggest some ways we show we are sorry for having done something wrong. Remind the students that words are one good way to show we are sorry. They may be a spoken apology or a promise to do better.

2. Briefly explain that "contrition" is a word that means "sorrow for sin." An Act of Contrition is a prayer telling God we are sorry, and promising to do better. (These definitions will be expanded upon in the lesson.)

3. Remind the students that the prayer on this page follows our confession, or admission of sin. Read the priest's part aloud, and have the students respond by reading the penitent's prayer.

4. If time allows, have the students turn to page 78 of their texts and review the different forms of the Act of Contrition. Encourage the students to memorize these prayers, or at least the form most commonly used in your diocese.

MY OWN BOOK

If the students are working on "I Celebrate Reconciliation" as an ongoing project, you may have them design a page for the Act of Contrition at this time. Suggest that the students copy the Act of Contrition that will be used at the First Reconciliation and elaborately decorate the borders of the page. You may wish to have the students leave room between the Confession page and this one to insert a page for Receiving a Penance (Lesson 6).

Guidelines for Using the Story

1. Before beginning the reading, let volunteers share examples of times when it was difficult for them to apologize.

2. Read aloud (or choose several good readers to read) the story on these two pages. If time permits, you may wish to pause in the reading at the point on page 39 when Joe asks, "What can I do to get out of this?" Have the students close their books and suggest possible courses of action for Joe. Then, return to the story to see how it comes out.

3. Distribute writing materials, and ask the students to respond briefly in writing to Thinking about the Story. Allow time for students to share their answers.

4. You may continue discussing the story, using the questions on page 39 as a model.

Making Peace

Joe loved to play baseball. He played at school and on an after-school team. He also played at home, even though there wasn't a lot of room in his backyard. Joe had been told over and over again not to play in the yard. But he did anyway.

One day, Joe's friend Eddie pitched him a perfect ball. Joe felt the bat meet the ball. He heard the crack. He saw the ball lift and sail out—a home run! The ball kept flying, over Joe's back fence. And then, with an awful crash, it smashed into the Mitchells' living-room window.

The excitement vanished, and Joe felt terrible. He knew right away that he had done something wrong.

Mr. and Mrs. Mitchell were really angry, and called Joe's parents to complain. "There's glass all over the living room!" Mr. Mitchell said. "And our cat jumped out through the broken window and ran away!"

MUSIC NOTE

You may wish to teach the song "Your Way, O God," student text page 76. Words and music notation can be found on page 137 in the Catechist's Edition. Use Benziger *Come, Follow Me* Grade 4 music cassette to help make the learning fun for all.

ENRICHMENT ACTIVITY

Distribute drawing materials to the students. Have the students use the top half of their papers to draw pictures of boys or girls their own age doing something to make peace after they have done something wrong. Then, ask the students to use the bottom half of the paper to write a short story about what happened. Have the students share their pictures and stories.

Making Good Again

Joe sat down with his parents. He felt like crying. "What can I do to get out of this?" Joe asked.

"You need to make peace with the Mitchells," Joe's dad answered.

"I really am sorry," Joe said.

"Show the Mitchells that you're sorry," Joe's mom added.

"How do I do that?" Joe asked.

"You can tell them you'll be more careful in the future," his mom said. "You can keep your promise not to play baseball in the yard."

"There's still the broken window," Joe's dad said.

"And the cat," Joe added, sighing. "I guess I should try to make up for the damage I did. Making peace is hard work!"

"Sometimes it is," his dad agreed. "But we've all had to do it at one time or another."

Joe took his parents' advice. He went out right away and looked around the yard. He found the Mitchells' cat curled up under the Barkleys' car. Joe coaxed the cat into his arms and walked nervously over to the Mitchells' house.

"I'm really sorry," Joe told Mr. and Mrs. Mitchell. "I promise it won't happen again. And I'll save the money I get for my paper route to pay for a new window."

Mr. and Mrs. Mitchell understood. They told Joe that they forgave him. Mr. Mitchell even offered to help Joe with his batting practice—at the park!

Thinking about the Story

- Why was the broken window not an accident?
- What did Joe do to make peace with the Mitchells?

Talking about the Story

About the Story:

1. What was the first thing Joe's parents told him he had to do to get out of the trouble?

2. What was the second thing?

3. What does it mean to make peace?

4. Should Joe have apologized to the Mitchells even if breaking the window was an accident? Why or why not?

About You:

1. What have you done to show someone you were sorry about something?

2. How do you feel after you have apologized?

WHAT IS THE LESSON?

Be sure the students understand these key ideas:

- When we have done something wrong, it is important to make peace.
- Sometimes feeling sorry is not enough to make peace. Special words or actions are also needed.

ENRICHMENT ACTIVITY

If you did not do so during the course of the reading, you may wish to have the students form small groups to role-play alternative endings to the story. What are some other courses of action Joe might have taken? What if he refused to apologize? What if the Mitchells refused to accept Joe's apology?

Guidelines for Using the Text

1. Read the first three paragraphs of the text to the students. Write the term "selfish" on the chalkboard, making sure the students understand how this term is used in the text. Ask, "Why is selfishness often a cause of sin?"

2. Next, write the word "peace" on the chalkboard, and ask volunteers to define it. Continue reading the text section, Disturbing the Peace.

3. Read aloud the text section Making Peace. This material is critical to the students' understanding of the sacrament of Reconciliation. Offer as much time as necessary for questions and clarifications.

Asking for Forgiveness

Sin is a kind of selfishness. When we are selfish, we think only about ourselves. We know what we want, and we want it right now. We don't think about how our actions may hurt us, or hurt others. Or, we simply don't care.

Joe was being selfish when he disobeyed his parents and played baseball in the yard. He didn't think about what would happen if he disobeyed. He didn't wonder how his actions might affect his neighbors.

Every time we choose sin, we become less sensitive—less aware and caring—of others. We build a kind of wall of selfishness between ourselves and others, and between ourselves and God's love. That wall disturbs the peace. That is what Joe learned.

Disturbing the Peace

The word peace has many meanings. There is the type of inner peace that comes when a person feels a sense of well-being or security. There is another type of peace in which two enemies settle their conflicts without using any weapons. There is a third type of peace that results when a person has a good relationship with God.

Sin hurts all these kinds of peace. **Forgiveness** is the way to make peace again. Forgiveness begins with the desire to be forgiven. It has to be asked for. That's why saying "I am sorry" is so important. To say "I'm sorry" is to say "I was wrong. Please forgive me." It also means "I really do care. I want us to be at peace again."

To admit to being wrong takes a certain amount of **humility**—the ability to be honest. Being humble is not always easy. That is why Jesus helps the members of God's Family through the sacrament of Reconciliation.

ENRICHMENT ACTIVITY

Distribute small cards or bookmark forms and have the students choose an Act of Contrition from page 78 to print onto the cards and decorate. Have the students take their cards or bookmarks home to use as reminders while preparing to celebrate their First Reconciliation.

ENRICHMENT ACTIVITY

Distribute drawing materials and have the students illustrate the idea of peace. You may wish to play some quiet instrumental music as a background for this activity. Display the students' artwork in the classroom, perhaps on a bulletin board entitled "Peace Has Many Faces."

Making Peace

In the sacrament of Reconciliation, the priest, who stands for Jesus and for the Christian **community**, welcomes you with kindness. He shares a story of God's forgiveness from the Bible. Then, you talk to the priest about the sins you have committed. You say that you are sorry for your sins. Before God and before the priest, you say "I am sorry" in an **Act of Contrition**. You promise to try not to sin again. Once you have said "I am sorry," you are on your way to being forgiven.

Learning to be thoughtful of others is a way to keep the promise to be better. Jesus shows us how in these words: "Do to others whatever you would have them do to you." We call this way of living the **Golden Rule**.

We Catholics Believe

Forgiveness is the act of pardoning someone who hurt you.

Humility is the ability to be honest about yourself and to accept your good points and bad points. Humble people can admit when they are wrong. They have the courage to say "I'm sorry."

A group of people who share something in common is called a **community**. The Church is a community because its members believe in and follow Jesus.

Contrition is sorrow for sin and the promise to do better. In the sacrament of Reconciliation, you say you are sorry by praying an **Act of Contrition**.

Around two hundred years age, people gave the **Golden Rule** its name because it is so precious.

DEVELOPMENT: WE BELIEVE

We Catholics Believe

Read aloud We Catholics Believe. Ask volunteers to name some members of the various communities they belong to who are humble. These may include family, school, parish, or church members. You might also ask students if they can name people (historical or fictional characters) who are noted for their humility. If students have a difficult time, spend a few moments discussing the reason why often popular heroes of TV and movies are not depicted as humble. How has humility gotten such a bad name? Help the students understand that humility should not be confused with passivity or "wimpiness."

FUN WITH NEW WORDS

Play a game of "Vocabulary Jeopardy" to challenge the students. Prepare a chart of twenty-five squares from which the players can select a vocabulary word. Across the top of the chart, label five columns Lesson 1, Lesson 2, Lesson 5 in the center, Lesson 3, and Lesson 4. Number the squares in each column from one to five. Print the vocabulary words from each of the lessons on the columns in the chart. Each student selects a lesson and a number. The vocabulary word is read, and the student recites the definition as a question. Play until all the words are defined and each student has had at least one turn.

Development: We Believe

Guidelines for Using the Scripture Story

1. Read aloud (or retell in your own words) the story of Peter's denial, from John 18:15, 25–27.

2. After the reading, allow time for comments and responses to Thinking about Scripture.

3. You may continue discussing the story using the questions below as a model.

Talking about Scripture

About the Story:

1. When Jesus said that Peter would deny him three times, what was Peter's response?

2. What did Peter do when he was asked about Jesus?

3. Why do you think Peter wept?

About You:

1. Have you ever hurt a friend or a family member because you were afraid?

2. How did you make up with that person?

Peter's Denial

On the night before He died, Jesus ate supper with His friends. "Tonight, your faith in Me will be shaken," He told them.

Peter refused to believe it. "Mine will never be," he claimed.

But Jesus knew better. "I say to you, this very night before the rooster crows, you will deny Me three times."

"Lord," Peter protested, "you know I would rather die than deny You!"

That night, soldiers arrested Jesus and took him to the court of the high priest. Peter was very afraid, but he followed them to the courtyard.

He was sitting by the fire when one of the maids came over to him. "You were with Jesus," she said to him.

"I don't know what you are talking about!" Peter answered.

Another girl recognized him. "You were with Jesus," she said.

Again Peter denied it. "I do not even know the man," he lied.

A little later, a crowd of people came over and said to Peter, "Surely, you are one of the followers of Jesus. You even talk like His friends."

Peter began to curse and swear. "I do not know the man!" he insisted.

Just then, a rooster began to crow. And Peter remembered the words Jesus had spoken. Peter was very sorry for what he had done. He went out of the courtyard and began to cry. In his heart, he asked Jesus to forgive him.

(*based on John 18:15–18, 25–27*)

Thinking about Scripture

- Why do you think Peter pretended he didn't know Jesus?

What Is the Lesson?

Be sure the students understand these key ideas:

- Like Peter, we may swear we will never do anything wrong, but everyone is tempted to sin.
- No matter how much we think we have hurt someone, we can be sorry and ask for forgiveness.

Enrichment Activity

Distribute writing materials, and have the students compose brief prayers asking Jesus' help in times when they are tempted.

Peace Puzzle

There are many words that have to do with repentance. Complete each sentence with the correct word. Write the word in the numbered spaces. What message do you read in the boxes?

1. When we __________, we hurt the peace between ourselves and God, and between ourselves and others.
2. Mr. and Mrs. Mitchell were __________ because Joe broke their window.
3. Joe needed to ______ ______ with Mr. and Mrs. Mitchell.
4. We are __________ when we think only about ourselves, and not about others.
5. __________ is the attitude of being sorry for sin.
6. "Do to others whatever you would have them do to you" is the Golden ______.
7. "I am sorry" is a way to ask someone to __________ you for what you did wrong.
8. "I am sorry" also means "I will ______ to do better."

1. _ _ _
2. _ _ _ _ _
3. _ _ _ _   _ _ _ _ _
4. _ _ _ _ _ _ _
5. _ _ _ _ _ _ _ _ _ _
6. _ _ _ _
7. _ _ _ _ _ _ _
8. _ _ _

Vocabulary

Write your own definitions for the following words:

Peace ____

Humility ____

APPLICATION: WE LIVE OUR FAITH

Guidelines for Reviewing the Lesson

1. Have the students read the directions for the puzzle section of the Review. Make sure they understand that they are to find the correct word that goes in each blank and transfer that word to the numbered spaces. If you feel the students will need help, you can print a Word Bank on the chalkboard in the following order: forgive, sin, make peace, angry, try, selfish, rule, contrition. Remind the students that they can use this Word Bank for hints to solve the puzzle.

2. Have the students work independently on the puzzle activity. When all the students have completed the exercise, ask how many have found the secret message. Students can point it out to any who might have missed it. Answers: (1) sin; (2) angry; (3) make peace; (4) selfish; (5) contrition; (6) Rule; (7) forgive; (8) try. Secret message: I am sorry.

3. Have the students complete the definitions for peace and humility at the bottom of the puzzle activity.

ENRICHMENT ACTIVITY

Read or retell the story of the next time Peter meets Jesus (John 21:15–17). Explain to the students that this conversation took place after Jesus rose from the dead. Discuss how Peter must have felt and what Jesus' words to him meant. Ask the students if they believe that Jesus forgave Peter.

Application: We Pray

Guidelines for Prayer

1. If the students will not be taking their texts home, you may adapt this page for classroom use. Distribute writing or drawing materials and have the students work independently to draw or write their answers to the three questions on this page. Encourage the students to take their completed work home to share with family members.

2. Have the students work in small groups to compose their own Act of Contrition. Students should copy their group's prayer into the space on this page.

3. If students have written individual prayers as an enrichment activity for this lesson, close the lesson by inviting volunteers to pray their prayers aloud. Or, groups may pray the Acts of Contrition they composed in class. Close your prayer by playing or singing together "Your Way, O God."

Showing Contrition

Find a time when the members of your family can meet together. Then ask each person to write or tell answers to the following questions:

What was one time when I was not
at peace with another family member?
What happened to restore the peace?
What is one way I have been forgiven?

Then, in the space below, write your own Family Act of Contrition. Ask God to help you forgive one another. You can pray your prayer together.

Family Note: Lesson 5 stresses contrition as an important part of the sacrament of Reconciliation, as well as a necessary part of everyday living. Help your child see the importance of being sorry for wrong choices. Model forgiveness in your home. To write the Family Act of Contrition, you may wish to refer to the prayers found on page 78.

Family Connection

If possible, the students may take their texts home to work with their families on this activity. Point out the Family Note on this page, and ask the students to bring this note to their parents' attention. Send one Family Letter home to each family.

6 Changing Your Life

Focus

We receive a penance in the sacrament of Reconciliation.

Catechetical Objectives

- To define conversion as a turning away from sin and a sincere attempt to do better.
- To explain that doing penance shows that we want to repair the damage we have done by our wrong choices.
- To teach that prayer is an important source of strength in the lifelong process of conversion.

Lesson Overview

Lesson 6 focuses on the necessity to make amends:

"Many sins wrong our neighbor. One must do what is possible in order to repair the harm (e.g., return stolen goods, restore the reputation of someone slandered, pay compensation for injuries). Simple justice requires as much. But sin also injures and weakens the sinner" *(Catechism of the Catholic Church, #1459).*

INTRODUCTION: WE CELEBRATE

- Receiving a penance in the sacrament of Reconciliation is another wonderful gift. The story of a little girl who works to change her ways shows how penance can bring us to peace.

DEVELOPMENT: WE BELIEVE

- Accepting a penance means we are ready to change and make better choices. The Scripture story of "The Woman Who Changed" can help us understand the meaning of conversion, of turning toward God's love and forgiveness.

APPLICATION: WE LIVE OUR FAITH

- The students determine ways to make up for wrong choices.

APPLICATION: WE PRAY

- A prayer service celebrating forgiveness brings the students together to express sorrow for sin and to show a willingness to forgive others for the wrong choices they may have made.

The Church's Wisdom

Here is the theology supporting Lesson 6.

"Penance means 'the inmost change of heart under the influence of the Word of God and in the perspective of the Kingdom' *(Matthew 4:17).* But penance also means changing one's life in harmony with the change of heart . . . It is one's whole existence that becomes penitential, that is to say, directed toward a continuous striving for what is better. Doing penance is something authentic and effective only if it is translated into deeds and acts of penance" *(Reconciliation and Penance, #4).*

The church's understanding of penance is that of action rather than of private remorse. If a child is hungry, food will satisfy the hunger more quickly than prayer. Once the child has eaten, pray a prayer of thanksgiving for the gift of the meal.

God's desire for humankind is to be in union with Jesus, through the Holy Spirit for the glory of God. God does not require anything less than love from all creatures. God calls us all to be family together. Penance is a positive restoration of any unloving act.

Penance is also a response to the Holy Spirit, who dwells within us and leads us to conversion of heart. It is never a "once and for all" occasion. Conversion is the journey of life, which is total gift from God, toward perfect union with God. We are truly pilgrim people.

Catechist Resources

AUDIOVISUAL:

- "Loving Your Neighbor as Yourself" (V/Adults/Two 25 min. segments/Christian Morality and Forgiveness #5/St. Anthony Messenger Press and Franciscan Communications) Part one of this video presents family morality in the home, as a place of sin and healing. Part two looks out of the home and discusses who our neighbor is and what responsibility we have toward our neighbor.

BOOK:

- Rohr, Richard. *Radical Grace.* (St. Anthony Messenger Press) This book is a collection of 408 daily meditations which follow the liturgical cycle. The author challenges readers to hear the gospel in a new way and to respond in a new way.

Classroom Resources

AUDIOVISUAL:

- "The Hoarder" (V/Intermediate/8 mins./Benchmark Films) This fable tells the story of a greedy blue-jay. In his secret hideaway he hoards whatever his eyes behold and his beak can carry. Not even the sun escapes his greed, but not without consequences. Finally, the bird is made to see the error of his ways. The video is stylized cut-out animation.

BOOK:

- Peters, Russell M. *Clambake, A Wampanoag Tradition.* (Lerner Publications Company) This nonfiction book is full of information about the Wampanoag people of Massachusetts and one of their special ceremonies, the "appanaug," or clambake. This is a very spiritual book, and describes a feast that begins with prayer and thanksgiving for the gifts of life.

Before Beginning the Lesson

TO DO:

- Be prepared with all the materials necessary to present Lesson 6.
- Resolve any problems with certificates, scheduling, student readiness, and the like.

TO HAVE ON HAND:

- Student texts
- Writing and drawing materials
- Bibles or New Testaments
- Chalk

FOR OPTIONAL ENRICHMENT ACTIVITIES:

- Booklet or folder materials, magazine pictures, paste or glue, fine tip markers (page 45)
- Poster materials, fine tip markers (page 47)
- Benziger *Come, Follow Me* Grade 4 music cassette and cassette player (page 48)
- Blank audio tape, cassette player/recorder (page 49)
- Light colored construction paper crosses or flowers, writing materials, yarn, jar, bulletin board (page 51)

New Words

Look at the wrap on page 49 for a suggestion to introduce new vocabulary words to the students. The vocabulary words are italicized or boldfaced in the student's text. All vocabulary words are also defined in the Glossary pages 69–71.

- **conversion:** Making a change for the better and turning toward God's love and forgiveness.
- **penance:** An action that is done in order to show sorrow and a willingness to change.
- **prayer:** Words or actions that share our love for God.
- **repent:** To feel sorry for sin; to change one's life.
- **Works of Mercy:** Actions that serve others physically and spiritually.

Catechist Prayer

A moment of quiet reflection just for you.

"Behold, half of my possessions, Lord, I shall give to the poor, and if I have extorted anything from anyone, I shall repay it four times over" *(Luke 18:8).*

Gracious God, Who would never give a stone when it is bread we need, help me teach the students the joy of penance done willingly out of love. Bless me with patience with the students, as You are patient with me. Amen.

Half of giving is receiving. You give so generously of your time. If you wish, ask for a gift of time for yourself. Perhaps time to sit quietly in the yard, to take a stroll on the beach, work on a hobby, or to meander through the grocery store without a list is what you'd like. Ask, and receive joyfully!

Changing Your Life

Receiving A Penance

Priest: Have you confessed all your sins?

Penitent: Yes.

Priest: Will you try to change what you were doing wrong?

Penitent: Yes.

Priest: For your penance, then, I ask that you say a prayer (or do something to make up for your wrong choices). This will help you to make peace and to grow as a follower of Jesus.

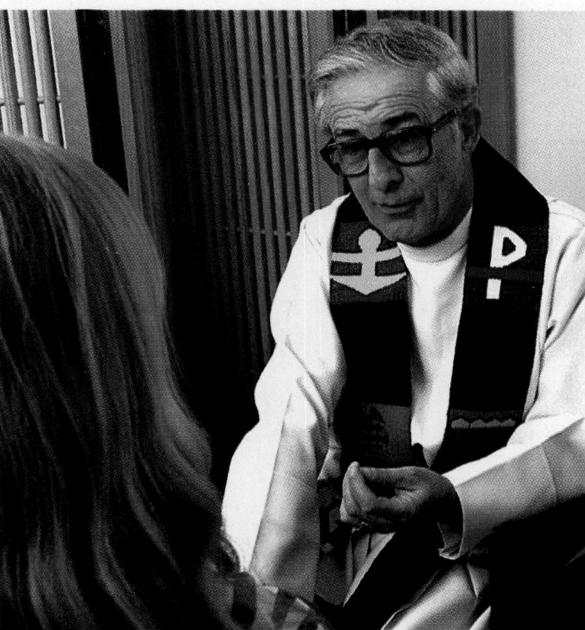

45

Lesson Plan

INTRODUCTION: WE CELEBRATE

Guidelines for Using the Text

In the actual order of the rite, the giving of the penance precedes the Act of Contrition, which was treated in the last lesson. The lessons appear in this sequence in the text because it is easier for the students to comprehend the motivation for doing penance when they understand contrition.

1. Before beginning the reading, you may give the students a brief definition of the term penance as it is used in the Rite of Reconciliation. A penance is a prayer or action assigned by the priest which helps us make up for what we have done wrong and learn to follow Jesus more closely.

2. Read aloud the text on this page. You might tell the students that this part of the rite of Reconciliation is a kind of conversation; the priest uses his own words. The words on this page are just one example of how the priest might explain the penance.

3. Allow time after the reading to discuss any questions or comments the students might have about this part of the rite. Keep this conversation brief, as the idea of penance will be more fully explored later in the lesson.

MY OWN BOOK

If the students are working on "I Celebrate Reconciliation" as an ongoing project, you may have them design a page for Receiving a Penance at this time. Suggest that the students title this page "Receiving A Penance." Provide preselected magazine pictures of helping activities, such as raking leaves, people embracing, or reading to a child or household tasks. The students may select the picture that best describes an act of penance to them. Suggest that the students print "This will help you make peace and grow as a follower of Jesus." If the students will not be confused, you may have them insert this page before the page on the Act of Contrition in order to more accurately follow the order of the rite.

Guidelines for Using the Story

1. Have the students read the story on these two pages.

2. When the students have completed the reading, ask volunteers to respond to the two Thinking about the Story questions.

3. You may continue discussing the story using the questions on page 47 as a model.

Changing

Jody Phillips had a problem. Every time she got angry, she would yell at her younger sister, Anne. Sometimes, she would even hit Anne.

Mrs. Phillips didn't like the situation. One day, Mrs. Phillips sent Jody to her room. "Stay there," Jody's mom said, "until you're ready to live in peace with Anne."

"Mom," Jody asked, "can't I just say I'm sorry to Anne?"

"Saying you're sorry is the first step," her mother replied. "If you say you're sorry now, and then tomorrow you start yelling and hitting again, you haven't changed anything. I think you need some time out to come up with a better way to treat your sister."

Jody sat staring out the window. She thought about what her mother had said. It would be a lot easier just to tell Anne she was sorry. Changing was hard.

WHAT IS THE LESSON?

Be sure the students understand these key ideas:

- Achieving peace and reconciliation involves changes in behavior.
- We can learn new, positive ways to deal with problems.
- Change is not easy, but we have choices about our behavior.

ENRICHMENT ACTIVITY

Distribute writing materials. Ask each student to think of one bad habit or wrong choice that he or she would like to change. Have the students make lists, like Jody's, of alternative ways to behave. Assure the students that these lists are private. Encourage them to keep their lists to look over later.

The Next Step

Jody got a sheet of paper and a pencil from her desk. She thought for a long time. Then, she made a list of all the things she could do when she got angry. And even though she knew it would be difficult, Jody left yelling and hitting off her list.

Mrs. Phillips smiled and gave her a hug when Jody showed her the list. "This is a good start," she said. "We'll all try to help you."

Jody told Anne she was sorry. She promised to try very hard not to take her anger out on Anne. Jody even played a game with Anne, without quarreling.

The next day, Jody came home from school in a bad mood. Her bus was late. She had extra homework. And then she saw that someone had taken the last chocolate chip cookie from the jar. Jody ran to her room and slammed her books down.

Anne was waiting. She had game pieces spread out all over Jody's room. And she had the last cookie in her hand. Anne took one look at Jody's angry face, and then, she ran.

Without thinking, Jody started to yell. She turned to run after Anne. Then, Jody's eyes fell on the list she had made. She took a deep breath. She took a pillow from her bed and began to punch it over and over.

Soon, she began to feel silly, and started to laugh. Jody wasn't angry any more. She even felt proud that she had begun to change her ways.

"Anne," Jody called. "I've got time for one quick game."

"I saved you half a cookie," Anne said, coming back. Jody laughed and hugged her little sister. Changing wasn't easy—but for now, it felt very good.

Thinking about the Story

- Why did Jody have to do more than just say she was sorry?
- How did Jody prove she was really sorry for what she had done to Anne?

INTRODUCTION: WE CELEBRATE

Talking about the Story

About the Story:

1. What behavior did Jody need to change?

2. What did her mother do about Jody's behavior?

3. What did Mrs. Phillips say was the first step for reaching peace and reconciliation?

4. What did she say the next step was?

About You:

1. Do you think everyone has behavior that needs to change?

2. When you get angry, what are some good ways you can deal with your anger?

ENRICHMENT ACTIVITY

Distribute poster materials. Have the students work in small groups to design posters listing the steps in making a change for the better. You may wish to list the steps on the chalkboard, as follows:

- Say "I'm Sorry."
- Think about what you have done wrong.
- Find a way to do better.
- Practice better ways to act!

Groups can decorate or illustrate their posters. Display the finished artwork in the classroom.

Development: We Believe

Guidelines for Using the Text

1. Read the first two paragraphs of the text to the students. Write the term "conversion" on the chalkboard and ask volunteers to define it in their own words.

2. Then, read the text section Doing Penance to the students. Go through this material carefully, making sure the students understand the several functions of doing penance. Also, be sure the students clearly understand that the penance is to be carried out as soon as possible after receiving the sacrament.

3. Read the text section Always Growing to the students. After the reading, ask the students to close their books. Ask volunteers to name some of the helps they have been given to live a good Christian life. List these on the chalkboard as they are offered.

Conversion

Jesus began His teaching with this message: "Reform your lives. Turn away from sin. Try to be better." This is a message that members of God's Family still need to hear. It is a message of change, a message of **conversion.** Whenever we choose to do wrong, we need to change, or reform, our lives. Like Jody Phillips, we need to try to act in better ways.

Contrition is only the first step we take. We want to show we are truly sorry and want to do better. And so we choose to prove this.

Doing Penance

This is what receiving a **penance** in the sacrament of Reconciliation is all about. The penance is an outward sign that you want to **repent,** or make up for any hurt you have caused. It is an outward sign that you want to change and to make better choices. The penance can even be a way to practice making better choices.

After you have confessed your sins to the priest, he will give you a penance to do. He may ask you to say several prayers, asking God to help you change the way you act. Sometimes, your penance may be to do something for someone who has been hurt by your actions. For example, if you have been fighting with your brother, the priest may ask you to spend some time playing with your brother peacefully, or helping with his chores. Or the priest may tell you to do one of the **Works of Mercy** as a penance. The Works of Mercy are ways that the followers of Jesus show they care for one another. You can find a list of these helping actions on page 78 of this book.

Enrichment Activity

The Works of Mercy are listed on page 79 of the student book. If time allows, you may wish to review this list with the class, asking volunteers to give examples of how each work of mercy might be practically carried out by young people.

Music Note

You may wish to review the song "Your Way, O God," student text page 76. Words and music notation can be found on page 137 in the Catechist's Edition. Use Benziger *Come, Follow Me* Grade 4 music cassette to reinforce the review. You may wish to play the song during one of the quiet Enrichment Activities.

It is important to remember that penance is not magic. It doesn't make a person never do wrong again. Real change, real conversion, is a life-long process. It takes time and continual work.

Always Growing

Conversion means growing to be as much like Jesus as we can. That's a big responsibility. But we're not alone.

We have the Ten Commandments, the Great Commandment, and the example of Jesus to follow. We have the sacraments to give us strength. And we have the other members of God's Family to help us.

We also have **prayer.** Whenever and wherever we wish, we can talk to God, knowing that God listens and will give us what we need to grow and change.

We Catholics Believe

Conversion is making a change for the better in the way you think, choose, and act. Conversion is turning toward God's love and forgiveness.

Penance is something you agree to do to show that you are willing to make peace and to change your life. It is also a step in Reconciliation.

To **repent** is to feel sorry for your sins and to want to change to be better.

The **Works of Mercy** are actions that serve others physically or spiritually.

Prayer is words or actions that share our love for God. Four kinds of prayer are praise, thanksgiving, petition, and sorrow for sin. We can also pray to Mary and the saints.

Development: We Believe

We Catholics Believe

Ask five different students to read aloud the five paragraphs of this text. Pause after each paragraph for questions or clarifications.

Encourage students to add to the list of helps on the chalkboard using the vocabulary words from We Catholics Believe.

Fun with New Words

Try "News Anchor" for a change of pace. You are the news program director. Using a cassette player/recorder to record the activity, proceed as follows. The director excitedly reads a definition from the vocabulary list found on the Lesson 6 Background pages. The first volunteer to correctly respond with the vocabulary word that matches the definition is allowed to "report" the word and definition into the recorder. Continue play until everyone has had an opportunity to "report." If time permits, play the cassette tape back to the students.

Development: We Believe

Guidelines for Using the Scripture Story

1. Before beginning the reading, ask for student response to this question: "How can you tell whether someone is willing to change his or her actions for the better?" Look for specific examples.

2. Read (or retell in your own words) the story of the Woman Who Changed, based on Luke 7:36–50. By way of explanation, you may want to tell the students that washing the feet of a guest was a typical sign of care and hospitality in Jesus' time.

3. Ask volunteers to respond to the Thinking about Scripture question. You may continue discussing the story using the questions below as a model.

Talking about Scripture

About the Story:

1. Why was Simon angry at the woman? What did he think Jesus should do?

2. What did Jesus mean when He said that the woman's life was saved?

About You:

1. How do you feel when you get a second chance at something?

2. How can showing real love help you follow Jesus?

The Woman Who Changed

Once, Jesus was invited to have supper with one of the teachers of the Law. Just as they were getting ready to eat, a woman pushed her way into the room. She was carrying a jar of perfumed ointment.

The woman threw herself down in front of Jesus and began to weep. She washed His feet with her tears, and dried them with her long hair. She poured the precious ointment on Jesus' feet. Then, she knelt quietly.

Simon, the teacher, was outraged. He recognized the woman. The whole town knew her as a sinner. Surely, if Jesus knew anything at all, Simon thought to himself, He would not let this bad woman touch Him!

Jesus knew what Simon was thinking. "Don't be so quick to condemn this woman," Jesus told Simon. "She has shown by her love and care for Me that she is sorry for her past and is trying to change her life. Simon, that is the best sign of reconciliation: love."

Jesus turned to the woman. "Your sins are forgiven," He told her gently. "Go now, and live in peace."

(*based on Luke 7:36–50*)

Thinking about Scripture

- How could Jesus tell that the woman was willing to change her life?

What Is the Lesson?

Be sure the students understand these key ideas:

- Doing penance by caring and helping is a way to thank God for forgiveness.
- We should not judge or condemn others, but encourage them to follow Jesus.

Choosing to Change

Imagine that the sentences below describe you and a choice you made. For each, write an action you could do that shows you want to do better.

1. The last time you went to the grocery store, you put some gum in your pocket without paying for it.

____

____

2. Along with everyone else, you've ignored the new girl in class.

____

____

3. Math is confusing, so you count on Tony to give you homework answers.

____

____

4. You blamed your younger brother for doing something you actually did.

____

____

5. Everyone teases Beth, so you do, too.

____

____

6. Your Grandma calls you on the phone every Sunday, but you never feel like talking to her.

____

____

Vocabulary

Write your own definitions for the following words:

Prayer ______________________________

Penance ______________________________

APPLICATION: WE LIVE OUR FAITH

Guidelines for Reviewing the Lesson

1. Read the directions for the Choosing to Change activity on this page.
2. Tell the students to think quietly and carefully before writing what action they would choose to show that they want to do better.
3. Have the students form small groups to share their answers.
4. If time allows, students may remain in small groups to think of other choice-making situations. Groups may tell about or role-play their situations and let other students suggest appropriate choices.

Vocabulary

Have the students read the directions for this section and work independently on writing their definitions. Be sure they understand that they are to write the definitions in their own words, not the words from the text.

ENRICHMENT ACTIVITY

Have the students form small groups to brainstorm ideas for simple actions that will help them follow Jesus more closely. Distribute small pieces of paper (these might be crosses or flowers cut from construction paper). Ask the students to write one idea on each piece of paper. Collect these, and place them in a jar or pin them to a bulletin board inside a cross-shaped outline made of yarn. As an ongoing activity, encourage students to choose one idea from the jar or bulletin board of each session and share how they have carried out the idea.

Guidelines for Prayer

1. First look over the prayer "Celebrating Forgiveness" and provide the proper pronunciation of the response "Kyrie eleison, Christe eleison, Kyrie eleison." Then, ask for three volunteers to read the appropriate parts of the litany.

2. Gather the students around the prayer table if one is available or in an open space. Lead the "Celebrating Forgiveness" prayer. If you wish, play the song "Your Way, O God" and join in the singing.

Celebrating Forgiveness

Leader: Let us gather together in the name of the Father, and of the Son, and of the Holy Spirit.

All: Amen.

Leader: We are here to ask for God's forgiveness for the wrong choices we've made and the times we have turned away from God's love.

Reader 1: Lord, there have been times when we have refused to forgive someone. We didn't even forgive when they wanted us to. We're sorry.

All: Lord, have mercy. Kyrie eleison.

Reader 2: Lord, sometimes we have told people we have forgiven them. But, we didn't let go of our anger or hurt. We're sorry.

All: Christ, have mercy. Christe eleison.

Reader 3: Lord, sometimes we have gotten back at someone who has hurt us. We're sorry.

All: Lord, have mercy. Kyrie eleison.

Leader: We end with this prayer:

All: Lord, we are sorry for all our sins. We want to be like You—understanding and forgiving. Because we are forgiven by You, help us to be generous in forgiving others. Let our actions speak for our sorrow. Amen.

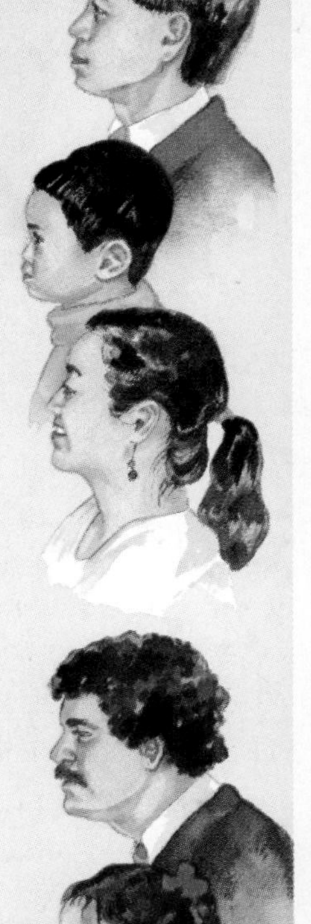

Family Note: Lesson 6 reminds us that contrition is not enough to make up for a wrong doing. Proof, or the desire for conversion, is needed. In Reconciliation, this proof is in the form of a penance. You can guide your child to practice conversion at home. When an action calls for forgiveness, help your child go beyond saying "I'm sorry" and actually do something that shows remorse. For example, if a younger brother was teased, the older child can offer to spend some one-on-one time with the brother. In the prayer service, Kyrie eleison and Christe eleison are Latin for Lord have mercy and Christ have mercy.

Family Connection

If possible, the students may take their texts home to pray the "Celebrating Forgiveness" prayer with the family. Point out the Family Note on this page, and ask the students to bring this note to their parents' attention.

7 I Am Forgiven

Focus

The meaning of absolution in the sacrament of Reconciliation is explained.

Catechetical Objectives

- To describe reconciliation and forgiveness in terms of healing and well-being.
- To remind the students that the sacrament of Reconciliation restores them to God's grace, or friendship.
- To explain the ways we can receive absolution in the sacrament of Reconciliation.

Lesson Overview

Lesson 7 will attempt to draw the students to a maturing attitude of forgiveness.

"Christ has willed that in her prayer and life and action His whole Church should be the sign and instrument of the forgiveness and reconciliation that He acquired for us at the price of His Blood. But He entrusted the exercise of the power of absolution to the apostolic ministry" *(Catechism of the Catholic Church, #1442).*

INTRODUCTION: WE CELEBRATE

- In the sacrament of Reconciliation, we receive absolution. We are healed and restored to God's love and friendship. A story of a little girl who broke her arm gives an example of the healing process.

DEVELOPMENT: WE BELIEVE

- In the Gospels of the New Testament, Jesus tells us over and over again of God's loving forgiveness. The Scripture story of The Lost Coin helps us realize how God rejoices when a sinner repents.

APPLICATION: WE LIVE OUR FAITH

- In this exercise, the students think of some ways to heal a relationship that has been injured. Then, the students are given a space in which to write or draw what it feels like to be forgiven.

APPLICATION: WE PRAY

- In this prayer service, you and the students will pray for God's mercy and ask God for spiritual healing.

The Church's Wisdom

Here is the theology supporting Lesson 7.

"Those who approach the sacrament of Penance obtain pardon from the mercy of God for offenses committed against Him. They are at the same time reconciled with the Church, which they have wounded by their sins, and which by charity, example, and prayer seeks their conversion" *(The Church, #11).*

The absolution of sin can be described as a most generous mystery. We say yes to the invitation of God to be incorporated into the Body of Christ. We accept for ourselves, or as an infant someone accepts in our behalf, the privilege of membership in the family of God. We are blessed with the indwelling of the Holy Spirit and become temples of the Holy Spirit. But we are human. We mess up. We use poor judgment. We sin.

The responsibility to our baptismal commitment is great. The compassion and understanding of God is greater. Reconciliation, penance, absolution, and our willingness to avail ourselves of this opportunity brings humanity and divinity intimately together. We may enjoy living the faith that we accept for ourselves and our families. We are Christ-bearers to the world.

Catechist Resources

AUDIOVISUAL:

- "A History of Christian Sacramental Forgiveness" (V/Adults/Two 25 min. segments/Christian Morality and Forgiveness #2/St. Anthony Messenger Press and Franciscan Communications) Part one of this video presents the evolution of penance and moral theology in the first six centuries of the church. Part two discusses the evolution of penance and moral theology from the Monastic period to the present.

BOOK:

- Puls, Joan. *Seek Treasures in Small Fields.* (Twenty-Third Publications) The author encourages readers to tap into the "treasures" that lie beneath the "small fields" of everyday life circumstances to find God. The opportunities, the lessons, the limitations and doubts, the profound significant moments and events, the deeper challenges and motivations can all provide us insight into everyday holiness.

Classroom Resources

AUDIOVISUAL:

- "God's People are Sorry" (V/Intermediate/Three 16 min. segments/Understanding the Sacrament of Reconciliation for Children #2/Paulist Press) This video is an interplay of scenes from children's lives, scripture, and reflection to help the students see sin as ignoring opportunities to love one's neighbors.

BOOK:

- Paulsen, Gary. *Nightjohn.* (Delacorte) This is a riveting short novel set in the 1850s and features a 12-year-old female slave and Nightjohn, once a free man, who returns to slavery to teach reading.

MUSIC:

- "The Best of Wolfgang Amadeus Mozart" (AC/LaserLight) One of an inexpensive series of great composers, this audio cassette contains selections from Mozart's operas, symphonies, and piano concertos.

Before Beginning the Lesson

TO DO:

- Be prepared and enthusiastic
- If possible, be available for scheduled meetings or rehearsals.
- Reproduce the Family Letter, pages 119–120, and send one home for each family.
- Check with the catechetical office to be sure that there are no scheduling changes.
- You are doing your best, God will do the rest.

TO HAVE ON HAND:

- Student texts
- Writing and drawing materials
- Bible
- Chalk

FOR OPTIONAL ENRICHMENT ACTIVITIES:

- Booklet or folder materials, fine tip markers, audio cassette tape of classical music, cassette player (page 53)
- Poster materials, tag-board or large sheets of white or light-colored construction paper, one for each student, colored markers or crayons (page 54)
- Several small jigsaw puzzles (page 55)
- Large puzzle pieces made from colored construction paper, black marker, clear contact paper, scissors (page 57)
- Benziger *Come, Follow Me* Grade 4 music cassette and cassette player (page 59)

New Words

Look at the wrap on page 57 for a suggestion to introduce new vocabulary words to the students. The vocabulary words are italicized or boldfaced in the student's text. All vocabulary words are also defined in the Glossary pages 69–71.

- **absolution:** A word that means "to wash."
- **Gospels:** The Good News that tells the life and teachings of Jesus.

Catechist Prayer

A moment of quiet reflection just for you.

"One thing I do know is that I was blind and now I see" *(John 9:25).*

God of mercy, You have shown me a taste of the joy of heaven in the healing of Reconciliation. Help me bring that same light, happiness, and peace to the students. Amen.

If you wish, do something joyful this week. Fly a kite, blow some bubbles, try a hula-hoop, or just be real silly! We all have lots of time to be adult; God calls us to be childlike, too.

7 I Am Forgiven

Absolution

Priest: God, the Father of mercies, through the death and resurrection of His Son, has reconciled the world to Himself and sent the Holy Spirit among us for the forgiveness of sins; through the ministry of the Church may God give you pardon and peace. I absolve you from your sins in the name of the Father, and of the Son, and of the Holy Spirit.

Penitent: Amen.

Lesson Plan

INTRODUCTION: WE CELEBRATE

Guidelines for Using the Text

1. Before using the text, ask if any of the students know the meaning of the word absolution. You may wish to provide a simple definition now (see We Catholics Believe, page 57) and remind the students that they will be learning more about this term during the lesson.

2. Direct the students to read the text on this page silently.

3. After the reading, allow time for student response and questions. You may wish to point out that these words convey the forgiveness of sin that is at the heart of the sacrament of Reconciliation. Point to the priest's words to show who grants forgiveness (God—Father, Son, and Holy Spirit), how forgiveness is granted (through the ministry of the Church), and who administers the sacrament (the priest—"I absolve you . . ."). Point out, too, the connection between this sacrament and the sacrament of Baptism, symbolized by the repetition of the Sign of the Cross ("In the name of the Father . . ."). You may also want to point out the two effects of the sacrament: pardon (coming back to God's friendship) and peace (a feeling of wholeness and community).

MY OWN BOOK

If the students are working on "I Celebrate Reconciliation" as an ongoing project, you may have them design a page for the Absolution at this time. The students may title the page "Absolution: I Am Forgiven." Ask the students to be quiet for a moment and to ask the Holy Spirit to help them. Suggest that the students draw a picture that represents the feeling of absolution, whatever the imagination dictates. Help this to be a reflective time for the students by playing classical music as they complete the activity.

Guidelines for Using the Story

1. Before beginning the reading, ask students to share any experiences they may have had with recovering from a long illness or waiting for a broken bone to mend.

2. Read the story on these two pages to the students. Allow time for reactions, and ask volunteers to respond to the Thinking about the Story questions.

3. You may continue discussing the story using the questions on page 55 as a model.

Healing

Every day after school, Amy took her dog, King, for a walk. Actually it was more of a run. Amy would ride her bike, and King would run along beside her.

This afternoon, Amy was very excited. For her birthday, her grandfather had given her an antique watch with a moon dial. Amy loved the watch. She kept glancing at it as she rode.

All of a sudden, King saw a cat. In chasing after it, he ran right in front of Amy's bike. Amy slammed on the brakes, but lost her balance. She toppled over onto the concrete.

Amy groaned as she felt a sharp pain in her left arm. She was almost afraid to look. Moving hurt so much! But Amy didn't really start to cry until she saw the pieces of her antique watch scattered all over the street.

Amy's parents rushed her to the hospital where x-rays were taken. They showed a break in Amy's forearm. "To help the bone come together again in just the right way," the doctor said, "we're going to put your arm in a cast."

A Slow Process

At first, Amy enjoyed the attention the cast caused. But as the weeks went by, the cast became a real bother. She couldn't play volleyball or basketball. She had a hard time riding her bike. And, since she could never get the cast wet, Amy couldn't wash her arm.

"It itches," Amy complained to her mother, "and I can't even scratch it."

"You'll just have to be patient," her mother said. "Healing takes a long time."

54

ENRICHMENT ACTIVITY

Distribute drawing materials, and have the students create posters that show the steps in physical healing. Refer the students to the story for this information, or list the following steps on the chalkboard:

1. Amy breaks her arm.

2. Amy goes to the hospital.

3. The doctor takes x-rays.

4. The arm is put in a cast, which grows uncomfortable.

5. The cast is removed, and Amy's arm is washed.

6. Amy's family helps her celebrate.

Have the students keep their posters to use on page 59.

Finally, the day came for the cast to come off. Amy's parents and her grandfather took her to the doctor's office. When the doctor sawed the cast open and broke it apart, Amy looked down at her arm and wiggled her fingers.

"How does it feel?" the doctor asked.

"The arm feels great!" Amy replied. "Now, everything's back the way it was."

"Not quite," Amy's grandfather remarked. "You still need this."

Amy looked at the watch he was buckling on her wrist. "Grandpa, my watch! But how did you...?"

"Your dad gathered up all the pieces," he explained. "I took them to a jeweler. It took almost as long to be fixed as your arm did to heal!"

Amy smiled. She raised her wrist to the light. The moon face on her watch seemed to be smiling back.

Thinking about the Story

- Why did Amy need patience after breaking her arm?

INTRODUCTION: WE CELEBRATE

Talking about the Story

About the Story:

1. How did Amy hurt herself?

2. What did Amy's parents do when they found out what had happened?

3. Why did the doctor put a cast on Amy's arm?

4. How did Amy feel about the cast at first? Later?

5. What made Amy's happiness complete?

About You:

1. Have you ever lost or broken something special to you? How did you feel?

2. Were you able to get it back or have it fixed? How did you feel?

WHAT IS THE LESSON?

Be sure the students understand these key ideas:

- When things are not the way they should be in our lives, we are not comfortable.
- When things are not right with us we can take steps to heal the situation. Whether we are sick or simply unhappy because something is wrong, we can change.

ENRICHMENT ACTIVITY

To illustrate the ideas of putting something together again and teamwork, bring several small jigsaw puzzles to class. Have the students form small groups. Give each group the jumbled pieces of a puzzle. Do not show the covers. As the groups work (or after they have completed the puzzles), talk about any feelings of frustration or impatience with the process, or about the sense of accomplishment that comes from working together.

Development: We Believe

Guidelines for Using the Text

1. Read the first three paragraphs of the text to the class. Write the term "reconcile" on the chalkboard, making sure the students understand the definition provided. Then, change the word reconcile to Reconciliation, so that students see the connection. Be sure, too, to stress that Amy's broken arm was an accident. To make the parallel with sin more direct, Amy would have had to break her arm—or her watch—on purpose. Help the students understand the use of the term "effect of sin."

2. Read the text section Signs of Healing to the students. Ask:

- Why do you think being forgiven is a cause for celebration?
- Can you name any other stories Jesus told or actions He performed to show God's forgiving love?

3. Read the text section God's Love to the students. This section contains important information on the different ways to celebrate the sacrament of Reconciliation. Allow time for questions or comments.

Becoming Whole Again

Reconciliation is a process that is much like healing a broken bone. In fact, the word reconcile means "to heal or to bring together again."

What does it mean to be healed? It is to be whole and well. It is a feeling that everything is the way it should be. Sometimes healing occurs physically, like the bone in Amy's arm. Healing can also be spiritual and help us to be the kind of person God wants us to be.

Amy's broken arm was an accident. Sin is something you choose on purpose. There is a way the effect of sin is similar to the effect of Amy's accident. Sin causes a kind of "break" in our relationship with God and with others. We need spiritual healing.

Signs of Healing

The **Gospels** tell us that Jesus often healed sick people, spiritually and physically. He did this to show God's mercy and love. Over and over again, Jesus explained that God is a loving Father. "God will not hand you a stone when you ask for bread. Likewise, He will not punish you when you ask for forgiveness" (*Matthew 7:9,11*).

Since the people found it hard to believe that God could be so merciful and forgiving, Jesus also told them many stories and parables about God. Jesus said that God is like the shepherd who searches after each lost sheep and brings it safely back to the pasture. God is like the father who gives a big party when his runaway son returns home at last.

God's Love

The sacrament of Reconciliation is a celebration of healing. In this sacrament, you take the time to mend your relationship with God. You make peace with others, and you make peace with yourself. When you say that you are sorry and need forgiveness, the priest gives you **absolution.** Your relationship with God and with other members of God's Family is whole once again. Healing has taken place.

56

Enrichment Activity

This point in the lesson offers an excellent opportunity to help the students walk through the sacrament. If you are planning a number of practice times, you may wish to make this one of them, involving the priest and the students' parents, if possible. At the very least, have the students visit the church and familiarize themselves with the Reconciliation room and/or confessional if you have not already done so. The students can refer to the outline of the rite on pages 73–74 of their texts or to their Reconciliation booklets for review.

There are three ways you can receive absolution in the sacrament of Reconciliation. You can receive this sacrament in a confessional, where you and the priest are separated by a screen. Or, you can confess your sins to the priest face-to-face. You can also attend a parish Reconciliation service that includes individual confession and absolution. Each of these ways restores you to God's grace. Each of these ways gives you the joy of being healed.

We Catholics Believe

The **Gospels** are the New Testament accounts of the life and teachings of Jesus. The word gospel means "good news." Jesus often use parables to teach about God's kingdom.

The word **absolution** means "to wash." After you have confessed your sins and prayed an Act of Contrition in the sacrament of Reconciliation, the priest prays a prayer of absolution as a sign that God has forgiven you.

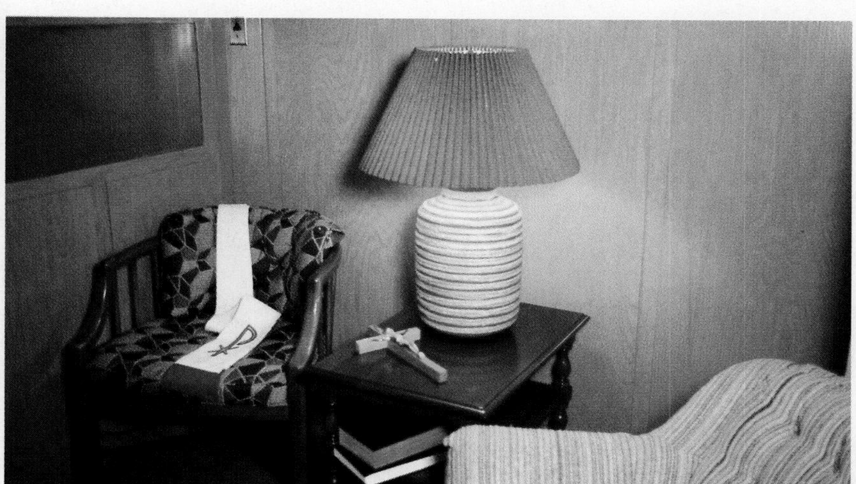

DEVELOPMENT: WE BELIEVE

We Catholics Believe

Choose two good readers to read aloud the two paragraphs of this section. If necessary, refer the students back to page 53 of their texts to review the prayer of absolution.

FUN WITH NEW WORDS

To keep with the theme of the puzzle activity, the students may enjoy "Puzzle-Up" for a bit of variety. Using a variety of colors, prepare puzzle pieces by cutting construction paper into puzzle shapes. Print the vocabulary word on one puzzle piece, and the definition on the matching puzzle piece. For a challenge, include the words from previous lessons for review. If you wish, protect the prepared puzzle pieces with clear contact paper. Shuffle the puzzle pieces, and allow each student to select one piece of puzzle. Then the students find the matching puzzle piece, and recite together the vocabulary word and definition. There are no winners, only learners.

Development: We Believe

Guidelines for Using the Scripture Story

1. Ask a student to read aloud the story of The Lost Coin, based on Luke 15:8–10.

2. After the reading, distribute writing materials and have the students respond in writing to the two Thinking about Scripture questions. Allow time for volunteers to share their responses.

3. You may continue discussing the story using the questions below as a model.

Talking about Scripture

About the Story:

1. What did the woman do when she lost one of her coins?

2. What did she do when she found the coin?

3. What did Jesus say about His story?

About You:

1. How do you feel about the idea that God will never give up on you?

2. What are some feelings or events that make you feel like having a party?

The Lost Coin

Jesus told this story to His friends.

Once, there was a poor woman who had only ten coins. She kept these coins in a secret place in her house. She could not afford to lose any of them.

But one day, she discovered that one of the coins was missing. The woman was very upset!

She lit a lamp and swept the entire house. She looked under the bed and behind each chair.

Finally, she found the coin she had lost.

The woman was so happy, she called together all her friends and neighbors. "Rejoice with me," she told them, "because I have just found the coin that I lost."

Then, Jesus said to His friends: "In just the same way, I tell you, there will be rejoicing among the angels of God over one sinner who repents."

(*based on Luke 15:8–10*)

Thinking about Scripture

- How is the lost coin like a person who sins?
- How is the woman in the story like God?

What Is the Lesson?

Be sure the students understand this key idea:

- God's love and forgiveness are very great gifts that should never be taken for granted.

Enrichment Activity

Distribute drawing materials to the students. Have them draw pictures of the woman celebrating with her friends. The students can copy Jesus' words (from the last paragraph of the story) onto their drawings.

Healing Solutions

In each of the following situations, sin has disturbed the peace of a relationship. Imagine that these choices were yours. Then, think of a way to heal each situation.

1. You didn't go home when you were supposed to.

   Healing Solution: ______________________________

   ____

2. You made fun of your younger brother and called him names.

   Healing Solution: ______________________________

   ____

3. You stole a book that belongs to the library.

   Healing Solution: ______________________________

   ____

In this space, draw or write about how you feel when you are forgiven.

Vocabulary

Write your own definitions for the following words:

Absolution ______________________________

Healing ______________________________

APPLICATION: WE LIVE OUR FAITH

Guidelines for Reviewing the Lesson

1. Have the students read the directions for the first part of Healing Solutions. Then, direct them to work independently on writing the activity.

2. Have the students choose partners to share their solutions. Allow time for volunteers to share with the class what they have written.

3. Next, have the students complete the writing or drawing section of the review. Make art materials available as necessary. Encourage the students to take their texts home to share with family members what they have drawn or written.

MUSIC NOTE

You may wish to teach the song "More Joy in Heaven," student text page 77. Words and music notation can be found on page 138 in the Catechist's Edition. Use Benziger *Come, Follow Me* Grade 4 music cassette to help the students learn the song.

ENRICHMENT ACTIVITY

If the students have made posters on the steps of physical healing, have them take these out now. Ask volunteers if they can name similar steps in the spiritual healing that occurs in Reconciliation. The students can add these steps to their posters or make a Reconciliation poster on the reverse side. Help the students see the parallels between the physical and spiritual healing processes.

Application: We Pray

Guidelines for Prayer

1. Choose a good reader to proclaim the Gospel (Matthew 18:12–14).

2. Gather the students together around the prayer table or in an open space. Lead the litany "Have Mercy on Us." End the prayer with the song "More Joy in Heaven." You may sing together or listen to the audio cassette.

Have Mercy on Us

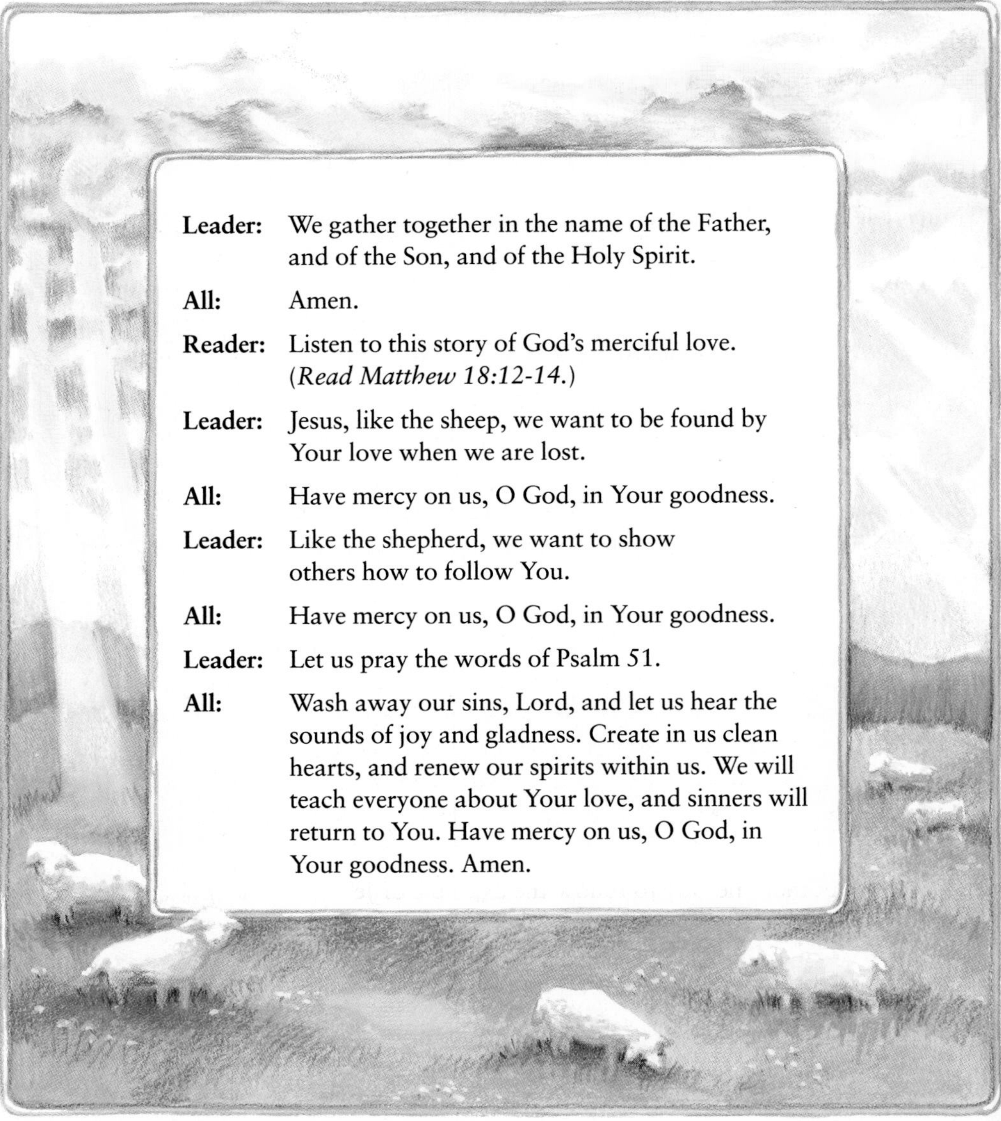

Leader: We gather together in the name of the Father, and of the Son, and of the Holy Spirit.

All: Amen.

Reader: Listen to this story of God's merciful love. (*Read Matthew 18:12-14.*)

Leader: Jesus, like the sheep, we want to be found by Your love when we are lost.

All: Have mercy on us, O God, in Your goodness.

Leader: Like the shepherd, we want to show others how to follow You.

All: Have mercy on us, O God, in Your goodness.

Leader: Let us pray the words of Psalm 51.

All: Wash away our sins, Lord, and let us hear the sounds of joy and gladness. Create in us clean hearts, and renew our spirits within us. We will teach everyone about Your love, and sinners will return to You. Have mercy on us, O God, in Your goodness. Amen.

Family Note: Lesson 7 explains the meaning of absolution in Reconciliation. Forgiveness is described as a spiritual healing that restores us to God's grace. You may wish to light a candle as a symbol of God's presence when saying the prayer on this page.

Family Connection

If possible, the students may take their texts home to pray "Have Mercy on Us" with their families. Point out the Family Note on this page, and ask the students to bring this note to their parents' attention. Send one Family Letter home to each household.

8 Forgiving Others

Focus

The sacrament of Reconciliation challenges us and gives us the grace to build peace and to forgive others.

Catechetical Objectives

- To point out that one way to follow the example of Jesus is to forgive others.
- To introduce the Beatitudes and how the students can begin to use these principles in their own lives.
- To encourage the students to be peacemakers in all of their relationships.

Lesson Overview

Lesson 8 introduces the Beatitudes to the students and what the results of reconciliation can be.

"Reconciliation with God is thus the purpose and effect of this sacrament. For those who receive the sacrament of Penance with a contrite heart and religious disposition, reconciliation is usually followed by peace and serenity of conscience with strong spiritual consolation. Indeed, the sacrament of Reconciliation with God brings about a true 'spiritual resurrection,' restoration of the dignity and blessings of the life of the children of God, of which the most precious is friendship with God" *(Catechism of the Catholic Church, #1468).*

INTRODUCTION: WE CELEBRATE

- At the end of the sacrament of Reconciliation we are forgiven and ready to start anew. The story of twin boys introduces the idea that now we must follow God's example and learn to forgive others.

DEVELOPMENT: WE BELIEVE

- Just as we have the free will to sin or not to sin, we also have the choice whether or not to forgive someone. The Scripture story of Jesus' command to the Apostles to share His peace with others teaches us what we, too, must do.

APPLICATION: WE LIVE OUR FAITH

- A review of the sacrament of Reconciliation is a fun way to reinforce the facts of the sacrament. The students are also given space to write what the sacrament of Reconciliation means to them.

APPLICATION: WE PRAY

- You and the students can share a Franciscan prayer that asks for God's help to be peacemakers.

The Church's Wisdom

Here is the theology supporting Lesson 8.

"In a world where alienation and loneliness seem to be the norm, it is an expression of one's Christian faith to forgive others and to seek forgiveness when necessary" *(National Catechetical Directory, #125).*

In a perfect universe, there is no concern for forgiving or for reconciling. In a perfect universe, justice and peace, love and cooperation, and blissful happiness eliminate the need for such concerns. Christian people refer to this perfect universe as heaven.

Our faith tells us that we are created in the image of God. Our faith leads us to the baptismal font. Our human nature is not always perfect, however. We sin.

Our faith tells us that we are never totally "out of the loop." God always and ever draws us back to the Image in which we are created. We are that perfect Image when we forgive others, when we forgive ourselves, and when we ask forgiveness. Christ has come to live with us, and will come again. And again. And again. . . .

Catechist Resources

AUDIOVISUAL:

- "Touching God through the Celebration of Forgiveness" (V/Adults/Two 25 min. segments/Christian Morality and Forgiveness #8/St. Anthony Messenger Press and Franciscan Communications) Part one of this video presentation examines the Reconciliation rites as we celebrate in today's church. Part two presents the sacrament of Anointing of the Sick.

BOOK:

- Huebsch, Bill. *Rethinking Sacraments: Holy Moments in Daily Living.* (Twenty-Third Publications) The author presents sacraments as Christian service, or grace lived out in our daily lives. This book is a challenge to old ideas and a nurturance to new ideas on what sacraments mean to Catholic people today.

Classroom Resources

AUDIOVISUAL:

- "St. Francis of Assisi" (V/Intermediate/28 mins./St. Anthony Messenger Press and Franciscan Communications) This video tells the story of St. Francis in lively animation from his partying teenage years to the final blessing of his community before his death.

BOOK:

- Bettigole, OSF Brother Michael, Robert Muccigrosso, and Gregory Rossicone. *Stories of God.* (Brown-Roa) This is an anthology of literature for Catholic children that seeks to make students aware of their Catholic literary heritage. The presence of God and God's involvement in the lives of men and women are portrayed in classic and contemporary stories, drama, poems, biography and narrative literature.

Before Beginning the Lesson

TO DO:

- Have all necessary materials at hand to teach Lesson 8.
- Be especially peaceful and calm. The students may be excited or apprehensive about celebrating First Reconciliation.
- Find the snapshots you took of the students at the first class meeting!
- Invite the pastor to visit your students, if a presentation of the stole is to be made.
- The students are prepared. Just be there for them.

TO HAVE ON HAND:

- Student texts
- Writing and drawing materials
- Bible
- Chalk

FOR OPTIONAL ENRICHMENT ACTIVITIES:

- Booklet or folder materials, preselected magazine pictures, paste or glue, fine tip markers, snapshots of the individual students, if possible (page 61)
- Blank notes and envelopes or drawing paper, writing materials (page 63)
- Benziger *Come, Follow Me* Grade 4 music cassette and cassette player (page 64)
- Appropriate materials for special stole (page 64)
- Squares of felt or burlap, scissors, fabric glue, fabric scraps, stencils, laundry marker or fabric paint (page 66)

New Words

Look at the wrap on page 65 for a suggestion to introduce new vocabulary words to the students. The vocabulary words are italicized or boldfaced in the student's text. All vocabulary words are also defined in the Glossary pages 69–71.

- **Apostles:** Twelve close friends and followers of Jesus who were sent by Him to work in His name.
- **Beatitudes:** Short sayings that Jesus told the people in His Sermon on the Mount.
- **heaven:** Being happy with God forever.
- **ministry:** Another word for service.

Catechist Prayer

A moment of quiet reflection just for you.

"May the eyes of your hearts be enlightened, that you may know what is the hope of His call" *(Ephesians 1:18).*

Forgiving and compassionate God, thank you for allowing me this time with these students. Holy Spirit, lead these young people to wholeness and peace through the grace of the sacrament. Now and forever, Jesus, open our hearts to love and serve in Your Name! Amen.

If you wish, carve out some quiet time for yourself. Sit in a busy place for a while, such as a shopping mall or a reception office, and just watch. Watch the people, all created in the image of God, pass by. See how grand and diverse is the handiwork of the Creator. Be at peace, for you are loved.

Forgiving Others

Praise and Dismissal

Priest: Give thanks to the Lord, for He is good.

Penitent: His mercy endures forever.

Priest: May the Passion of our Lord Jesus Christ, the intercession of the Blessed Virgin Mary and of all the saints, whatever good you do and suffering you endure, heal your sins, help you grow in holiness and reward you with eternal life.

Penitent: Amen.

Lesson Plan

Introduction: We Celebrate

Guidelines for Using the Text

1. Before beginning the reading, remind the students of the Dismissal of the Mass, which is meant to be more than just a simple "The End." As the Mass concludes, we are sent forth with an instruction to "Go in Peace to love and serve the Lord." Like the Mass, the sacrament of Reconciliation concludes with formal words of dismissal.

2. Read the priest's words aloud. Have the students read the penitent's responses. You may wish to explain that the first two lines of this text come from Psalm 106 (among others), an ancient sung prayer of the Hebrew people which asks for God's forgiveness for the whole community. You may also need to define the term "Passion" as it is used here, meaning the sufferings and death of Jesus, and the term "intercession," which means the prayers and good works of Our Lady and the saints on our behalf.

3. Ask the students what the priest's prayer reminds them to do (to continue to grow in holiness).

My Own Book

If the students are working on "I Celebrate Reconciliation" as an ongoing project, you may have them design a page for the Praise and Dismissal at this time. Suggest that the students print "Praise and Dismissal" at the top of the page. Provide the students with a selection of magazine pictures depicting examples of serving or loving. They may select one and paste it onto the page. The words "to love and serve" may be printed on the bottom of the page. If a snapshot of the student is available, paste the snapshot in an appropriate place on the booklet. The booklet may be collected and bound, if you wish, to be returned to the students at the closing prayer service of the class, or distributed at First Reconciliation.

Guidelines for Using the Story

1. Before beginning the reading, discuss this question: Which is more difficult to say—"I'm Sorry" or "You're Forgiven"? Why?

2. Read the story on these two pages to the students.

3. You may discuss the story using the questions on page 63 as a model.

Forgiving

Kevin and Kenny were twins, but they were very different. Kenny was good in sports but not in studies. Kevin was a good student, but he couldn't play baseball or basketball.

One day, their teacher announced an essay contest with a brand-new computer as the prize.

The boys spent an entire week on their papers. Kevin had no trouble at all. He knew how to express himself, and spelling came easy. But Kenny had a difficult time. He felt that he couldn't write anything that sounded right.

The night before the papers were due, Kenny found Kevin's essay and read it. It was really good. Then he got an idea. Carefully, he copied the paper in his own handwriting and put his name on it. Then he put his pages underneath Kevin's title page. The next day, he handed in both sets.

The teacher liked Kevin's paper the best. Since Kenny's name was on it, he won the computer.

For a week, Kenny did nothing but play computer games. But soon, he got bored. He began to feel sorry that he had sw.tched papers with his brother. Finally, Kenny told Kevin what he had done.

Kevin was more than angry. Kevin was furious. "I hate you!" he yelled. "I wish you weren't my brother!"

Making Up

For days, Kevin didn't speak to Kenny nor would he sit with Kenny at lunch time. If Kenny walked into a room, Kevin walked out. When the two boys went to bed in the room they shared, Kevin turned out his light without saying "Good night."

Kenny couldn't stand it any more. He went to the teacher and told her what he had done. He asked her to announce the real winner in class the next day. The teacher was disappointed in Kenny, but she could see that he was sorry.

Kenny raced home after school. He moved the computer to Kevin's side of the room. Then, he left a note on

ENRICHMENT ACTIVITY

Have the students form small groups. Direct the groups to make up stories in which someone needs forgiveness and is initially refused. Have the students end their stories with the people making peace. You may want to have the students use one of the following forms for their stories:

- A skit
- A short story
- A series of drawings

Allow time for groups to share their work.

the computer screen.

"Kevin," he wrote, "I'm really sorry. I told our teacher what I did. I told Mom and Dad, too. But I need you to forgive me. I'd rather have a brother than a computer. How can I make it up to you? Your brother, Kenny."

When Kevin got home, he read the note, but he was still very angry. Then he began to think how quiet it was without Kenny to talk to. He thought about the good times they had. Kevin felt his anger melting away. He knew Kenny would feel bad enough when the class found out what he had done.

Kevin found Kenny in the yard. "Hey," he said. "There's only one way you can make up for what you did."

"How?" Kenny asked, sadly.

"You can teach me how to play computer basketball!" Kevin laughed.

Talking about the Story

About the Story:

1. How were Kevin and Kenny different from each other?

2. Why did Kenny cheat on the contest? Which commandment did Kenny break?

3. How did Kenny feel after he won the computer?

4. Why did Kevin finally decide to forgive Kenny?

About You:

1. Have you ever held a grudge? How did it make you feel?

2. Has anyone ever given you the "silent treatment"? How did it make you feel?

3. Is there ever a time when you should not forgive someone? Why or why not?

What Is the Lesson?

Be sure the students understand these key ideas:

- We need to do whatever is necessary in order to make peace with someone we have hurt.
- When someone asks for forgiveness, we need to offer it even though it may be difficult for us to do.

Enrichment Activity

Distribute materials for making greeting cards. Have the students design and make "I'm Sorry" and "You're Forgiven" cards to be used when necessary with family members or friends. Encourage the students to take their cards home.

Guidelines for Using the Text

1. Have the students read the first two paragraphs of the text. After the reading, ask volunteers for examples of other choices we have in hurtful situations.

2. Next, read the text section We Are Called to Forgive aloud. You may wish to discuss this material in depth using these or similar questions.

- How is forgiving others a way to say "Thank You" to God?
- Why do you think Jesus made the power to forgive an important part of His Apostles' ministry?
- Where do bishops and priests receive the power to grant absolution in the sacrament of Reconciliation?
- Why do we need the sacrament of Reconciliation?

3. Read the text section Following Jesus to the students. If time allows, have the students turn to page 79 of their texts. Go through each of the Beatitudes with the students. Ask for examples of how each Beatitude can be used as a guideline for forgiveness. (If time is short, you may assign this exercise as homework, to be shared during the next class session.)

Forgiving Is a Choice

When someone cheats you, when a friend acts selfishly, when a parent breaks a promise, you experience many feelings. You may feel hurt, or you may feel angry. Like Kevin, you may feel that you never want to trust that person again.

These feelings are not unusual. But it is important to remember that in these situations, if you are the one who is hurt, you decide how to respond. You can choose to be resentful and angry. Or you can choose to be merciful and forgiving.

We Are Called to Forgive

Members of God's Family know that forgiving others is one way to follow the example of Jesus. Even when He was dying on the cross, Jesus prayed for those who had hurt Him. "Father, forgive them for they do not know what they are doing" (*Luke 23:34*). Forgiving others is a way to say thank you for the love and mercy God has shown us. Because God has forgiven our sins, we have the grace and strength to forgive others.

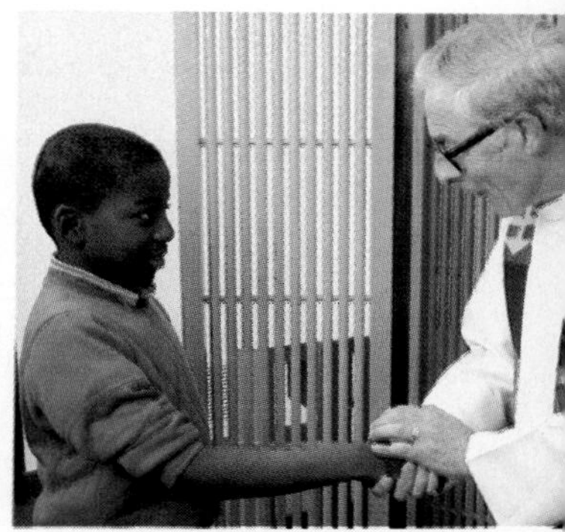

Before He ascended into heaven, Jesus gave the **Apostles** a mission. He told them that He wanted them to be ministers of forgiveness. "Whose sins you forgive are forgiven them, and whose sins you retain are retained" (*John 20:23*). From this mission of Jesus, priests and bishops are called to an ordained **ministry.** They receive the power to give absolution in the sacrament of Reconciliation.

Following Jesus

Of course, not all of the followers of Jesus are ordained ministers. But they are all called to follow Jesus through a ministry of service to others.

MUSIC NOTE

You may wish to teach the song "Oh, Happy One," student text page 77. Words and music notation can be found on page 141 in the Catechist's Edition. Use Benziger *Come, Follow Me* Grade 4 music cassette to help the students learn the song.

ENRICHMENT ACTIVITY

The students may wish to work together to make (or raise funds to buy) special stoles for the priests who will be participating in their First Reconciliation celebration. Your parish staff may have suggestions about appropriate materials and decorations. Invite the priests to come to class so that the students can formally present their gifts.

Jesus gave us some guidelines for leading happy, forgiving, and serving lives. We call these the **Beatitudes,** because the word beatitude means "blessed" or "happy." You can find these words of Jesus on page 79 of this book.

Learning to forgive others is an important part of seeking true happiness. People who can forgive do not carry around the weight of their anger. They do not hold grudges. They are not always looking for ways to "get even." They are free to be happy.

When we live the Beatitudes, we grow in our ability to forgive others and to restore peace. Above all, we put serving others before everything else.

We Catholics Believe

The **Apostles** were special friends of Jesus sent by Him to carry on His work.

Ministry is another word for service. In the sacrament of Holy Orders, bishops, priests, and deacons are given special grace and strength to serve the Church as **ordained ministers.** All Christians are called by the sacrament of Baptism to use their gifts and talents to serve others.

The **Beatitudes** are eight short sayings that Jesus told the people in His Sermon on the Mount. They tell us how to live a happy life on earth that will bring us everlasting happiness in **heaven.**

DEVELOPMENT: WE BELIEVE

We Catholics Believe

Ask three different students to read these three paragraphs aloud. After the reading, ask the students to close their books. Write the terms "Apostles," "ministry," and "Beatitudes" on the chalkboard. Distribute writing materials, and ask the students to use these terms in original sentences. Allow time for volunteers to share what they have written.

FUN WITH NEW WORDS

Play "Tag Along" for a review of all the vocabulary words.

To play "Tag Along" invite the students to seat themselves in groups of three. Begining with the vocabulary words from Lesson 8, player number one may read or recite from memory one vocabulary word and definition. Next, "Tag Along" with player two adding another word and definition to make the sentence more complex. Player three adds a third word to the growing sentence. Play continues until one group is able to "Tag Along" at least five words together. (Example: The "Apostles" were special friends of Jesus, who all had a "ministry," a special service in the "community," which is a group of people who share something in common, who were "humble," honest about oneself, and followed the "Ten Commandments" which are the laws God gave to Moses. . . .)

Development: We Believe

Guidelines for Using the Scripture Story

1. Before beginning the reading, remind the students of the Greeting of Peace that takes place during the Mass. What do we say to those standing near us? What do these words mean?

2. Next, read aloud (or retell in your own words) the story of Jesus' appearance to the apostles, taken from John 20:19–23.

3. Take a few moments to remind the students of the importance of the Holy Spirit in their lives and the life of the Church. Help them see the connection to the sacrament of Confirmation.

4. Discuss the story using the Thinking about Scripture questions and the questions below as a model.

Talking about Scripture

About the Story:

1. When Jesus appeared to the apostles, what did He say to make them feel better?

2. What did Jesus ask them to do?

About You:

1. How can you bring the peace of Christ to others?

2. Who helps you follow Jesus' example of forgiveness and peace?

Peace Be with You

Several days after Jesus died, the Apostles gathered together in a secret place. They locked the door because they were afraid that the people in Jerusalem might kill them, too.

The Apostles weren't happy. They felt guilty that they had run away when Jesus was arrested. They felt sad that most of them had not stayed by Jesus when He was on the cross.

Suddenly, Jesus came and stood among them. "Peace be with you," He said. "Do not be afraid. I am Jesus."

The Apostles touched Jesus. They knew that God had raised Him from the dead, just as He had promised.

"Peace be with you," Jesus said again. This time, the Apostles began to feel better. They knew that Jesus loved them even though they made mistakes. They knew that God would be with them always in the days to come.

"I want you to share this peace with others," Jesus said to them. "Go out to all people and tell them how much God loves them. Forgive others, and I will forgive them, too."

The Apostles did this. They told people that God wanted them to be His children. They baptized people and shared Eucharist with them. They forgave those who had sinned. They also taught people to be at peace with one another.

(*based on John 20:19–23 and Acts 2:37–47*)

Thinking about Scripture

- Why were the Apostles afraid when they saw Jesus?
- How did the Apostles share the peace of Christ with others?

What Is the Lesson?

Be sure the students understand these key ideas:

- Jesus left us a gift of peace.
- One important way to be at peace is to forgive and to be forgiven.
- The Holy Spirit helps us share the peace of Christ with others.

Enrichment Activity

The students will need a small square of felt or burlap, scissors, glue, fabric markers, and fabric scraps. Ask the students to think of a symbol for Reconciliation (a heart, the word "PAX" which is Latin for "peace," two hands clasping). Cut out the symbols from fabric scraps and glue them to the felt squares. The students can work individually or in pairs. The students may sign their names to the squares. Stitch the squares together into a patchwork pattern that may be used as an altar hanging or lectern banner for the students' First Reconciliation celebration.

Sacrament Review

Here's what a person preparing for Reconciliation has to say about the sacrament. Circle **Yes** for every correct statement and circle **No** for every incorrect statement.

1. "Reconciliation helps me make better choices and follow Jesus more closely." Yes No
2. "Before I receive Reconciliation, I say a penance." Yes No
3. "The priest may tell others what he hears during confession." Yes No
4. "Some sins are accidents or mistakes." Yes No
5. "Absolution is a sign of God's loving forgiveness." Yes No
6. "I can receive Reconciliation only once a year." Yes No
7. "The priest takes the place of God." Yes No
8. "I can receive Reconciliation in a confessional or in a Reconciliation room." Yes No

In the space below, write one or two sentences about what the sacrament of Reconciliation means to you.

APPLICATION: WE LIVE OUR FAITH

Guidelines for Reviewing the Lesson

1. Have the students read the directions for the activity. Explain that this activity draws on information the students have learned from the whole text. You may wish to allow the students to look back through the text if they have difficulty with a question.

2. Allow the students time to complete the activity independently.

3. If you wish, have the students exchange books to correct their answers. Answers: (1) Yes; (2) No; (3) No; (4) No; (5) Yes; (6) No; (7) Yes; (8) Yes.

4. Direct the students to work independently on the writing exercise. Allow sufficient time for the students to develop thoughtful answers. You may wish to have the students copy their sentences onto separate sheets, which may be collected and read as part of the students' First Reconciliation service, if possible.

ENRICHMENT ACTIVITY

Distribute writing materials, and ask the students to write short prayers asking the Holy Spirit to help them live and share the peace of Christ. Suggest that the students take their prayers home and share them with family members.

Application: We Pray

Guidelines for Prayer

1. If time permits, you may view the video "St. Francis of Assisi." Following the video, pray the Franciscan prayer together.

2. Because this may be the last prayer experience you will be sharing as a class, you may wish to make it a real culminating celebration. If possible, celebrate this service in the parish church or in a small chapel. Invite the pastor and the students' families.

3. You may wish to include a simple commissioning ceremony. Read 1 John 4:7–21 (Love One Another) aloud. Present each student with a memento of the class: a cross or the completed and bound Reconciliation booklets the students have made themselves. As each student comes forward, ask God to bless the child with the gifts of love, forgiveness, and peace. Sing together "Oh, Happy One."

4. Conclude the service with a simple party.

One way we experience the peace Jesus promised us is through the sacrament of Reconciliation. We want to share this peace with others. Here is the Franciscan prayer that asks for God's help to be peacemakers.

Lord,
Make me an instrument of Your peace;
Where there is hatred, let me plant love;
Where there is injury, pardon;
Where there is doubt, faith;
Where there is despair, hope;
Where there is darkness, light;
Where there is sadness, joy.
Grant that I may not so much seek to be
comforted as to comfort;
To be understood as to understand;
To be loved as to love.
For it is in giving that we receive,
it is in pardoning that we are pardoned,
and it is in dying that we are born to eternal life.

Family Note: Lesson 8 tells us that Reconciliation challenges us to live more like Jesus. It also gives us grace to build peace and to forgive others. Try to use your everyday family situations to guide your child to be a peacemaker.

Family Connection

If possible, the students may take their texts home to pray the Franciscan prayer with their families. Point out the Family Note on this page, and ask the students to bring this note to their parents' attention.

Absolution A word that means "to wash." After you have confessed your sins and prayed an Act of Contrition in the sacrament of Reconciliation, the priest prays a prayer of absolution as a sign that God has forgiven you. (*page 57*)

Apostles Twelve close friends and followers of Jesus who were sent by Him to work in His name. (*page 65*)

Baptism This sacrament of initiation washes away sin, gives new life, and joins us to God's Family. (*page 9*)

Beatitudes Short sayings that Jesus told the people in His Sermon on the Mount. The word beatitude means "blessed" or "happy." The Beatitudes tell us how to gain eternal happiness by living Jesus' Way. (*page 65*)

Blessed Trinity Our name for one God who is Father, Son, and Holy Spirit. (*page 9*)

Catholic A word meaning "for everyone." The members of the Catholic Church are baptized and follow the authority of the pope and the bishops. (*page 9*)

Community A group of people who share something in common. A family is a community because the members are all related to one another. A school is a community because people go there to learn and to grow. A parish is a community because its members believe in and follow Jesus. (*page 41*)

Confession The act of telling your sins to a priest in the sacrament of Reconciliation. To confess means "to tell honestly or to admit something about yourself." This word is sometimes used as another name for the sacrament of Reconciliation. (*page 33*)

Conscience God's gift that helps us know right from wrong. (*page 25*)

Consequences The effects of your choices or actions. Consequences can affect both you and other people. Responsible people think about the consequences of their actions before they act. (*page 33*)

Contrition A feeling of sorrow for sin and the promise to do better. (*page 41*)

Conversion Making a change for the better and turning toward God's love and forgiveness. (*page 49*)

Covenant A solemn agreement. God's covenant with the Israelites was sacred and loving. God would be with them always; in return, they promised to follow the Ten Commandments. We continue to live this covenant. (*page 17*)

Disciple Someone who believes in and follows Jesus. (*page 10*)

Forgiveness The act of pardoning someone who hurt you. (*page 41*)

Free will God's gift that allows us to choose to walk with Jesus or away from God. (*page 25*)

Using the Glossary Section

The Glossary contains an entry for each of the text vocabulary words, which are either religious terms, such as "rite," or familiar terms with a new religious context, such as "contrition." In the student text, these words are boldfaced or italicized. They have been featured in the We Catholics Believe section of each lesson or defined within the reading text.

For each word, a definition based on the text is given, along with the page on which the word is used. Sometimes a word is used often in *Reconciliation*. The page given refers to the page that defines the word.

Using the Glossary Section

Use the Glossary to either preview or review the vocabulary. If possible, preview the vocabulary before each lesson. Then, the vocabulary will already be familiar when you are teaching. Also, review the vocabulary after each lesson. This reinforces the material that has been taught. Simple flash cards might help in either vocabulary preview or review.

The vocabulary given should be understood by each student who is ready to celebrate Reconciliation for the first time.

Glossary

Golden Rule "Do to others whatever you would have them do to you" (*Matthew 7:14*). (*page 41*)

Gospels The Good News that tells the life and teachings of Jesus. (*page 57*)

Grace A share in God's life and love. (*page 25*)

Great Commandment "You shall love the Lord, your God, with all your heart, with all your being, with all your strength, and with all your mind. And, you must love your neighbor as yourself" (*based on Matthew 22:34-40*). (*page 17*)

Heaven Being happy with God forever. (*page 65*)

Hell Total and lasting separation from God's love. (*page 33*)

Humility The ability to be honest about oneself. Humble people know both their good points and their bad points. They can admit when they are wrong. They have the courage to say "I am sorry." (*page 41*)

Israelites Another name for the Jewish people. They are called Israelites because they are the children of Jacob, whose name was also Israel. Moses led the Israelites out of slavery and into freedom. (*page 9*)

Jesus The Son of God and our Savior. (*page 10*)

Messiah The Savior; the person picked by God to help the people of Israel live the way God wanted them to live. Christians believe that Jesus is the Messiah. (*page 33*)

Ministry Another word for service. Bishops, priests, and deacons are ordained ministers. Through Baptism, all Christians are called to serve others. (*page 65*)

Original sin The first sin. Only Jesus and His Mother, Mary, were born without original sin. Jesus saved us from original sin, but its effects are still with us. (*page 25*)

Parable A special story used by Jesus to teach His Way. There are many parables in the four Gospels. (*page 26*)

Penance An action that is done in order to show sorrow and a willingness to change. Also, a step in Reconciliation. (*page 49*)

Penitent A person who is sorry for sinning. (*page 5*)

Prayer Words or actions that share our love for God. Four types of prayer are praise, thanksgiving, petition, and sorrow for sin. (*page 49*)

Reconciliation One of the seven sacraments of the Catholic Church. In this sacrament, a person confesses his or her sins to a priest, expresses sorrow for these sins, and promises to do better in the future. The priest forgives the person, in the name of God and the members of God's Family. (*page 9*)

Repent To feel sorry for sin; to change one's life. Jesus asked His followers to repent and to turn toward God. (*page 49*)

Responsible The ability to be answerable for the wrong choices that are made. (*page 33*)

Sacrament One of the special signs and celebrations of God's love. Jesus gave us seven sacraments: Baptism, Confirmation, Eucharist, Reconciliation, Anointing of the Sick, Marriage, and Holy Orders. These sacraments give God's own life, or grace, to the members of the Church. They help the members grow. (*page 9*)

Sin Choosing to do wrong. Venial sin hurts our friendship with God. Mortal sin ruins our friendship with God. Mortal sin is sometimes called deadly sin, because it separates us from grace, our share in God's life. (*page 25*)

Ten Commandments The laws God gave Moses on Mount Sinai. These ten laws told the Israelites how to live in peace and love. We follow these commandments today. (*page 17*)

Works of Mercy Actions that serve others physically and spiritually. (*page 49*)

Using the Glossary Section

Suggested Uses

In addition to the vocabulary reviews provided within the regular lesson plan, the feature Fun with New Words makes an additional suggestion to help the student memorize the words. One suggestion is made in each lesson in the wrap.

Glossary words may also be worked with in the following ways.

The students may enjoy creating a Picture Glossary by illustrating major terms introduced in the text. Have students print a word and its definition on an 8½ x 11 sheet of unlined paper, and add an illustrative drawing or magazine photo. These pages can be bound to make a class Picture Glossary.

Because middle-grade children are fascinated by words, you may take this interest and build on it, to increase their religious vocabularies. One way to help the students sharpen their skills is to ask them to use new words and terms in context sentences, or to incorporate them into extra-credit stories or reports.

Using the Reconciliation Section

Because customs and practices for celebrating First Reconciliation differ widely by locality and culture, this section provides only general information.

Important Things to Know

This section offers a general overview of the knowledge required of young people preparing for First Reconciliation. Material in this section can be used for review throughout the teaching of Reconciliation.

Questions about the Sacrament of Reconciliation

This section contains a summary of the questions young people most commonly raise about Reconciliation, especially regarding the Church's requirements. Here are some ways you can use the section.

1. Read through the questions and answers with the students. Provide additional information where necessary.

2. You might ask the students to memorize these questions and answers one or two at a time.

3. Students may add their own questions to this list, for you to answer. You might also invite the pastor to go over these questions with the students and to answer any other questions the students may have.

4. You can use the entire page as a final quiz in preparation for the reception of First Reconciliation.

Reconciliation

Important Things to Know about Reconciliation

Sin is turning away from God by choosing to do wrong. Sin is a failure to respond with love to God and to others.

- **Venial sin** is choosing something that is wrong that hurts our friendship with God. To receive forgiveness for venial sin, we must be sincerely sorry and ask God, in prayer, to help us live better lives.
- **Mortal sin** is choosing something that is very seriously wrong. A person who chooses mortal sin is choosing to turn away from God's love and from God's Family. Mortal sin is sometimes called deadly sin, because it separates us from grace, our share in God's life.
- For a sin to be mortal, the action must be seriously wrong. The person must know that the action is seriously wrong and chooses to commit the action anyway. No one can commit a mortal sin by mistake or by accident.
- To receive forgiveness for mortal sin, it is necessary to confess the sin to a priest in the sacrament of Reconciliation. The person must be sincerely sorry for the sin and willing to make up for the serious wrong he or she has done. This is shown through the performing of the penance given by the priest. The priest, taking the place of Jesus, says a prayer of absolution as a sign of God's forgiveness and of our reconciliation with God's Family.

Questions about the Sacrament of Reconciliation

1. **When should I receive the sacrament of Reconciliation for the first time?** Most young Catholics who were baptized as babies will receive the sacrament of Reconciliation for the first time at about the age of seven—when they are old enough to know the difference between right and wrong. Usually, you will receive the sacrament of Reconciliation for the first time just before you make your First Communion.
2. **How often should I receive the sacrament of Reconciliation?** Catholics are required to confess any mortal sin at least once a year, during the Easter season. Because you cannot receive Holy Communion while you are in a state of mortal sin, it is important to confess any serious sins as soon as possible. But Reconciliation is not just important in times of mortal sin. Regular, frequent confession of venial sin will help you overcome bad habits and bring you closer to God.
3. **What if I have committed a serious sin, and I cannot get to the sacrament of Reconciliation?** In a grave emergency (such as the danger of death), you can receive absolution from mortal sin by praying a sincere Act of Contrition and by promising God you will try to change your life. You should try to receive the sacrament of Reconciliation as soon as you possibly can.

4. **What if the priest is angry with me, or tells my sins to someone else?** In confession, the priest takes the place of Jesus. He is not there to judge you or to yell at you, but to offer you God's forgiveness. If you have difficulty talking to a particular priest, you may choose to make your confession to another priest. All priests are bound by a sacred promise to keep what they hear in confession private. Anything you say in confession remains a secret.

How to Go to Confession

Before Receiving the Sacrament

- Spend some time quietly thinking about what you will confess. You can use the Examination of Conscience on page 75 of this book to see how you are living the commandments.
- Say a prayer to the Holy Spirit. Ask the Holy Spirit to help you make a good confession.
- Wait quietly until it is your turn to enter the Reconciliation room or confessional. Be courteous to others who are waiting.

Steps in the Sacrament of Reconciliation (*Individual*)

1. The priest greets you in the name of the Father, and of the Son, and of the Holy Spirit.
2. The priest says a prayer to help you trust in God. You answer, "Amen."
3. The priest may read a passage from Scripture to remind you of God's love and forgiveness. You listen quietly.
4. You tell your sins to the priest. Then, he talks with you about how you might make better choices.
5. The priest gives you a penance—something you agree to do in order to make up for your sins and to show that you want to change your life.
6. The priest invites you to tell God how sorry you are. You pray an Act of Contrition.
7. The priest prays the prayer of absolution. If you are making your confession face-to-face, the priest will extend his hands over your head while he prays. You say, "Amen."
8. The priest prays: "Give thanks to the Lord, for He is good." You answer, "His mercy endures forever."
9. The priest says, "The Lord has freed you from your sins. Go in peace."

How to Go to Confession

This simple outline reviews the steps in the Rite of Reconciliation and provides some guidelines for what to do before and after going to confession. You can use this outline in rehearsing the students for their First Reconciliation. It should be introduced about midway through your presentation of the text (no later than Lesson 5).

Because the ceremonies surrounding individual confession may differ, this outline is concerned only with the order of sacramental confession itself. See page 130 of this Catechist's Edition for an outline of a sample penitential service.

How to Go to Confession

This page gives a simple outline of the steps involved in Reconciliation with a group. There is also a section on what follows the reception of the sacrament, whether received as an individual or as a group.

Reconciliation

(*With a Group*)

1. The Reconciliation service may begin with a hymn. The priest greets the penitents and prays the Opening Prayer. You respond, "Amen."
2. Listen to the Scripture readings.
3. Listen to the homily.
4. Participate in the Examination of Conscience, which may be silent or in the form of a litany.
5. Pray the Act of Contrition or Litany of Sorrow, followed by the Lord's Prayer.
6. Confess and receive absolution individually.
7. Gather again to sing or pray in thanksgiving for God's mercy.
8. The priest says the concluding prayer. You respond, "Amen."
9. The priest blesses all present in the name of the Father, and of the Son, and of the Holy Spirit.
10. The priest or deacon dismisses the assembly by saying, "The Lord has freed you from your sins. Go in peace." You respond, "Amen."

After Receiving the Sacrament

- Remain in the church for a few moments. Say a prayer of thanksgiving to Jesus for the grace and healing you have received.
- If the priest has asked you to say prayers as your penance, you may pray these prayers quietly now. If the priest has asked you to do something as your penance, plan how you can carry out this action soon.
- Do not talk with others about your confession. Do not ask others about their confessions.

74

An Examination of Conscience

You can use these questions to prepare for the sacrament of Reconciliation. The questions are based on the Ten Commandments.

1. Do I really love God above all other things?
   Do I put God first in my life?
   Do I trust in God's love for me?
   Do I avoid relying on supersition or "magic"?
2. Do I show respect for God's name?
   When I make promises, do I take them seriously?
   Do I show reverence for holy people, places, and things?
   Is my language respectful and clean?
3. Do I participate fully at Mass?
   Am I a part of my parish family?
   Do I take time for prayer and spiritual growth?
   How do I use my leisure time?
4. Do I contribute to my family's happiness?
   Am I obedient to my parents and others in authority?
   Do I show love for my brothers and sisters?
   How well do I show repect for older adults?
5. Do I respect God's gift of life?
   Do I take care of my health and the well-being of others?
   Am I able to avoid the temptation to use drugs or alcohol?
   Do I avoid violence and fighting in my life and in what I watch or read?
6. Do I show respect for the human body and for God's gift of sexuality?
   Do I avoid situations, entertainments, and conversations that make fun of God's gift of sexuality?
   Am I modest and chaste in my thoughts, my words, and my actions?
7. Do I avoid cheating and stealing?
   Do I take care of my possessions and respect the belongings of others?
   Am I careful to make sure that others get their fair share?
8. Am I honest with others and with myself?
   Can people put their trust in me?
   Do I avoid lying?
   Do I refuse to gossip about others or call them names?
9. Do I show respect for marriage and family life?
   Do I recognize that responsible sexuality requires the mature commitment of marriage?
   Am I jealous of my friends, or can I be open to new relationships and allow others that freedom, too?
10. Am I happy with what I have, or am I always asking for more?
    Do I run others down out of envy? Do I let material possessions run my life?
    Do I do my part in caring for God's creation?

An Examination of Conscience

This page is provided to enable the students to review their own lives in order to prepare for the sacrament of Reconciliation. Students are referred to this page at several points during their study of Reconciliaztion. In introducing this material to the students, you might:

1. Help the students make the connection between these questions and the commandments on which they are based.

2. Encourage the students to add their own questions to the list.

3. Remind the students that these questions are for their own personal reflection; answers are not to be shared. Encourage the students to reflect on these questions often, not only in preparation for the sacrament of Reconciliation but as an ongoing part of their personal prayer life.

Using the Music Section

This section of the student text contains the lyrics of the five Reconciliation songs introduced in the text, for the students' convenience in learning and practicing this music. These songs can be found on the Benziger *Come, Follow Me* Grade 4 music cassette. The musical notation for these songs can be found on pages 135–142 of this Catechist's Edition.

Learning the songs gives some variety to the lesson. Knowing the songs prepares the students to use the songs during the rite of Reconciliation.

Here is a list of the songs that go with *Reconciliation* and suggestions for using them.

Lesson 1
"We Are a Kingdom People"

This song reflects service, helping others, and what we do to build God's kingdom on earth. It is a good choice as a gathering or closing song.

Lesson 3
"Choices"

The theme of honesty and making choices is reinforced in this song. This song may be used to initiate a discussion of choices that the students make in their lives. It may be sung or played during the celebration of Reconciliation.

Lesson 5
"Your Way, O God"

This song may be used as a closing prayer. The theme of the song is to follow Jesus, and it is appropriate during a Reconciliation service or in liturgy as a Communion song.

Music

We Are a Kingdom People

Words and music by Christopher Walker

We are a kingdom people, kingdom people
Sent to love and serve our God.
We are a kingdom people, a kingdom
people sent to love and serve our God.

1. We serve Jesus ev'ry time we help our brothers and sisters, brothers and sisters.
2. We serve Jesus ev'ry time we share the good things God gives us, good things God gives us.
3. We serve Jesus ev'ry time that we are honest and truthful, honest and truthful.

Choices

Words by Cathy Ruff
Music by David Phillips

I am learning to make choices, and now's
the time to start
To listen and obey God's rule, the choice is
in my heart.
I am learning to make choices, and now's
the time to start
To listen and obey God's rule, the choice is
in my heart.

1. There's always rules to follow, at home,
at play.
God knew I'd need a helping hand each
and ev'ry day.
So God gave us commandments,
rules we must obey.

2. Gossiping and lying cause destruction
and despair,
But honesty and words of praise show
others that we care.
If somehow you have hurt someone,
don't think the pain will hide.

Your Way, O God

Words and music by Bob Hurd

Your way, O God, I want to follow,
Help me to walk the path of life.
You are the Shepherd, we are the sheep,
Teach us the sound of Your voice.

1. Help us to make this journey together,
Help us to share the Bread of Life.
We must be Christ for each other
For we are Your own.

2. Sometimes we hurt ourselves
And each other,
And we feel lost, ashamed and alone.
You sent us Jesus to find us
And lead us home.

76

More Joy in Heaven

Words and music by Marie Jo Thum

1. There once was a shepherd who loved
all his sheep.
They numbered on hundred fold,
But one little lamb wandered away,
Was frightened and lonely and cold.
With ninety-nine safe in the field
The shepherd set out to rescue his stray
And when he returned with his lamb in
his arms
He invited his neighbors to stay. He said,

(Refrain)
Come, share my happiness,
Feast at my table.
Join me with great jubilation.
Do you not know what was lost has been
found?

Rejoice in my glad celebration!
And there is more joy in heaven,
There is more joy in heaven,
There is more joy in heaven,
There is more joy in heaven
When the lost one has returned.

2. There once was a father who loved
both his sons,
But his younger son wanted to roam.
He squandered their money
and lived like a fool
And sadly he started for home.
Sorry and shameful he cried to his father,
"Your servant," he said. "Let me be."
But his father embraced him and said,
"You're my son,
and my son you'll
Always be."
He said, (*Sing the refrain.*)

Oh, Happy One

Words and music by Marie Jo Thum

Oh, happy one! Come and rejoice!
The kingdom of heaven belongs to you!
Oh, happy one! Come and rejoice!
The kingdom of heaven belongs to you,
Oh happy one!

1. God is your treasure, God knows all
your needs.
Blest are the poor in spirit.
Look for the good in ev'rything and
ev'ryone.
Blest are the clean of heart.

2. Say yes to God. Accept God's will with
courage.
Blessed are the meek.
Treat other people as you want them to
treat you.
Blest are those who hunger for justice.

3. Do the right thing, even when it is
not easy.
Blest are those who suffer in My name.
Give up power and instead bring peace.
Blessed are those who bring peace.

4. Show God's mercy. Be kind and
forgiving.
Blest are the merciful.
Suffer with those who hurt
And share their tears.
Blessed are those who mourn.

Lesson 7
"More Joy in Heaven"

This song has strong and specific Scriptural references, and is excellent for demonstrating the link between what we sing and what we read in the Bible. Jesus, the Good Shepherd, the prodigal son, self-esteem, reconciliation and forgiveness are some of the themes that this song reflects. The communal celebration of Reconciliation is a natural occasion for this song to be sung.

Lesson 8
"Oh, Happy One"

The focus of this song is the Beatitudes. This song is a good choice for classroom prayer services.

Using the Prayers Section

This page contains a compendium of traditional Catholic prayers. Although the students may already be familiar with many of these prayers, this page is intended as a review and resource. You may refer to this page throughout the teaching of *Reconciliation*. In addition, this resource page may be used in the following ways.

1. Help the students become more familiar with these prayers by using them at appropriate opportunities during the lesson.

2. The students can use this page for reference when writing their own prayers or planning classroom prayer and liturgy.

3. Students may wish to design their own prayer books or to add pages for these prayers to their ongoing Reconciliation project "I Celebrate Reconciliation."

4. Students may choose individual prayers to illustrate as prayer posters, bookmarks, and the like.

Prayers

The Sign of the Cross

In the name of the Father,
and of the Son,
and of the Holy Spirit.
Amen

The Lord's Prayer

Our Father, who art in heaven,
hallowed be Thy name.
Thy kingdom come; Thy will be done
on earth as it is in heaven.
Give us this day our daily bread,
and forgive us our trespasses
as we forgive those who trespass against us.
And lead us not into temptation
but deliver us from evil.
Amen.

The Hail Mary

Hail, Mary, full of grace,
the Lord is with thee.
Blessed art thou among women,
and blessed is the Fruit
of thy womb, Jesus.
Holy Mary, Mother of God,
pray for us sinners, now,
and at the hour of our death.
Amen.

Glory to the Father

Glory to the Father,
and to the Son.
and to the Holy Spirit.
As is was in the beginning,
is now, and will be forever.
Amen.

Acts of Contrition

My God, I am sorry for my sins with all my heart.
In choosing to do wrong and failing to do good,
I have sinned against You
whom I should love above all things.
I firmly intend, with Your help,
to do penance, to sin no more,
and to avoid whatever leads me to sin.
Jesus Christ suffered and died for us.
In His name, dear Father, forgive me.
Amen.

O my God,
I am heartily sorry for having offended Thee.
And I detest all my sins,
because of Thy just punishments,
but most of all because they offend Thee, my God,
who art all good and deserving of all my love.
I firmly resolve, with the help of Thy grace,
to sin no more,
and to avoid the near occasion of sin.
Amen.

Lord, Jesus Christ, Son of God,
have mercy on me, a sinner.

Lists Catholics Remember

The Ten Commandments

(*based on Exodus 20:2–17*)

1. I am the Lord, your God. You shall have no other gods besides Me.
2. You shall not take the name of the Lord, your God, in vain.
3. Remember to keep holy the Sabbath day.
4. Honor your father and your mother.
5. You shall not kill.
6. You shall not commit adultery.
7. You shall not steal.
8. You shall not lie.
9. You shall not desire your neighbor's wife.
10. You shall not desire anything that belongs to your neighbor.

The Rules of the Church

1. Take part in the Eucharist every Sunday and holy day. Do no unnecessary work on Sunday.
2. Receive the sacraments frequently.
3. Study about the Good News of Jesus Christ.
4. Follow the marriage laws of the Church.
5. Support the people of God.
6. Do penance on certain days.
7. Reach out to other people. Support the missionary effort of the Church.

The Works of Mercy

Corporal (*For the Body*)
Feed the hungry.
Give drink to the thirsty.
Clothe the naked.
Shelter the homeless.
Visit the sick.
Visit the imprisoned.
Bury the dead.

Spiritual (*For the heart, soul, and mind*)
Help the sinner.
Teach the ignorant.
Counsel the doubtful.
Comfort the sorrowful.
Bear wrongs patiently.
Forgive injuries.
Pray for the living and the dead.

The Beatitudes

(*based on Matthew 5:3–10*)

Blessed are the poor in spirit,
for theirs is the kingdom of heaven.
Blessed are they who mourn,
for they will be comforted.
Blessed are the meek,
for they will inherit the land.
Blessed are they who hunger and thirst for righteousness,
for they will be satisfied.
Blessed are the merciful,
for they will be shown mercy.
Blessed are the clean of heart,
for they will see God.
Blessed are the peacemakers,
for they will be called children of God.
Blessed are they who are persecuted for the sake of righteousness,
for theirs is the kingdom of heaven.

Using the Lists Catholics Remember Section

This section contains the fundamental core of Catholic morality and service. Throughout the text of Reconciliation, students are referred to this page as a resource. In addition to text-related uses, you may work with this material in the following ways.

1. Students may be asked to memorize this material in manageable sections.

2. At appropriate points during the course, you may have the students work with one or another of these lists, perhaps rephrasing statements in their own words or providing examples.

3. Lists may be illustrated as posters or class murals.

4. Lists may be rephrased as litany-type prayers for use in classroom prayer and liturgy.

Lists Catholics Remember

The Seven Sacraments

Sacraments of Initiation
- Baptism
- Confirmation
- Eucharist

Sacraments of Healing
- Reconciliation
- The Anointing of the Sick

Sacraments of Service
- Marriage
- Holy Orders

The Gifts of the Holy Spirit

(from the Rite of Confirmation)

Wisdom
Understanding
Right judgment
Courage
Knowledge
Reverence
Wonder and awe

The Fruit of the Spirit

(from Galatians 5:22–23)

Love
Joy
Peace
Patience
Kindness
Generosity
Faithfulness
Gentleness
Self-control

The Virtues

Theological Virtues
- Faith
- Hope
- Love

Cardinal Virtues
- Prudence
- Justice
- Temperance
- Fortitude

Days of Penance

The days of Advent
Ash Wednesday
The days of Lent, specially Fridays
Fridays throughout the year

80

Catechist's Manual

Contents

Introduction

Using Benziger *Reconciliation* . . . 82
An Overview of Benziger *Reconciliation* . . . 84
The Student Text
The Catechist's Edition
The Family Edition
Family Magazines
Music Cassettes

For You, the Program Director

Putting the Program in Place . . . 86
Implementing the Program in the Catholic School . . . 88
Implementing the Program in CCD . . . 88
Implementing the Program in the Family . . . 89
Implementing the Program in Neighborhood Clusters . . . 89
Implementing the Program on a Parishwide Basis . . . 90
Organizing a Catechist Orientation Meeting . . . 91
Organizing a Family Orientation Meeting . . . 96
Arranging Family Interviews . . . 100
Arranging a Family Mini-Retreat . . . 101
Arranging an Enrollment Ceremony . . . 102
Including Catechists and Families . . . 104
Sample invitations and letters for home and parish use
Sample family information sheets

For You, the Catechist

Preparing for Your Ministry . . . 111
Communicating with the Families . . . 113
Sample letters to send home in English and Spanish
Planning Prayer and Liturgies . . . 129
Sample Reconciliation and Eucharistic liturgies
Planning chart for a Eucharistic liturgy
Using Music with *Reconciliation* . . . 134
Lead sheets

Commissioning Certificate . . . 144

Introduction

Using Benziger *Reconciliation*

Reconciliation teaches intermediate-age students what we Catholics believe, celebrate, live, and pray.

A separate catechesis, or program of teaching, for the reception of the sacrament of Reconciliation is both appropriate and essential. This is true regardless of the age of the person being prepared. *Reconciliation* has been created to meet the needs and learning capabilities of the middle-grade student. The information taught adheres to the requirements set by Pope Saint Pius X.

In *Reconciliation*, there is *experiential* learning through hands-on activities, celebrations, and songs. There is *relational* learning through Scripture and stories that explore issues and concerns that guide students to an understanding of Christian living. There is *traditional* learning that stresses a knowledge of the Catholic teaching and vocabulary and information basic to an understanding of Reconciliation. And there is *internalized* learning that helps the student live what he or she learns.

The text is based on the essentials of Catholic belief and teaching about the Reconciliation. These are:

- Sin is freely choosing to do wrong.
- Sin hurts both the sinner and the community.
- Sin weakens or breaks friendship with God and community.
- Reconciliation pardons sins committed after Baptism and brings the sinner back to God and the community.
- Reconciliation brings an increase of spiritual strength for Christians.
- Followers of Christ are called to continual conversion and renewal.

The *Catechism of the Catholic Church* describes Reconciliation in this way: "To return to communion with God after having lost it through sin is a process born of the grace of God who is rich in mercy and solicitous for the salvation of men. One must ask for this precious gift for oneself and for others" *(#1489)*.

WORKS HAND IN HAND

Reconciliation is not intended to substitute for regular religious instruction given daily or weekly in the Catholic school or CCD situation. Rather, it is designed as an accompaniment that focuses on Reconciliation. While this focus necessarily includes much of the rich treasury of Catholic teaching and practice, it is impossible to include the whole body of doctrine. It is presumed that the children using *Reconciliation* are also involved in a regular religious education program that will supply the larger context for faith development. The material covered in *Reconciliation* coordinates well with the middle-grade books of all major religious education series in use today.

WHICH SACRAMENT FIRST?

Sometimes the question of which sacramental preparation to offer first—Reconciliation or Eucharist—comes up. The *Reconciliation* text unfolds as the sacrament does, and so it begins with a greeting. Eucharist begins with the greeting and a time for remembering our sins and asking forgiveness for them. The Penitential Rite tells us to put away selfishness, pride, and a lack of concern for others. A turning away from sin focuses us on being one with Jesus.

Therefore, the Church requires confession and sacramental absolution in the case of serious sin as a prerequisite for the worthy reception of the Eucharist. The Church also teaches that the sacrament of Reconciliation is a source of grace and spiritual growth, even in the absence of mortal sin.

In a letter to all bishops, dated May 19, 1977, the Vatican Congregation for the Sacraments and Divine Worship and the Congregation for the Clergy reaffirmed Pope Saint Pius X's insistence that children have the right to receive the sacraments of Reconciliation and Eucharist, provided that the children are sufficiently prepared. This letter stated the Church's preference for first reception of Reconciliation to precede First Eucharist, a practice that has been reaffirmed in recent years. Most dioceses in the United States have developed guidelines for the sacramental preparation of young people. In cooperation with those guidelines, Benziger also publishes *Eucharist*, a program geared for the preparation of First Eucharist for middle-grade students.

SCHEDULING THE PROGRAM: CATECHISTS

Each of the eight lessons of *Reconciliation* is organized with enough flexibility so that you can make it work for you and your particular schedule. You might choose to present the text in eight consecutive sessions, limiting the number of enrichment activities and additional resources you use. This would be a minimal presentation. As an alternative, you could break down each lesson into smaller segments, taught over a period of several months. In this arrangement, you might follow the lesson plan outline and break each lesson into four parts—We Celebrate, We Believe, We Live Our Faith, and We Pray. Or, you can divide the lesson into three parts—We Celebrate, We Believe, and We Live Our Faith—and send We Pray home with the students.

However you choose to present the material, keep the pace at a rate that works best for your students. Try to avoid doing too much too quickly.

SCHEDULING THE PROGRAM: FAMILIES

If you are using the Family Edition of *Reconciliation* to prepare a child for Reconciliation, the best scheduling advice is to do what works best for you. You should meet regularly with the parish staff and arrange to be included in parish celebrations throughout the year. However, home-teachers must remember to allow more, not less, time to explore the material. No home is actually a classroom, and there will be plenty of distractions. But the home is a friendly, loving and in fact, terrific place for learning about this sacrament. Using *Reconciliation* in the home is more than an opportunity to convey important material. It can unify the whole family and provide spiritual growth and enjoyment.

An Overview of Benziger *Reconciliation*

Because the preparation of young people for Reconciliation takes place under all kinds of circumstances, *Reconciliation* has been created as a comprehensive, easy to use, and flexible program. The components of this program include:

THE STUDENT TEXT

Attractive and colorful, the student text for *Reconciliation* is built around eight lessons. Each lesson follows the same format:

INTRODUCTION: WE CELEBRATE

- A one-page excerpt from the rite of Reconciliation that sets the theme for the lesson and helps the students learn the prayers and responses of individual and group Reconciliation.
- A one-page read-aloud or read-along story, drawn from everyday life experiences or Scripture, that explores the theme of the lesson.

DEVELOPMENT: WE BELIEVE

- Two pages of reading text that present the theme of the lesson in the context of Church teaching. A special feature of this part of the lesson is a highlighted section entitled "We Catholics Believe" that provides additional information on related Catholic beliefs, practices, and religious vocabulary.
- A one-page Gospel story exploring the theme of the lesson as it is found in the life and teachings of Jesus.

APPLICATION: WE LIVE OUR FAITH

- A one-page activity that focuses on verbal or art skills to review the lesson content. In all lessons, this page also provides a vocabulary review exercise.

APPLICATION: WE PRAY

- A one-page prayer that can be taken home and shared with the families. A Family Note tells what was learned in the lesson and how to apply the lesson at home. The Catechist's Edition also provides suggestions for adapting this page to classroom use.

The student text also contains several pages of resources, including a Glossary, the lyrics to the songs used with the text, traditional Catholic prayers, and summary material needed to celebrate Reconciliation.

During each lesson, the students do a My Own Book activity. At completion, the activities will compose the "I Celebrate Reconciliation" book that will include personal work, full-color photos, and simple Reconciliation Rite responses.

THE CATECHIST'S EDITION

Designed for practical use by catechists of all levels of experience—from the beginning volunteer to the professional DRE—the Catechist's Edition for *Reconciliation* provides everything you need to teach the program, under one cover!

LESSON BACKGROUND SECTION

Two overview pages precede each of the eight lessons and provide the following information:

- *Lesson Number* and *Title*
- *Focus*
- *Catechetical Objectives* Several key points within the lesson.
- *Lesson Overview* A brief quotation from the *Catechism of the Catholic Church* and simple explanations of each of the four lesson sections in the student text.
- *The Church's Wisdom* The theology supporting the lesson.
- *Catechist Resources* A list of annotated videos, books, and music cassettes that would enrich your teaching.
- *Classroom Resources* Videos, books, and music cassettes to use with your students.
- *Before Beginning the Lesson* A list of things you need to prepare the lesson.
- *New Words* A list of vocabulary and definitions you will cover.
- *Catechist Prayer* A prayer to help you prepare yourself spiritually.

LESSON PLANS

Lesson plans are presented in simple format, keeping time restrictions in mind.

- The student text is reproduced in full color. Running alongside each student page is a margin column containing the suggested lesson plan. You have the steps you need right in front of you.
- Along the bottom of the page are features with optional suggestions for enriching and extending the lesson.

RESOURCES

The back of the book has a section that is filled with resources for the program director and for the catechist.

- You will find plans for implementing *Reconciliation*, for organizing catechist and family meetings, and letters for communicating with those involved in the program. The letters are given in English and in Spanish.
- There are sample prayer services and background information on planning classroom liturgies, a Reconciliation liturgy, and the First Eucharist liturgy.
- The lyrics and lead sheets for songs that correspond to the *Reconciliation* music program are included.

THE FAMILY EDITION

Many parents are taking advantage of the opportunity to prepare their children, in the warmth and intimacy of the home setting, for Reconciliation. The Family Edition of *Reconciliation*—which echoes the Catechist's Edition in format—provides everything a parent needs to prepare his or her child for the sacrament. The lessons are presented in simple language that suits the home situation. The Family Edition is also recommended for use by small communities or neighborhood clusters.

FAMILY MAGAZINES

Two magazines are available for families whose children are in the primary and the middle-grade sacramental preparation programs.

- *The Reconciling Family* and *The Eucharistic Family* use inviting graphics and a popular layout to keep families in touch with the sacramental life of their children as well as the issues and concerns of today's families.

MUSIC CASSETTES

Music for *Reconciliation* has been chosen from the Benziger *Come, Follow Me* Grade 4 music program. A cassette is available. The wrap feature Music Note tells the catechist or family member which song to use and where to find the lyrics and notations.

For You, the Program Director

Putting the Program in Place

All of the Benziger sacramental preparation books—*First Reconciliation, First Eucharist, Reconciliation* and *Eucharist*—have been designed so they are simple to use. Whatever your catechetical situation, the Eucharist and Reconciliation programs meet your parish needs. Following this introduction, you will find models for implementing the program:

- in the Catholic school;
- in the CCD groups;
- in the home, taught by family members;
- in neighborhood clusters;
- as a total parish program.

The situations in most parishes require combining elements from a number of these models. Use the notes given as a starting point, and build from there according to your needs.

All models share some of the following common elements:

PLANNING

An initial planning session is key to the effective implementation of any of these models. This meeting should involve the pastor, the program director (coordinator of sacramental preparation or director of religious education), and principal catechists who will be presenting the program. If parents will be assuming primary responsibility for the formation of their children—as in home-based models—parents should be represented at the initial planning session.

The single most important question that should be addressed at this meeting is: "What do we want for the children and families of our parish with regard to the preparation and reception of the sacraments?"

In addition, practical considerations need to be addressed:

- Beginning and ending dates for catechesis
- The date/s and time/s for the sacramental celebrations (Does a large number of candidates make one central celebration difficult?)
- Dress for the celebrations
- Housekeeping details, such as arranging for a photographer, organist, choir, and servers
- Liturgical style of the celebrations (Will First Eucharist be celebrated as part of a regular Sunday Mass? Will Reconciliation be celebrated as part of a parish renewal service?)

Other considerations for this planning session include the establishment of a cut-off date for accepting candidates and the criteria for inclusion in the program. Some pastors feel that everyone old enough to receive the sacraments should be encouraged to do so, while others question the wisdom of admitting candidates whose families are uninterested or uninvolved in the parish. It is important to establish a consistent policy (presumably reflecting a high degree of pastoral sensitivity) and to make this policy known at the parish.

EXTENDING THE INVITATION

Regardless of whether a parish prepares its candidates together or in separate groups, in the classroom or at home, an invitation should be extended to all potential participants in the name of the parish community. A list of family names can be compiled by the program director, using family records from the Catholic school and/or parish school of religion. Use several means to extend the invitation:

- A letter written on parish stationery, signed by the pastor and program director, can be mailed or sent home with students. *See pages 104–105 for sample letters of invitation.*
- An announcement can be inserted into the parish bulletin.
- The invitation can be extended from the pulpit or read as part of the announcements at Sunday Masses.

There are two purposes for the invitation. First, it allows families to see clearly that sacramental preparation is a parish responsibility. Second, the invitation requests the presence of candidates and their families at a meeting or series of meetings, which eases logistical planning and brings families into the catechetical process.

Catechists and assistants should also be formally invited, in the name of the parish community, to participate in this ministry.

See page 106 for a sample catechist invitation letter.

CATECHIST ORIENTATION MEETING

At least one meeting for catechists and assistants should be scheduled before the program begins. Parents who will be teaching children at home or in neighborhood clusters should also be invited to the orientation meeting and should be considered catechists for the purposes of this meeting. Besides helping the catechists feel at home with the Benziger sacramental preparation texts and the Catechist's Editions, this meeting offers the program director an opportunity to evaluate the skills and needs of the catechists. A concluding prayer service can help build community among all the catechists and assistants, who may bring varying degrees of experience to the teaching situation. Your catechists may need additional formation in sacramental theology. Catechist enrichment may be provided in a pleasant and flexible way by using Benziger *Catechists in Formation, Book Two, Introduction to Theological Studies*, Chapter 7, entitled "Sacraments." Chapters 8 and 10 may also be helpful.

See pages 91–95 for a catechist orientation meeting outline, worksheets, and prayer service.

FAMILY ORIENTATION MEETING

You may wish to schedule one sacramental meeting that focuses on Reconciliation and on Eucharist. This meeting is an important one and should be scheduled to attract as many parents as possible. Give special consideration to the needs of parents who work outside the home, and if necessary, provide child care during the meeting. (You may be able to get the help of the Confirmation candidates.)

The families will be most concerned about the practical details of the sacramental celebrations. But this orientation meeting will serve other purposes as well. By inviting the families of the Catholic school and the CCD classes to meet together, you will help strengthen the parish community. Through discussions and worksheets, you will guide the families to reevaluate the role of Eucharist and Reconciliation in their lives. You will help them see that they actually participate in the faith journey of their children. A concluding prayer service will join the families together in celebration.

If needed, schedule additional family meetings that coincide with practices or liturgies.

See pages 96–99 for a family orientation meeting outline, worksheets, and a prayer service.

FAMILY INTERVIEWS

Whenever possible, the initial family orientation meeting should be supplemented by family interviews. These are lead by the pastor and/or the program director before catechesis begins.

See page 100 for a family interview outline and sample questions.

FAMILY MINI-RETREAT

If you feel the families would enjoy and benefit from a mini-retreat that introduces them to the sacramental preparation program, you may spend a weekend morning together. End with a pot luck lunch.

See page 101 for a sample mini-retreat.

ENROLLMENT CEREMONY

Scheduling a formal enrollment ceremony helps to celebrate sacramental preparation as a parish event.

See pages 102–103 for an enrollment ceremony and handout sheet.

PLANNING FOR SPECIAL NEEDS

When orientation meetings or family interviews reveal special needs among the candidates and even their families, parish staff must determine a policy for handling these.

The most common special need encountered in parishes is age-appropriate catechesis. Benziger offers separate, complete catechesis for Reconciliation and for Eucharist on both the primary grade level (1–3) and the middle grade level (4–6). For junior-high students who have not yet received First Eucharist or Reconciliation, you may wish to consider Benziger *Christian Initiation* and Benziger *Confirmation.* These two texts are catechetical components that can be used with a catechumenate-based program.

The next special need encountered is a common language. Where large numbers of candidates lack facility in English, special programs need to be developed to meet their needs. In many cases, however, the children have a grasp of English that their parents lack. Translation of parent materials into other languages and the presence of interpreters at the family meetings and family interviews may be all that's needed.

Children with special needs of a physical, emotional, or intellectual nature can (and in most cases, should, for pastoral reasons) be accommodated within the regular program or programs. Where special-needs candidates are prepared in separate groups or individually at home, they and their catechists should be brought together at regular times with the parish's other candidates for prayer and celebration.

Implementing the Program in the Catholic School

ENROLLMENT

Within the parochial school system, it is often assumed that all baptized students who have reached the appropriate grade level, usually Grade 2, will be prepared for Reconciliation and First Eucharist. It's important to remember that not all students fit this norm. There may be students in the intermediate grades who have not received these sacraments. Also, students from Eastern rite churches may have received First Eucharist as infants, and the catechesis of transfer students may have to be evaluated. So the families of all eligible students should be contacted in advance of the program.

IMPLEMENTATION

In the parochial school, sacramental catechesis will most often take place within the setting of the regularly scheduled religion class. When this is done, it's important to coordinate use of the sacramental texts with the presentation of the core religion curriculum. Some adjustments, such as shortening or replacing core lesson plans, will need to be made. These adjustments are more common with middle-grade students, as most second-grade religion texts allow for sacramental preparation.

The simplest way to implement Benziger *Reconciliation* and *Eucharist* in the Catholic school is to substitute one core religion class per week with a sacramental class. The sacramental texts may be taught consecutively (usually eight weeks of Reconciliation followed by eight weeks of First Eucharist), or classes may overlap, in which case two days per week will need to be devoted to sacramental preparation.

Other scheduling options include devoting all religion classes to sacramental preparation over a suitable period of time (breaking each lesson into four sessions), or requiring students to attend sacramental preparation sessions outside the regular school day. (In the latter instance, parochial school students may attend classes with students from non-parochial schools.)

INVOLVING FAMILIES

Families of candidates in the parochial school should be involved in their children's sacramental formation by attendance at meetings, practices, and liturgies. You may send home the We Pray pages in the student texts and the Family Letters in this Catechist's Edition, and encourage the use of the family magazines *The Reconciling Family* and *The Eucharistic Family*.

See pages 113–128 for Family Letters in English and in Spanish.

Implementing the Program in CCD

ENROLLMENT

Sacramental preparation provides an excellent opportunity to involve children who do not attend the parochial school in the life of the parish. It is also the best way to involve the families of these students. Recruitment for sacramental preparation programs should not be limited to those families who already have children enrolled in CCD classes, but should be extended to the whole parish through the use of invitation letters, parish bulletin inserts, and announcements at Sunday Masses. Often, families who enroll their children in sacramental preparation classes will encourage them to continue in the regular CCD religion program.

IMPLEMENTATION

In the CCD situation, the key factor is the time limit. Most religion classes of nonparochial-school students meet only once a week for an hour or less. During sacramental catechesis, for maximum efficiency class time should be devoted only to working with the sacramental text. This is most commonly done by devoting the second semester of the year to sacramental preparation, with the regular core religion program being "telescoped" or adapted to fit this schedule. In cases, such as with older candidates, where it is deemed important to maintain continuity in the core religion program, sacramental preparation may necessitate adding special class sessions. If necessary, the sacramental preparation program may be covered in two to four expanded half-day or full-day sessions. Whatever you choose, keep in mind that the sacramental preparation texts do not take away from the core religion program; they enrich it.

Whenever possible, students preparing for the sacraments in the CCD situation should be brought together with their parochial-school peers for prayer and fellowship. A single celebration of the sacrament, with candidates from both programs, is another good sign of parish unity.

The catechist in the CCD situation may be the regular religion teacher or a special sacramental catechist. Close communication between you and the catechists will add to the success of the program.

INVOLVING FAMILIES

Families of candidates in CCD classes should be involved in their children's sacramental formation by attendance at meetings, practices, and liturgies. You may send home the We Pray pages found in the student texts and the Family Letters, and encourage the use of the family magazines *The Reconciling Family* and *The Eucharistic Family*.

See pages 113–128 for Family Letters in English and in Spanish.

Implementing the Program in the Family

ENROLLMENT

The Church teaches that parents have the primary responsibility for the religious formation of their children. Parental involvement in sacramental preparation has always been encouraged. Today, however, in many parishes, families have taken on the full responsibility for that preparation. The parish staff becomes the support system for family-centered catechesis. The role of the pastor and program director is to coordinate families, to offer background and resources, and to provide opportunities for group exchange and celebration. Whether home-centered catechesis is the rule or the exception in your parish (as in the case of one or two families with older candidates or special needs), it's important to draw parent-catechists into the process from the beginning, to involve and support them throughout, and to schedule the celebration of the sacraments as parishwide events.

IMPLEMENTATION

For home-centered catechesis, Benziger *Reconciliation* and Benziger *Eucharist* offer complete Family Editions, identical in format to the Catechist's Editions, but with lesson plans tailored to parent-child interaction. Scheduling of home-centered catechesis is the most flexible implementation model of all, with families themselves determining how much time to spend on a particular lesson, and when and where to meet. The responsibility of the parish staff is to determine the dates for the sacramental celebrations and to provide parent-catechists with texts and teaching materials far in advance to allow for adequate catechesis. Opportunities for parent-catechists to "check in" with one another and with the parish staff should be available frequently.

The catechist in the home-centered model will most often be one or both parents. Other possible catechists include grandparents, godparents, or siblings of high-school or college age. The Family Edition provides sufficient background material that helps the average Catholic adult feel comfortable and secure in working with his or her child.

INVOLVING FAMILIES

In the home-centered model of sacramental catechesis, family members are involved by definition in their children's formation. However, opportunities for involvement with other families and with the parish community as a whole should be part of this model. In addition to the Family Edition of the text, parent-catechists will find the use of the family magazines an enriching experience.

Implementing the Program in Neighborhood Clusters

ENROLLMENT

The neighborhood-cluster model of sacramental preparation combines features of several other models. Catechesis takes place in homes rather than in classrooms, but in groups rather than in individual families. This model is often utilized in larger, widespread parishes that have begun to develop basic Christian communities (small groups that meet to study Scripture, to carry out Christian social action, and so on). Because this model does carry the risk of isolating groups from the parish mainstream, it is suggested that the neighborhood-cluster model only be used when it is a parishwide policy—not in combination with other implementation models. Recruitment of candidates and their families for this model follows the same guidelines as for the others: by invitation, through parish bulletin inserts, and by announcement.

IMPLEMENTATION

Because the neighborhood-cluster model is not limited by classroom timeframes, scheduling can be flexible. Neighborhood clusters, like CCD classes or prayer groups, generally meet once a week, but the length and frequency of the sessions can be varied to meet the groups' needs. Where several neighborhood clusters are engaged in sacramental preparation at the same time, opportunities should be made available for bringing all candidates and their families together at regular intervals. The celebration of the sacraments should be scheduled for the same dates.

In the neighborhood-cluster model, the catechist may be a teacher (a special sacramental catechist) or a parent, or responsibilities may be shared among any combination of the two. Either the Catechist's Edition, with its emphasis on group activities, or the Family Edition, with its home-centered approach, may be used to present the program.

INVOLVING FAMILIES

Family members tend to be quite involved in the neighborhood-cluster model—whether or not they serve as catechists—simply because a larger part of the preparation takes place in the home setting. As with the family-centered model, opportunities for exchange and celebration with other clusters and with the parish community as a whole should be made available. Families of candidates involved in a neighborhood-cluster model will find the use of the family magazines valuable.

Implementing the Program on a Parishwide Basis

ENROLLMENT

Of course, the entire Benziger sacramental preparation program is parish-centered. A specifically parish-based model, however, combines all of the aforementioned approaches. There is one central preparation program for all students, no matter where they are enrolled for regular religion classes. The families of all eligible students are recruited in advance of the program, which may be scheduled to run concurrently with other parishwide sacramental preparation programs, such as programs for the baptismal or Confirmation candidates.

IMPLEMENTATION

A parish-based implementation model presumes the scheduling of sacramental preparation sessions outside of the regular school or CCD setting. These sessions may take place in classrooms or in homes or both; they may be led by a catechetical team that includes the pastor or a staff member, a sacramental catechist, interested parents, and even other adults of the parish who act as sponsors. Length and frequency of the sessions are flexible in a parish-based model.

Parish staff carry the responsibility for implementing a parish-based model, and the coordination of schedules will be of utmost importance. Once dates are chosen for the celebration of the sacraments themselves, catechetical sessions may be scheduled accordingly. The parish community as a whole should be kept up to date on the candidates' progress, as parishioners will be involved to varying degrees. One good way to involve interested parishioners is to ask individuals or families to become prayer partners of candidates and their families.

INVOLVING FAMILIES

A parish-based model offers families the chance to become more involved, not only in their children's catechetical formation, but also in the ongoing life of the parish. In addition to encouraging parents to serve as part of the catechetical team, family members should be invited to participate in meetings and liturgies. Opportunities for family involvement are increased through the use of the We Pray pages in the student texts, the Family Letters, and the family magazines.

ORGANIZING A CATECHIST ORIENTATION MEETING

PURPOSE

The purpose of the catechist orientation meeting is to gather together the catechists involved in preparing children for First Reconciliation and Eucharist, to relate the scheduling and enrollment information, to introduce the texts and teaching materials, and to celebrate the sacramental preparation program with prayer.

WHO SHOULD ATTEND

Parish staff (the pastor and the presider for the first sacraments celebrations and the program director, who will most likely facilitate the meeting) and all catechists, school and CCD, involved in presenting the program, should be invited. If parents are to assume responsibility for preparing their children for Reconciliation and First Eucharist at home, in neighborhood clusters, or as part of a catechetical team, they should be present at this meeting.

See page 106 for a sample catechist invitation letter for this meeting.

SCHEDULING

The catechist orientation meeting should be scheduled from four to six weeks in advance of the enrollment ceremony or the first catechetical session, and at least two weeks prior to the family orientation meeting. The time and place of the catechist orientation meeting should be convenient for all those involved. Depending on the needs of the catechists, this meeting should last from two to two and a half hours.

MEETING MATERIALS

You may wish to check off the items you will need as you organize them:

__ Copies of the meeting agenda
__ Copies of the four catechist worksheets (see pages 92–95)
__ A copy of the student text, Catechist's Edition, and/or Family Edition that pertains to each catechist's teaching level
__ Copies of the Family Invitation Letter (see pages 107–108)
__ Lists of prospective candidates, drawn from class lists
__ A Commissioning Certificate for each catechist (see page 144)
__ Refreshments

AGENDA/OUTLINE

1. Open the meeting with a prayer.
2. Welcome the participants and have informal introductions.
3. Share the following basic information with your catechists, and if possible, allow for their input.
   - Dates, times, places, dress for the Reconciliation and First Eucharist celebrations
   - Criteria for accepting candidates
   - Model/s for implementing the program in your parish
4. If necessary, the pastor or program director may provide a brief summary of the theology of Reconciliation and Eucharist. Or, you may wish to share an audiovisual resource on the sacraments.
5. Distribute copies of Catechist Worksheet #1, "Let's Talk." Break into small discussion groups, and set a time limit for completing the sharing. The catechists may remain in groups until the completion of the meeting.
6. Distribute texts and teaching materials. Give a brief overview of the sacramental preparation program (see pages 84–85). Allow sufficient time for everyone to look over the materials; accept questions and comments.
7. Collate lists of prospective candidates. Add other names, if necessary. Distribute copies of the Family Invitation Letter, with instructions for mailing or delivering the invitations.
8. Distribute copies of Catechist Worksheets #2 and #3, "Let's Get Organized." Allow time for participants to complete these schedule sheets; one is for Reconciliation and one is for Eucharist. Say that the catechists will be given specific information sheets on the sacramental celebrations (see pages 109–110) to distribute to parents at a later date.
9. Distribute copies of Catechist Worksheet #4, "Let's Pray." Close the meeting by celebrating the prayer service together. The Commissioning Certificates are distributed during the service.
10. You're now ready for simple refreshments!

1 Catechist's Worksheet

Let's Talk

Use these questions to help you focus on your role as catechist for sacramental preparation. Jot your ideas in the space at the bottom of the page. If you wish, share your answers with your group.

1. The Church reminds us that "the Eucharist is the sum and summary of our faith" *(Catechism of the Catholic Church, #1327)*. What part does the Eucharist play in your own life?
2. Reconciliation is the sacrament of God's forgiving love. How have you experienced this unconditional love in your life?
3. What attitudes and understandings about the Mass would you most like to communicate to your students?
4. What special gifts and qualities do you bring to the privilege of preparing children for receiving the sacraments?
5. What kind of help do you feel you need with your catechetical work?
6. How can you encourage the families' involvement in the sacramental preparation of their children?
7. How can you help your students see the importance of Reconciliation and Eucharist in their everyday living?

2 Catechist's Worksheet—Eucharist

Let's Get Organized

Use this worksheet to schedule all the elements of your particular Eucharist program. Keep the completed sheet handy as a reminder.

First Eucharist Celebration/s

Date/s ______________________ Time/s ______________________

Place/s ______________________

Presider/s ______________________

Catechetical Program

Send home Family Letter #1 ______________________

Teach Lesson 1 ______________________ Teach Lesson 2 ______________________

Send home Family Letter #2 ______________________

Teach Lesson 3 ______________________ Teach Lesson 4 ______________________

Send home Family Letter #3 ______________________

Teach Lesson 5 ______________________ Teach Lesson 6 ______________________

Send home Family Letter #4
and Family Information Sheet ______________________

Teach Lesson 7 ______________________ Teach Lesson 8 ______________________

Family Involvement

Family Orientation Meeting

Date ______________________ Time ______________________

Place ______________________

Other Family Meetings/Family Interviews

Date/s ______________________ Time/s ______________________

Place/s ______________________

Family Mini-Retreat

Date ______________________ Time ______________________

Place ______________________

Group Liturgies

Date/s ______________________ Time/s ______________________

Sacramental Practices

Date/s ______________________ Time/s ______________________

Place/s ______________________

3 Catechist's Worksheet—Reconciliation

Let's Get Organized

Use this worksheet to schedule all the elements of your particular Reconciliation program. Keep the completed sheet handy as a reminder.

First Reconciliation Celebration/s

Date/s ______________________ Time/s ______________________

Place/s ______________________

Presider/s ______________________

Catechetical Program

Send home Family Letter #1 ______________________

Teach Lesson 1 ______________________ Teach Lesson 2 ______________________

Send home Family Letter #2 ______________________

Teach Lesson 3 ______________________ Teach Lesson 4 ______________________

Send home Family Letter #3 ______________________

Teach Lesson 5 ______________________ Teach Lesson 6 ______________________

Send home Family Letter #4
and Family Information Sheet ______________________

Teach Lesson 7 ______________________ Teach Lesson 8 ______________________

Family Involvement

First Reconciliation Family Orientation Meeting

Date ______________________ Time ______________________

Place ______________________

Other Family Meetings/Family Interviews

Date/s ______________________ Time/s ______________________

Place/s ______________________

Family Mini-Retreat

Date ______________________ Time ______________________

Place ______________________

Group Liturgies

Date/s ______________________ Time/s ______________________

Sacramental Practices

Date/s ______________________ Time/s ______________________

Place/s ______________________

4 Catechist's Worksheet

Let's Pray

Leader: Let us gather together in the name of the Father, and of the Son, and of the Holy Spirit.

All: Amen!

Leader: God, our Creator, You have made us in Your loving image, and we are good. You sent Your Son, Jesus Christ, to live among us, to share our suffering and our joy. As a sign that we would never be alone, He left us the gift of Himself in the Eucharist. As we prepare to call Your children to the Table of the Lord, strengthen us with the Bread of Life. Through Your Spirit, give us the knowledge to guide our students and the humility to share honestly with them. Whenever we gather, let us feel Your presence with us.

All: Amen!

Reader: A reading from the Holy Gospel according to John:

[Read John 6:47–#51]

Pause for quiet reflection.

Leader: Let us pray for our students and their families, that they may know Jesus in the Eucharist and find God's compassion in Reconciliation.

All: Lord, come to us.

Leader: Let us pray for our parish community, that we may be nourished by the Eucharist and supported by one another in lifelong conversion.

All: Lord, be with us.

Leader: Let us pray for the Church around the world, for unity and for healing from sin and brokenness.

All: Lord, show us Your Way.

Leader: *[If you wish, present each catechist with a Commissioning Certificate.]*

All: May the Lord bless us and keep us; may He make His face to shine upon us and be gracious to us; may He lift up His countenance upon us and give us peace. Amen!

Organizing a Family Orientation Meeting

PURPOSE

The purpose of the family orientation meeting is to gather the families of the candidates preparing for Reconciliation and Eucharist, to share the scheduling and enrollment information, to provide a summary of sacramental theology, to introduce the texts and family materials, and to celebrate the sacramental program with prayer.

WHO SHOULD ATTEND

Parents of all children in the parish preparing for Reconciliation and Eucharist should be invited to this meeting. Parish staff (the pastor and/or principal celebrant/s for the sacramental celebration/s, and the program director) and all catechists involved in the program should also attend. This meeting is directed to adult family members; the candidates themselves need not attend. Perhaps there are parishioners who could provide voluntary child-care services during this meeting.

See pages 107–108 for sample Family Invitation Letters.

SCHEDULING

The family orientation meeting should be scheduled at least three weeks prior to the enrollment ceremony or the first catechetical session. Be sure families have received their invitation letters in sufficient time. The time and place of the meeting should be convenient for all those involved and conducive to a relaxed, comfortable atmosphere. This meeting should last around 90 minutes. It would be nice to have simple refreshments at the conclusion of the meeting.

If you feel it would be more beneficial to arrange a separate family meeting for Eucharist and one for Reconciliation, you may simply divide the resources given.

MEETING MATERIALS

You may use this checklist to prepare for the meeting:

__ An attendance sign-in sheet
__ Copies of the meeting agenda
__ A blank calendar page for families to fill in with the basic program information
__ Copies of the three family worksheets (see pages 97–99)
__ Sufficient copies of student texts and catechist materials for parents to peruse, and copies of the family magazines for each family to take home
__ Family interview appointment sheet

If not already requested, families should be encouraged to bring copies of the candidates' baptismal certificates.

AGENDA/OUTLINE

1. Open the meeting with a prayer.
2. Welcome participants and have informal introductions.
3. Hand out calendar sheets for the families to fill in with the basic program information:
   - Date/time/place of the enrollment ceremony and sacramental celebration/s
   - Schedule of practices
   - Schedule for the catechetical sessions
   - Information about further parent meetings and/or family mini-retreats
   - Dates of group liturgies

   Tell the families they will receive a Family Information Sheet on the sacramental celebrations nearer to the dates of the celebrations.
4. The pastor or program director should provide a brief talk, not a lecture, on the theology of Reconciliation and the Eucharist, tailored to the needs of the parents. Be sensitive to where they are coming from. Show them how important their involvement is in the program. You may wish to supplement this information with an audiovisual experience. Allow time for questions.
5. Distribute copies of Family Worksheet #1, "Let's Talk." Break into discussion groups, with each group of parents meeting with their children's catechist, to encourage the families to share their thoughts.
6. Provide a brief overview of the sacramental preparation program (see pages 84–85). Allow sufficient time for parents to look over the texts and teaching materials; invite questions or comments.
7. The families may remain in "class" groups. Try to record each child's baptismal information (and any other details needed for registration). Explain the purpose of the family interview, and ask parents to sign the family interview appointment sheet. Present each family with a copy of the appropriate family magazine/s to take home and enjoy.
8. Allow time for other questions or comments.
9. Distribute copies of Family Worksheets #2, "Let's Promise," and #3, "Let's Pray." Close the meeting by celebrating the prayer service together. The Pledge of Commitment on Worksheet #2 is used during the service.
10. Enjoy talking together and having refreshments.

1 Family Worksheet

Let's Talk

To help you feel an active part of your child's sacramental preparation, here are some questions for you to consider. Jot your thoughts in the space below. Share what you wish with your group.

1. The Church reminds us that "the Eucharist is the sum and summary of our faith" *(Catechism of the Catholic Church, #1327).* What part does the Eucharist play in your own life?
2. As Catholics, we gather at Mass to celebrate the Eucharist. What attitudes about the Mass would you most like to pass on to your child?
3. What are some ways forgiveness can be lived in the home?
4. What moral values and attitudes do you wish to communicate to your child?
5. What challenges does your family face in living out your Christian beliefs?
6. How can you help your child see beyond the special day of First Reconciliation and First Eucharist and understand the importance of these sacraments in everyday living?

2 Family Worksheet

Let's Promise

A Pledge of Commitment

Recognizing that my involvement is of special importance in helping my child prepare to receive the sacraments . . .

- I promise to see that my child celebrates Mass on Sundays and holy days, and to be with my child at Mass whenever possible.
- I promise to see that my child attends all catechetical sessions and does the assignments.
- I promise to support and encourage my child in preparation for the sacraments by participating in family activities.
- I promise to participate in the sacramental life of the parish, as a witness of my faith to my child.
- I promise to help my child learn the basic prayers of our faith and the Act of Contrition.
- I promise to pray for my child throughout this time of preparation.
- I promise, with God's help, to continue sharing the gift of myself and the gift of faith with my child, with our family, and with the parish community after this sacramental preparation has ended.
- I promise to oversee my child's continued religious education by supporting and encouraging attendance at religious classes or by providing the opportunity for a Catholic school education.

Signed: ______________________________

Date: ______________________________

3 Family Worksheet

Let's Pray

Leader: Let us gather as a family in the name of the Father, and of the Son, and of the Holy Spirit.

All: Amen!

Leader: Let us pray.

All: God, our Father, we thank You for entrusting us with the gift of our children, and for the great gift of Your Son in the Eucharist, which we will soon begin to share together. May Your forgiving love, celebrated in the sacrament of Reconciliation, be the mark of our family. Send Your Spirit to be with us on our lifelong journey of conversion. Help us to continue to grow in faith and unity. Amen!

Reader: A reading from the Holy Gospel according to Luke:

[Read Luke 9:46–48]

Pause for quiet reflection.

Leader: We offer these prayers to our Lord.

Group 1: Lord, You use the common and ordinary to reveal Your greatest mysteries.

Group 2: Flowing water, a grain of wheat, the juice of grapes.

Group 1: Lord, You are present in the smallest touch of Creation.

Group 2: And from these simple elements comes our understanding of Your presence in our lives.

Group 1: Give us childlike faith, that we may accept You in the people and events we experience.

Group 2: Give us childlike eyes, that we may see You in those we meet.

Group 1: Give us childlike hearts so that we will love without questioning.

Group 2: Nourish us through Your sacraments, now and forever.

All: Amen!

Leader: Let us end by reading together A Pledge of Commitment.

Arranging Family Interviews

PURPOSE

Family interviews allow the candidates and their families to meet the pastor (and, if possible, other parish staff members) in an informal, friendly setting. Families may express any special needs or questions about the program. The parish staff may get to know candidates and their families and assess their readiness and commitment.

The individual family interview is an opportunity for a conversation. It is not a test or a trial.

SCHEDULING

Family interviews should be scheduled in the time period between the family orientation meeting and the enrollment ceremony (or first catechetical session). The length of the interviews will be determined by the number of families and the interviewers' scheduling needs. A flexible schedule of interview appointments should be presented at the family orientation meeting. Keep in mind the availability of the families due to work schedules. Request that all parties involved should be conscientious about keeping appointments.

WHO IS INVOLVED

Each family with a child preparing for the sacraments should be interviewed. The child should be present along with the parent/s or guardian/s. Other family members may be present if this is necessary or desired. The family interview may be conducted by the pastor, the program director, the catechist, or any combination of these parish staff members. However, to avoid the appearance of a tribunal, the interviewers should not outnumber the family members. If family members are uncomfortable conversing in English, try to get bilingual interviewers or interpreters to help facilitate.

SETTING

Family interviews should be conducted in a relaxed, informal, private setting. The parish parlor or pastor's office, the program director's office, even a classroom or corner of the parish hall with chairs arranged comfortably will do. If the number of families to be interviewed is quite small, and geographical circumstances permit, interviews may be scheduled in families' homes.

Sample Questions for the Family Interviews

Use these sample questions as guidelines for the family interviews. To create a trusting atmosphere, phrase the questions in your own words, and add others that flow from the conversation. Adjust the number of questions you use to the amount of time you have. Use the names of the parties when addressing questions, and maintain eye contact. Most importantly, listen to the responses. If you need to make notes, do so after the interview has been concluded.

QUESTIONS DIRECTED TO THE CHILD

These questions are intended to provide non-threatening ways to get to know the individual child and his or her degree of readiness.

- Are you enjoying (looking forward to) school?
- What's your favorite subject in school?
- What do you like to do on the weekends?
- Are you looking forward to making your First Communion? Why?
- Do you know any prayers by heart?
- When you come to Mass, what do you enjoy most?
- Are you looking forward to the sacrament of Reconciliation? Do you have any questions about it?
- Do you know any stories about Jesus? What's your favorite?
- What are some of the ways that you help out at home?
- Is there anything you'd like to ask about the special religion classes you'll be starting soon?

QUESTIONS DIRECTED TO PARENT/S OR GUARDIAN/S

Before discussing these questions, summarize for the parent/s or guardian/s the goals and expectations of the program.

- Do you have any questions about what's expected of you and your child?
- Has your family lived in the parish long? What's the best part of living in this parish?
- Are you happy with your child's religious education?
- Would you be interested in learning more about the sacraments yourself?
- Would you like to be involved in teaching the program or carrying out the celebration?
- What would you most like to have your child understand about the sacraments?
- Do you anticipate any difficulties with what this program requires of you and your child? How can we be of help? (**Note:** The most frequently encountered difficulties have to do with parents' relationships to the Church. One or both parents may be non-Catholic or nonpracticing, or there may be marriage problems that prevent parents from approaching the sacraments. These issues call for much pastoral sensitivity and respect for family privacy. Be reassuring. Remember that the sacramental preparation of children is the single most significant factor in bringing parents back into active parish involvement and for healing a hurtful relationship with the Church. If necessary, arrange for further counseling at another time.)

Arranging a Family Mini-Retreat

PURPOSE

The purpose of a family mini-retreat morning is for the candidates, their families, and the catechists to explore Reconciliation as forgiveness and Eucharist as a sacred Meal. You may wish to schedule this morning on a Saturday, or include a Mass and plan the retreat for a Sunday. Have a comfortable and inviting setting and access to kitchen facilities for baking bread.

MATERIALS

Here's what you will need:

__Name tags and pens
__A large sheet of posterboard with "Jesus Is Our Light" printed along the top and candle flames, one for every participant, drawn on the board
__A paper candle for every participant
__Large Paschal candle or Christ candle, seven smaller candles, and matches, if fire regulations permit
__Television, VCR, and video: "Grandma's Bread" (17 min./Franciscan Communications) After her death, a family bakes Grandma's special bread to be used at the son's First Communion.
__A bread kit for each *group* of participants: greased baking sheet; rolling pin; bowl of unleavened dough (use the recipe below); paper cup of wheat grains; paper cup with white and whole wheat flours for rolling the dough; butter knife; slices of various breads; an unblessed host
__Juice, fruit, cups, and napkins
__Access to a large oven

THE MORNING

1. Welcome participants at the door. Distribute name tags.
2. Have participants write their names on the paper candle, and attach them to the flames on the posterboard.
3. Briefly explain the agenda for the morning, and then show the video, "Grandma's Bread." Divide the participants into small groups. While the groups take turns washing their hands to prepare for the bread making, they may talk about the video. You may use questions such as these: What are some special meals or foods your family shares? How is a meal a sharing? What does the father in the video come to appreciate about his mother? Why did Jesus use bread as a sign of His presence?
4. Next, the groups can enjoy their own bread making. Even the young can participate. Here's what to do: Let everyone examine the wheat grains; explain that wheat is ground to make flour. Tell the difference between leavened and unleavened bread and why unleavened is used in making Communion hosts. Then, let everyone taste and compare the different breads and the hosts. Next, give each group a ball of bread dough to knead and roll out. Mention that the dough is unleavened and therefore doesn't have yeast. Sprinkle the work surface with the mixture of white and wheat flours. Flour the rolling pins. Let participants take turns rolling out the dough to 1/4" thickness. Place the loaves on greased baking sheets. Use the butter knives to mark the loaves with crosses, initials, and so on. Place the dough in the ovens, and have a quick clean up.
5. While the bread bakes and cools, gather everyone to form a large circle. Dim the lights and light the Paschal candle. Say, "Jesus is the Light of the World. When we come together as His followers, He is with us. When we wander away, He calls us back to God's love. Sometimes, we forget to turn to the Light of the World." Then, read each of the following lines, having someone extinguish one of the smaller candles each time. Ask all to respond: ". . . there is less light in the world."

   "When we choose not to see what is good in life . . ."

   "When we argue and fight . . ."

   "When we are selfish with our time and our things . . ."

   "When we don't listen to one another . . ."

   "When we tell lies . . ."

   "When we ignore people who need us . . ."

   "When we care more for things than for people . . ."
6. Point to the Paschal candle and say, "Jesus, our Light, is with us. Let us forgive one another, so His light will always shine. Join hands and say the Lord's Prayer as a sign that we want to do better."
7. Share the juice and fruit, and enjoy the freshly-baked bread!

Unleavened Bread Recipe
For each loaf you will need:

1 1/2 cups whole wheat flour
1/2 cup white flour
3/4 tsp. baking soda
2 tbsp. shortening
3/4 tsp. salt
3/4 cup water

Mix flours, soda, and salt. Add shortening and water. Knead to a smooth dough. Roll and place on a greased sheet. Bake 20 minutes at 350 degrees.

Arranging an Enrollment Ceremony

The enrollment ceremony marks the beginning of formal catechesis for the sacraments. It acts as a sign to the children and to their families that they are part of the larger faith community. The parish community, in turn, sees that its prayers and support are needed for the candidates, their families, and their catechists throughout the preparation period.

SCHEDULING

The enrollment ceremony should be scheduled at least a week before the first catechetical session, and following the catechist and family orientation meetings and, if possible, after the family interviews.

SETTING

The ideal setting for the enrollment ceremony is within the Sunday Mass, following the homily. This setting encourages involvement by the whole parish community. If larger numbers of candidates are to be enrolled, ceremonies may be scheduled for more than one Sunday Mass, but all are held on the same day. If circumstances preclude scheduling the enrollment ceremony as part of the Mass, it should be celebrated in the parish church at a time when candidates and their families can gather.

WHO SHOULD ATTEND

All candidates for sacramental preparation, their parents or guardians and other family members, all sacramental catechists, and parish staff should be involved in the enrollment ceremony. If celebrated within the Mass, other parishioners will be present; if separate, other interested parishioners may be invited to attend. If possible, suggest that the candidates' godparents come as well.

ROLES FOR THE CEREMONY

As a sign of the parish's support and involvement, the pastor is the ideal leader of the enrollment ceremony. If the pastor is unable to take this role, the celebrant should lead the ceremony within a Mass. Outside the Mass, the pastor, a parish priest, or the program director may lead the ceremony. In addition to a leader, you will need to select a reader to proclaim the Scripture. If music is used, you may need the services of a cantor, choir, organist, or other musicians. Or you may play a cassette of selected hymns.

PREPARATION

You will need to prepare an enrollment book, scroll, or banner to be used during the ceremony. Ready-made enrollment books, used for the catechumenates, are available through religious bookstores. You can use any good-looking notebook or guest book with blank pages for signatures. A scroll may be made from artists' parchment or a roll of butcher paper. A large banner may also be used for enrollment; in this case, candidates and their families attach name tags to the banner. You will also need a small table for the book or scroll, a copy of the New Testament or a lectionary for the Scripture reading, copies of the ceremony for all participants, the Paschal candle or altar candles, and any other decorations.

See page 103 for the ceremony.

THE STEPS

1. Prepare the space for the celebration. The enrollment book or scroll should be placed on a table in front of the altar or just outside the sanctuary. An enrollment banner may be positioned in the same place. Light the Paschal candle or altar candles.
2. If celebrated outside of Mass, begin with an opening song. If celebrated during Mass, the candidates and their families should be seated in marked pews at the front of the church.
3. Follow the given ceremony. If the ceremony is within the Mass, omit the Scripture reading.
4. The leader begins with the greeting and then invites the candidates and their families to stand for the prayer.
5. All are invited to sit for the reading. The reader proclaims Scripture from the lectern.
6. Pause for brief reflection. All present stand and renew their baptismal promises.
7. The congregation may be invited to sit. The parents and guardians remain standing to proclaim their commitment.
8. The candidates and families are invited forward. The families present their children, saying, "We bring our child *[name]* who wishes to receive the sacraments of Eucharist and Reconciliation." After each child is presented, the child and family members sign the enrollment book or scroll, or attach name tags to an enrollment banner. The families return to their seats after they have enrolled.
9. All stand for a blessing.
10. If celebrated outside of Mass, close with a hymn. Otherwise, the offertory hymn follows. The enrollment book, scroll, or banner should remain displayed in the church or the parish hall throughout the period of preparation, as a reminder to the parishioners to pray for the candidates and their families.

Refreshments may be served after the ceremony or after the Mass.

Leader: Dear brothers and sisters in Christ, we have among us some young people who are preparing to receive the sacraments of Reconciliation and Eucharist for the first time. They have gathered here as a sign of the continuing faith of this community. They ask our prayers and support during this time of preparation. Let us pray for them now.

Candidates and families STAND at their places.

Leader: Creator God, You have blessed our parish with the gift of these children. Help them to come to appreciate the sacraments of Reconciliation and Eucharist, and to approach them often in faith. Help us as a parish community, as parents and guardians, as catechists and staff members to be examples of faith to these young people. We ask this in the name of Jesus Christ, Your Son, who lives and reigns with You and with the Holy Spirit, now and forever.

All: Amen!

SIT for the proclamation of God's Word.

Reader: A reading from the first letter of Paul to the Corinthians:

[Read 1 Corinthians 11:23–26]

Pause for a moment of quiet reflection. Then, all STAND for the renewal of Baptismal promises.

Leader: Do you promise to turn away from sin and selfishness and to live in a loving and caring way with those around you?

All: I do.

Leader: Do you promise to turn away from anger and meanness and to get along with your family and friends?

All: I do.

Leader: Do you promise to turn away from the devil and all temptations, and to turn toward God in prayer and good deeds?

All: I do.

Leader: Do you believe in God the Father, who created you and all that is?

All: I do.

Leader: Do you believe in Jesus Christ, God's Son, who died for our sins, rose from the dead, and will come again to bring us to God's kingdom?

All: I do.

Leader: Do you believe in the Holy Spirit, who guides us in the Way of Jesus and gathers us as a community of faith?

All: I do.

Leader: God the Father has given us a new life through Baptism. May this new life of faith help us prepare to receive Jesus through the sacraments of Eucharist and Reconciliation.

All: Amen!

Leader: Parents and guardians, are you willing to see that your child attends Mass on Sundays and holy days, to support and encourage your child in preparation for these sacraments, to participate in all meetings and activities, to help your child learn the basic prayers of our faith, to pray for your child, to continue to share the gift of your presence with this community, and to oversee your child's continued religious education?

Families: We are willing!

Leader: I now invite parents and guardians to come forward and present their children for enrollment.

Families: *[COME FORWARD.]* We bring our child *[name]* who wishes to receive the sacraments of Reconciliation and Eucharist. *[SIGN the enrollment book.]*

STAND for the blessing.

Leader: The Lord be with you.

All: And also with you.

Leader: Let us pray for God's blessing. May the blessing of almighty God—the Father, the Son, and the Holy Spirit—come upon you and remain with you forever.

All: Amen!

❖ ❖ Registration ❖ ❖

❖ ❖ ❖

______________________________ will be offering sacramental preparation
Parish

classes from ______________________ to ______________________.
Date *Date*

These classes are for baptized children, grades 2–6, who have not yet received the sacraments of Reconciliation or Holy Communion. For further details, please call: ______________________

Please indicate if you wish to enroll your child.

( ) I wish to enroll my child in the preparation class for Reconciliation.

( ) I wish to enroll my child in the preparation class for Eucharist.

______________________ ______________________
Child's name *Birth date*

____
Parent or Guardian

____
Address

____
Phone number

INVITATION TO THE PARISH

The children of our parish will be celebrating the sacrament of ______________________ for the first time on ______________________ at ______________________
Date *Time*

at ______________________
Place

As members of the parish community, you are invited to join us for this important celebration. We ask your prayers for the candidates, their teachers, and their families.

Note: You may type the appropriate information in the blanks, fold under this note, and reproduce the registration form and the parish invitation. Or, you may use these as models and write your own. The invitation on this page may also be read aloud during the announcements at Sunday Masses.

❖❖ ——— *Inscripción* ——— ❖❖

❖❖❖

________________________________ ofrecerà clases de preparación sacramental
La Parroquia

desde ____________________ hasta ____________________.
Fecha *Fecha*

Estas clases son para niños bautizados, que asisten a los grados 2–6 y gue aún no han recibido los sacramentos de la Reconciliación o la Sagrada Comunión. Para mayores detalles, sírvase llamar al

____

Por favor indicar si Ud. desea matricular a su hijo(a).

( ) Deseo matricular a mi hijo(a) en la clase de preparacion para Reconciliation.

( ) Deseo matricular a mi hijo(a) en la clase de preparacion para Eucaristia.

____________________ ____________________
Nombre de hijo(a) *Fecha de Nacimiento*

____
Madre/Padre o tutor(a)

____
Direccion de casa

____
Numero de Telefono

- -

INVITACIÓN A LA PARROQUIA

Los niños de nuestra parroquia celebrarán el sacramento de ____________________ por

primera vez el día ____________________ a las ____________________
Fecha *Hora*

en ________________________________.
Lugar

Como miembro de esta parroquia, le invitamos muy cordialmente a unirse a esta importante celebración. Le pedimos que eleve sus oraciones por los niños, sus maestros y sus familias.

- -

Note: These are the Spanish versions of the registration letter and the parish invitation. You may type the appropriate information in the blanks, fold under this note, and reproduce the forms. Or, you may use these as models and write your own. The invitation on this page may also be read aloud during the announcements at Sunday Masses.

Dear ____,

Thank you for your willingness to take part in the special catechetical ministry of preparing children to receive Reconciliation and Eucharist in our parish.

Your presence is requested at a Catechist Orientation Meeting to be held:

Place ____

Date ____

Time: From ________________________________ to ________________________________

At this meeting, you will meet other catechists, learn about the sacramental preparation program, set a schedule, and receive your teaching materials.

I look forward to working with you!

Sincerely,

____

Note: This is a sample invitation to the catechists. Copies of this letter may be reproduced on stationery with your parish letterhead; type or write in the necessary information. Or, you may use this form as a model for composing your own letter. Letters should be mailed or hand-delivered to prospective catechists, assistants, and parents who will be teaching the program to their children at home or in neighborhood clusters.

Dear ____,

I am happy to invite you to attend an important mandatory orientation meeting for the families of children who are in our parish sacramental preparation program.

Your presence is requested at a Family Orientation Meeting to be held:

Place ____

Date ____

Time: From ________________________________ to ________________________________

The purpose of this meeting is to explain the sacramental preparation program, give you scheduling information, introduce the catechists, and present you and your child with the books and materials that will be used during the teaching of the program. If possible, please bring a copy of your child's baptismal certificate with you to this meeting.

I look forward to seeing you.

Sincerely,

____

Note: This is a sample invitation to families that may be copied on stationery with your parish letterhead. Type or write in the necessary information, and sign the letter. Or, you may use this form as a model for composing your own letter. Letters should be mailed or hand-delivered to families of prospective candidates sufficiently in advance of the scheduled meeting.

Estimada Familia ______________________________,

Nos complace darles la bienvenida para que asistan a la primera reunión de las familias de los niños que recibirán, por primera vez, el sacramento de la Primera Reconciliación

en nuestra parroquia el próximo ____.

Fecha

La información referente a la reunión es la siguiente:

Lugar ____

Fecha ____

Hora: De ____________________________ hasta las ______________________________.

El propósito de la reunión es para explicar el programa de la Primera Reconciliación y mostrarles a ustedes y a sus hijos los libros y materiales que se usarán en el transcurso de las enseñanzas del programa. Si es posible le solicitamos el favor de traer una copia de la Fe de Bautismo de su hijo(a) a dicha reunión.

Esperamos tener el placer de contar con su presencia.

Cordialmente,

____

Note: This is a sample invitation in Spanish to families that may be copied on stationery with your parish letterhead. Type or write in the necessary information, and sign the letter. Or, you may use this form as a model for composing your own letter. Families should get the letter sufficiently in advance of the scheduled orientation meeting. If bilingual personnel will be available at the meeting, be sure to say so in the letter.

Everything You Want to Know about the Sacramental Celebrations*

*(But Are Glad We Didn't Have a Meeting to Discuss!)

Practice:

Seating:

When to Be There:

Offertory Gift:

Ways to Receive Communion:

Communion Fast:

Dress:

Pictures:

If you have any questions about anything regarding the sacramental celebration, please call:

Note: This is the Family Information sheet. It's a simple form that alerts parents to the practical details of the sacramental celebrations. Type in the necessary information, duplicate the form, and send copies to the candidates' families in advance of the final practice. If you wish, use one form for each sacrament.

Practica:

Asiento:

Llege a las:

Colecta:

Formas de recibir la Comunion:

Ayuna de Comunion:

Vestimenta:

Fotografias:

Si tiene preguntas con respecto a la celebraciones sacramental, por favor llame:

____

____

Note: This is the Spanish version of the Family Information sheet given on the previous page. Type in the necessary information, duplicate the form, and send copies to the candidates' families in advance of the final practice. If you wish, use one form for each sacrament.

For You, the Catechist

Preparing for Your Ministry

The ministry of the catechist is one of the most important gifts in the Church. Whoever you are—parent, beginning volunteer, or experienced DRE—the most important qualities you can bring to this ministry are a positive attitude, sincere convictions, a good feeling for the material, an understanding of Catholic Christian life, and a real sense of enjoyment in being with children. A well-developed sense of humor is an added plus!

Specifically, an effective catechist professes and practices his or her Catholic faith, desires to continually develop a relationship with Jesus in Reconciliation and in the Eucharist, and guides children to encounter Jesus at home and in the classroom, and in the Blessed Sacrament.

The *Catechism of the Catholic Church (#1697)* lists eight characteristics that all moral catechesis must have. Benziger *Reconciliation* and *Eucharist* develop each of these:

1. **A Catechesis of the Holy Spirit.** The Holy Spirit is our Helper and Guide.
2. **A Catechesis of Grace.** God's grace is needed to lead a good life.
3. **A Catechesis of the Beatitudes.** These Ways of Christ are the way to happiness with God forever.
4. **A Catechesis of Sin and Forgiveness.** Human beings do sin, but Christ and the Church forgive.
5. **A Catechesis of the Human Virtues.** There are good human habits that help us counteract the evil influences in our world.
6. **A Catechesis of the Christian Virtues.** The virtues show us the way to Christian living.
7. **A Catechesis of the Commandment of Love.** In following the Ten Commandments and the New Commandment, we live our covenant with God.
8. **An Ecclesial Catechesis.** It is in the context of the believing community that we find the best way to lead a good life.

FOLLOWING THROUGH

1. *Creating the Environment:* Your teaching environment should be warm, inviting, and cheerful. Good religious art, calendars, and comfortable, easily movable seating help provide a good atmosphere for learning. You will need access to a chalkboard or a large newsprint pad for display material, and an audiocassette player for music tapes.

   If you plan on incorporating audiovisual resources, make sure that good equipment, electrical outlets, and extension cords are available, and that the room lighting can be dimmed sufficiently to provide clear viewing of videos or slides.

   You and your students might want to set up a prayer corner or table in an area of your room. During the course, you can gather there for the prayer services. Items place in the prayer area can reflect the themes you're covering in class.

   If you are teaching in a CCD situation, when the teaching space is yours for a limited time period, try to meet regularly with the teacher with whom you share space. You might be able to set aside a bulletin board, a desk drawer, and some boxes or cupboard space for your own supplies. You also may want to take turns setting up the prayer area.
2. *Getting to Know the Students:* In a classroom setting, use seating charts or name tags to familiarize yourself with the children's names as quickly as possible. If you can, spend the time before and after class, getting to know your students, their families and friends, their likes and dislikes. These informal times give you an insight into all that influences your students' learning.
3. *Talking about the Material:* Much of the content of *Reconciliation* is communicated through talking about the reading text. It's important that the children feel comfortable during these talks. Encourage participation from everyone, no matter how inarticulate, but never pressure someone who does not want to talk. Help everyone to develop respect for one another's opinions. Correct frankly erroneous statements gently, without sarcasm or comparison.

   Many of the discussions in *Reconciliation* center around family customs and practices. In the classroom, it is extremely important to preserve family privacy. A student should not be pressured into sharing details of his or her home life. Where sensitive family situations exist—separation, divorce, widowhood, illness or handicap, extreme poverty or parental joblessness, non-Catholic or non-religious parents—tread lightly. Be sure no child is made to feel different or slighted because of a family situation.
4. *Enjoying the Enrichment Activities:* Activities designed to enhance the Benziger *Reconciliation* text are suggested in the wrap at the bottom of the teaching page throughout the lesson plans. Feel free to adapt these to your own situation. Many suggested activities are based on art and craft experiences. Try to encourage each child's best efforts without being overly critical of the level of skills evidenced. All children enjoy seeing their work displayed, so if you can, hang it everywhere—in the hallways, in the church area, in the parish hall, and even in other classrooms.

5. *Memorizing:* If you received your own religious education from the traditional catechism method, you know the value of memorization as a teaching tool. Vocabulary definitions and the prayers and lists in the back of the student text lend themselves well to memorization, which is especially effective when practiced with a partner. It's very important, however, that the children clearly understand what is being memorized.
6. *Using the Text Illustrations:* The student texts—*First Reconciliation, First Eucharist, Reconciliation,* and *Eucharist*—are richly illustrated. Occasionally, you can incorporate the illustrations into your teaching using such questions as:
   - What does this picture tell you about Jesus?
   - What does this picture tell you about a character in the story?
   - What does this picture tell you about what we are learning?

Dear Family,

Your child will be using Benziger *Reconciliation* to prepare for the reception of Reconciliation. There are a number of ways for you to share in your child's preparation. If your child brings home the *Reconciliation* text, you may enjoy looking through the book, talking about the lessons, and doing the We Pray pages together.

Another way to participate and to increase your own understanding of the sacrament is to use *The Reconciling Family*, a special family magazine designed just for families like you. This magazine contains interesting articles, parenting tips, Catholic prayers and customs for families, and even simple games—all tied to the material your child is learning in class.

At regular times during your child's preparation, you will be receiving letters like this one to update you on your child's sacramental preparation. There are eight lessons in your child's text. Each family letter will review the previous two chapters your child studied and will explain the upcoming two chapters. It will also give some simple suggestions on reinforcing the themes of the lessons with your child.

Lesson 1, "Welcome," reminds your child that Baptism welcomed him or her into membership in the Catholic Church and introduces the idea of God's forgiving love. If you wish, you can help your child understand this lesson by exploring the similarities between belonging to your family and belonging to the Church. You can talk about the ways family members welcome one another.

Lesson 2, "Rules of Love," refers to the Ten Commandments, signs of our response to God's faithfulness and love. At home, you can help your child discover the role that love plays in the family rules you follow.

I hope your child's preparation for First Reconciliation is an enriching experience for the whole family. Please contact me if you have any questions or ideas to share during this important preparation time.

Sincerely,

____

Catechist Note: Give this letter to students' families at registration time, or send it home on the first day of class.

Estimada Familia,

Con el fin de preparase para su Reconciliación, su hijo(a) estará utilizando la obra *Reconciliación* de Benziger. Hay varias maneras en las cuales usted puede participar en la preparación de su hijo(a). Si su hijo(a) trae consigo a casa el texto *Reconciliación*, tal vez usted disfrute hojeando el libro y participando conjuntamente en las Actividades Familiares que se sugieren.

Otra forma de participar y de aumentar su propia comprensión del sacramento, es utilizando *La Familia Reconciliada*, una revista familiar creada para complementar el texto de su hijo(a). La revista contiene artículos de interés, sugerencias para la crianza de los hijos, oraciones y costumbres católicas para las familias e incluso juegos sencillos—todo relacionado con lo que su hijo(a) está aprendiendo en clase.

Periódicamente, durante el tiempo que dure la preparación de su hijo(a), usted recibirá cartas como ésta, que lo mantendrán al tanto sobre la preparación sacramental de su hijo(a). El texto de su hijo(a) consta de ocho capítulos; cada una de las cartas repasará el contenido estudiado en los dos capítulos anteriores y esbozará el contenido de los dos siguientes. En cada carta encontrará sugerencias sencillas que le ayudarán a reforzarle a su hijo(a) los temas tratados a lo largo de los capítulos.

La Lección 1, "Bienvenidos," le recuerda a su hijo(a) que el Bautismo fue la beinvenida que lo convirtió en miembro de la Iglesia Católica e introduce la idea del amor de Dios que todo lo perdono. Si lo desea le puede ayudar a su hijo(a) a comprender estas lecciones explorando las semejanzas entre pertenecer a su familia y pertenecer a la Iglesia. Pueden hablar sobre las distintas formas en que los miembros de una familia se dan mutuamente la bienvenida.

La Lección 2, "Reglas de Amor," se refiere a los Diez Mandamientos, señales de nuestra respuesta a la fidelidad y el amor de Dios. En casa le puede ayudar a su hijo(a) a descubrir el papel que juega el amor en las reglas familiares que los rigen a ustedes.

Espero que la preparación de su hijo(a) para la Primera Reconciliación sea una experiencia enriquecedora para toda la familia. Por favor comuníquese conmigo en caso de que tenga preguntas o ideas que desee compartir durante este importante período de preparación.

Cordialmente,

____

Catechist Note: Give this letter to students' families at registration time, or send it home on the first day of class.

Dear Family,

As you recall, Lesson 1 in *Reconciliation* was about Baptism, the celebration bringing us to a special, loving relationship with God. Lesson 2 explained that the Bible tells us about Jesus and God's rules of love, the Ten Commandments.

In Lesson 3, "Right and Wrong," your child will be introduced to important terms and concepts. He or she will begin to understand that sin is a failure to respond to God's love. Conscience formation, introduced in this lesson, is very important for children, who need help determining the morality of their actions and choices. You can assist your child by providing clear, consistent standards and by affirming his or her good choices and actions.

In Lesson 4, "I Confess," your child will begin to see sacramental confession as a gift from God to help us take responsibility for our actions and choices. Your child is now able to see the consequences of his or her actions. This lesson also carefully delineates the difference between sin and accidents or mistakes, an important distinction for children. You can help your child by making yourself available to talk about difficult choices.

A reminder: The family magazine, *The Reconciling Family*, offers suggestions for exploring these two lessons at home.

I hope you are enjoying your participation in your child's sacramental preparation. If there is anything I can do to assist you, please let me know.

Sincerely,

____

Catechist Note: Send this letter home with the students upon completion of Lesson 2, "Rules of Love."

Estimada Familia,

En las Lecciones 1 y 2 de *Reconciliación,* su hijo(a) aprendió que el pertenecer a la Iglesia Católica comienza con el sacramento del Bautismo, que nos da la bienvenida a una relación muy especial con un Dios lleno de amor. Esa relación o alianza se exploró más ampliamente por medio de ólas reglas de amor, los Diez Mandamientos. Estos capítulos introductorios le ayudaron a su hijo(a) a prepararse para comrpender los conceptos básicos del pecado, el perdón y la moral, que tienen gran importancia en la preparación para el sacramento de la Reconciliación.

En la Lección 3, "El Bien y el Mal," se le presentarán a su hijo(a) importantes términos y conceptos. El o ella empezará a comprender que el pecado es una falta de respuesta al amor de Dios. La formación de la conciencia, que se introduce en esta lección, es muy importante para los niños, los cuales necesitan ayuda para determinar la moralidad de sus acciones y decesiones. Usted puede ayudar a su hijo(a) brindándole parámetros claros y constantes, y afirmando aquellas acciones y decisiones suyas que sean correctas.

En la Lección 4, "Yo Confieso," su hijo(a) comenzará a mirar el sacramento de la confesión como un don de Dios para ayudarnos a asumir la responsabilidad de nuestras acciones y decisiones. Su hijo(a) está agira capacitado para prever las consequencias de sus acciones. Esta capítulo también delinea cuidadosamente las diferencias entre pecado y accidetes o errores, una distinción que es de gran importancia para los niños. Usted puede ayudar a su hijo(a) poniéndose a su disposición para hablar sobre las decisiones difíciles.

La revista familiar, *La Familia Reconciliada*, ofrece sugerencias sobre cómo profundizar en estos dos capítulos en el hogar.

Espero que esté disfrutando de la preparación sacramental de su hijo(a). Si existe alguna manera en que pueda prestarle mi colaboración, no dude en comunicármelo.

Cordialmente,

____

Catechist Note: Send this letter home with the students upon completion of Lesson 2, "Rules of Love."

Dear Family,

Your child has completed Lessons 3 and 4 in *Reconciliation.* In Lesson 3 your child learned the importance of knowing the difference between right and wrong—a key stage in your child's moral development and in his or her preparation for the sacrament of Reconciliation. Lesson 4 presented sacramental confession as a means of helping us grow in responsibility for our actions.

Now your child is ready to begin Lesson 5, "Being Sorry." This lesson presents the importance of expressing contrition, or sorrow for sin, and the desire to do better. Your child will learn an Act of Contrition to pray as part of his or her participation in the sacrament. Sincere sorrow for sin helps us ask forgiveness and begin to make peace with God and with people we have hurt. You can reinforce this lesson by talking with your child about the ways that members of your family say "I'm sorry" to one another.

Lesson 6, "Changing Your Life," introduces the concept of doing penance as an outward expression of sorrow for sin. In the sacrament of Reconciliation, accepting a penance is also a sign of continuing conversion—bringing our lives more into line with the example of Jesus. You can help your child understand that the penance is not an empty punishment, but a sign of our willingness to make up for doing wrong and a way to practice doing better.

Many of these themes are further explored and brought to life in the family magazine, *The Reconciling Family*. I hope you will continue to use this and other resources to enrich your participation as a family. Please let me know if I can be of help.

Sincerely,

____

Catechist Note: Send this letter home with the students upon completion of Lesson 4, "I Confess."

Estimada Familia,

Su hijo(a) ha terminado las Lecciones 3 y 4 de *Reconciliación*. En la Lección 3 aprendió la importancia de conocer la diferencia entre el bien y el mal—una etapa clave en la formación moral de su hijo(a) en su preparación para el Sacramento de la Reconciliación. La Lección 4 presentó la confesion sacramental como un medio para ayudarnos a crecer en responsabilidad por nuestros actos.

Ahora su hijo(a) se encuentra preparado para comenzar la Lección 5, "Estar Arrepentido." Esta lección presenta la importancia de expresar nuestra contrición, o la pena por haber pecado y el deseo de enmendarnos. Su hijo(a) aprenderá un Acto de Contrición para rezarlo como parte du su participación en el sacramento. El arrepentimiento sincero por haber pecado nos ayuda a pedir perdón y a comenzar a hacer la paz con Dios y con las personas a quienes hemos herido. Usted puede reforzar la lección aprendida en esta lección hablando con su hijo(a) acerca de las formas en que los miembros de su familia se dicen mutuamente "Lo siento."

La Lección 6, "Cómo Cambiar Nuestra Vida," introduce el concepto de hacer penitencia como una expresión externa del arrepentimiento por haber pecado. En el sacramento de la Reconciliación, el aceptar una penitencia es también una señal de permanente conversión—igualando más nuestras vidas con el ejemplo de Jesús. Usted puede ayudarle a su hijo(a) a comprender que la penitencia no es un castigo carente de sentido, sino una señal de nuestra intención de compensar el mal hecho y una forma de practicar haciendo el bien.

Muchos de estos temas se exploran más profundamente y cobran vida en la revista familiar *La Familia Reconciliada*. Espero que continúen usando éste y otros recursos para enriquecer su participación como familia. Por favor infórmeme si puedo serle de alguna ayuda.

Cordialmente,

____

Catechist Note: Send this letter home with the students upon completion of Lesson 4, "I Confess."

Dear Family,

Your child has completed Lessons 5 and 6 in *Reconciliation*. In Lesson 5 your child was introduced to the idea of sorrow for sin as a necessary condition for proper reception of the sacrament. He or she learned an Act of Contrition, a prayer of sorrow for sin. Lesson 6 explored the doing of a penance as a way to make up for wrongdoing and to practice conversion—changing our lives for the better.

Your child is now moving into the last stages of preparation for Reconciliation. In Lesson 7, "I Am Forgiven," your child will learn that Reconciliation is a sacrament of healing. He or she will review the several ways in which the sacrament can be celebrated. You can help by making sure that your child is familiar with the steps for receiving Reconciliation (face to face or anonymously in a Reconciliation room or confessional, individually or as part of a parish Reconciliation service) and by making it possible for your child to attend all necessary practices. Most importantly, you can give your child a beautiful example by your own participation in the sacrament itself and by your family's attendance at parish penitential services.

Lesson 8, "Forgiving Others," will help your child see that there is a connection between being forgiven and offering forgiveness. Each person is called to share God's forgiving love with others in Jesus' name. The Beatitudes are presented as ways to live out this call. In addition to helping your child plan for the celebration of Reconciliation, you can lead your child to see that participation in the sacrament is a lifelong source of grace and peace. The family magazine, *The Reconciling Family*, contains a number of suggestions for continuing your spiritual growth as a family.

It has been a pleasure for me to work with you and your child during this special time. I look forward to seeing you at the celebration!

Sincerely,

____

Catechist Note: Send this letter home with the students upon completion of Lesson 6, "Changing Your Life." At this time, you might want to attach the Family Information sheet.

Estimada Familia,

Su hijo(a) ha terminado las Lecciones 5 y 6 de *Reconciliación.* La Lección 5 se le hizo a su hijo(a) una introducción del concepto del arrepentimiento por haber pecado como condición necesaria para recibir adecuadamente el sacramento. El o Ella aprendió un Acto de Contrición, que es una oración de arrepentimiento por el pecado. La Lessión 6 examinaba el cumplimiento de la penitencia como forma de enmendar el mal cometido y de practicar la conversion—cambiando y mejorando nuestro modo de vivir.

Su hijo(a) entrará ahora en las últimas etapas de su preparación para la Reconciliación. En la Lección 7, "Estoy Perdonado," su hijo(a) aprenderá que la Reconciliación es un sacramento de reparación. Repasará las diversas maneras en que se puede celebrar el sacaramento. Usted puede ayudar a su hijo(a) asegurándose de que esté familiarizado con los pasos necesarios para recibir la Reconciliación (cara a cara o en forma anónima en un confesionario o Sala de Reconciliación, individualmente o como parte de un servicio parroquial de Reconciliación) y facilitando la asistencia de su hijo(a) a todas las praticas necesarias. Más importante aún, usted puede brindarle a su hijo(a) un bello ejemplo participando personalmente en el sacramento y mediante la asistencia de la familia a las actividades de penitencia de la parroquia.

La Lección 8, "Perdonando a los Demás," le ayudará a su hijo(a) a observar la conexión que existe entre perdonar y ser perdonado. Aprenderá que cada persona está llamada a compartir con los demás y en nombre de Jesús, el amor de Dios que todo lo perdona. Se presentan las Bienaventuranzas como formas de vivir esta llamada. Además de ayudarle a su hijo(a) a planear la celebración de la Reconciliación, puede guiarle para que vea su participación en el sacramento como una fuente de gracia y de paz a lo largo de su vida. La revista familiar, *La Familia Reconciliada*, contiene una serie de sugerencias para continuar creciendo espiritualmente como familia.

Ha sido un placer para mí trabajar con usted y su hijo(a) durante esta época tan especial. ¡Aguardo con anticipación verle en la ceremonia!

Cordialmente,

____

Catechist Note: Send this letter home with the students upon completion of Lesson 6, "Changing Your Life." At this time, you might want to attach the Family Information sheet.

Dear Family,

Your child will be using Benziger *Eucharist* to prepare for First Communion. There are a number of ways for you to share in your child's preparation. If your child brings home the *Eucharist* text, you may enjoy looking through the book and participating together in the suggested Family Activities.

Another way to participate and to increase your own understanding of the sacrament is to use *The Eucharistic Family,* a special family magazine that contains interesting articles, parenting tips, Catholic prayers and customs for families, and even simple games.

At regular times during your child's preparation, you will be receiving letters like this one to update you on your child's sacramental preparation. There are eight lessons in your child's text; each letter will review the content studied in the previous two lessons and outline the content of the upcoming two lessons.

Lesson 1 of the text, "Gathered Together," reminds your child that he or she belongs to a family of faith, the Catholic Church. The sacrament of Baptism, the sign of belonging, is explored in this chapter, which helps prepare your child for fuller participation in the Church through reception of the Eucharist. If possible, spend some time with your child recalling his or her baptism.

Lesson 2, "We Ask Forgiveness," uses the Penitential Rite of the Mass to present the importance of forgiveness and unity as part of the Eucharist. At home, you can talk with your child about the signs of family unity and reconciliation.

I hope your child's preparation for First Communion is an enriching experience for the whole family. Please contact me if you have any questions or ideas to share during this important preparation time.

Sincerely,

____

Catechist Note: Give this letter to students' families at registration time, or send it home on the first day of class.

Estimada Familia,

Con el fin de preparase para su Primera Comunión, su hijo(a) estará utilizando la obra *Eucharistia* de Benziger. Hay varias maneras en las cuales usted puede participar en la preparación de su hijo(a). Si su hijo(a) trae consigo a casa el texto *Eucharistia*, tal vez usted disfrute hojeando el libro y participando conjuntamente en las Actividades Familiares que se sugieren.

Otra forma de participar y de aumentar su propia comprensión del sacramento, es utilizando *La Familia Eucharistia*, una revista familiar creada para complementar el texto de su hijo(a). La revista contiene artículos de interés, sugerencias para la crianza de los hijos, oraciones y costumbres católicas para las familias e incluso juegos sencillos—todos relacionado con lo que su hijo(a) está aprendiendo en clase.

Periódicamente, durante el tiempo que dure la preparación de su hijo(a), usted recibirá cartas como ésta, que lo mantendrán al tanto sobre la preparación sacramental de su hijo(a). El texto de su hijo(a) consta de ocho lecciones; cada una de las cartas repasará el contenido estudiado en los dos lecciones anteriores y esbozará el contenido de los dos siguientes.

La Lección 1, titulado "Todos Reunidos," le recuerda a su hijo(a) que él o ella pertenece a una familia de fe, la Iglesia Católica. En esta lección se explora el sacramento del Bautismo, como el signo que nos hace miembros o pertenecientes a esa familia, esto ayuda a su hijo(a) a prepararse para participar más a fondo en la Iglesia, recibiendo la Eucaristía. Si es posible, dedique algún tiempo a recordar con su hijo(a) su bautismo.

La Lección 2, "Pedimos Perdón," utiliza el rito penitencial de la Misa para presentar la importancia que tiene el perdón y la unidad como parte de la Eucaristía. En casa, usted puede hablar con su hijo(a) acerca de los signos de la unidad familiar y la reconciliación.

Espero que la preparación de su hijo(a) para la Primera Comunión sea una experiencia enriquecedora para toda la familia. Por favor comuníquese conmigo en caso de que tenga preguntas o ideas que desee compartir durante este importante período de preparación.

Cordialmente,

____

Catechist Note: Give this letter to students' families at registration time, or send it home on the first day of class.

Dear Family,

In Lessons 1 and 2 of *Eucharist*, your child learned that membership in the Catholic Church begins with the sacrament of Baptism and is fully expressed by participation in the Eucharist, "the source and center of Christian life." Because Holy Communion is a sign of unity, the attitudes of forgiveness and peace celebrated in the Penitential Rite of the Mass are an important part of our preparation for this sacrament.

In Lesson 3, "Meeting Jesus in God's Word," your child will explore the meaning of the Liturgy of the Word at Mass. He or she will learn that by careful listening, we encounter Jesus in the inspired words of Scripture. We get to know Him better, so that we can welcome Him into our hearts in Holy Communion. At home, you can help your child become more familiar with the Bible and its stories of Jesus. You can talk with your child about the meaning of the readings you hear at Sunday Mass.

In Lesson 4, "All That We Have," your child will learn that the Eucharist is a sacrifice as well as a sacred Meal. Just as Jesus gave Himself to the Father for us, we give of ourselves at Mass when we offer the gifts of bread and wine. Talk with your child about the importance of unselfish giving.

A reminder: The family magazine, *The Eucharistic Family*, offers a number of suggestions for exploring these two lessons at home.

I hope you are enjoying your participation in your child's sacramental preparation. If there is anything I can do to assist you, please let me know.

Sincerely,

____

Catechist Note: Send this letter home with the students upon completion of Lesson 2, "We Ask Forgiveness."

Estimada Familia,

En las Lecciones 1 y 2 de *Eucharistía*, su hijo(a) aprendió que el pertenecer a la Iglesia Católica comienza con el sacramento del Bautismo, y se expresa en toda su plenitud por medio de la participación en la Eucaristía, "la fuente y el centro de la vida cristiana." Debido a que la Santa Comunión es un signo de unidad, las actividades de perdón y de paz que se celebran en el Rito Penitencial de la Misa son parte importante de nuestra preparación para este sacramento.

En la Lección 3, "Encontrando a Jesús por medio de la Palabra de Dios," su hijo(a) explorará el significado que tiene la Liturgia de la Palabra en la Misa. El o ella aprenderá que escuchando cuidadosamente, podemos encontrar a Jesús en las inspiradas palabras de las Sagradas Escrituras. Llegamos así a conocerle mejor, para que podamos darle la bienvenida en nuestros corazones a través de la Sagrada Comunión. En el hogar, usted puede ayudarle a su hijo(a) a familiarizarse más con la Biblia y con sus historias acerca de Jesús. Usted puede hablar con su hijo(a) acerca del significado de las lecturas que escucha en la Misa dominical.

En la Lección 4, "Todo lo que Tenemos," su hijo(a) aprenderá que la Eucaristía es un sacrificio a la vez que un sagrado Alimento. Así como Jesús se entregó a Sí Mismo al Padre por nosotros, nos entregamos en la Misa cuando ofrecemos las ofrendas del vino y del pan. Hable con su hijo(a) acerca de la importancia de dar sin egoísmo.

La revista familiar *La Familia Eucharistía*, ofrece sugerencias sobre cómo profundizar en estos dos capítulos en el hogar.

Espero que esté disfrutando de la preparación sacramental de su hijo(a). Si existe alguna manera en que pueda prestarle mi colaboración, no dude en comunicármelo.

Cordialmente,

____

Catechist Note: Send this letter home with the students upon completion of Lesson 2, "We Ask Forgiveness."

Dear Family,

Your child has completed Lessons 3 and 4 of *Eucharist*. In Lesson 3, your child learned the importance of listening carefully to the Word of God in Scripture, of coming to know Jesus better, and of following His example. Lesson 4 used the Presentation of the Gifts at Mass to teach the sacrificial dimension of the Eucharist and reminded your child of the importance of unselfish giving in everyday life.

Now your child is ready to begin Lesson 5, "Remember and Give Thanks." This lesson focuses on the Eucharistic Prayer, the central prayer of the Mass. In this lesson, your child will learn that Jesus instituted the sacrament of the Eucharist at the Last Supper on the night before He died. In the Mass, we remember Jesus' life, death, and resurrection, and we give thanks to the Father for His saving gift. You can talk with your child about the importance of keeping memories alive and showing gratitude to one another and to God.

Lesson 6, "Give Us This Day," uses the Lord's Prayer to explore the many kinds of prayer that come together in the Mass. Your child will learn that prayer is a natural and loving response to God. In prayer, we praise God; we thank God for all gifts; we show sorrow for sin; and we ask God's help for ourselves and for others. You can help build your child's spiritual life by praying together at home, especially the Lord's Prayer and the family rosary.

Many of these themes are further explored and brought to life in the family magazine, *The Eucharistic Family*. I hope you will continue to use this and other resources to enrich your participation as a family. Please let me know if I can be of help.

Sincerely,

____

Catechist Note: Send this letter home with the students upon completion of Lesson 4, "All That We Have."

Estimada Familia,

Su hijo(a) ha terminado las Lecciones 3 y 4 de *Eucharistía*. En la Lección 3 aprendió la importancia de escuchar cuidadosamente la Palabra de Dios en las Sagradas Escrituras, de llegar a conocer mejor a Jesús y de seguir su ejemplo. La Lección 4 utiliza la Presentación de las Ofrendas en la Misa para enseñar la dimensión del sacrificio de la Eucaristía y le recordó a su hijo(a) la importancia de dar con generosidad en la vida cotidiana.

Ahora su hijo(a) está preparado para comenzar la Lección 5, "Conmemoremos y Demos Gracias." Esta lección se concentra en la Oración Eucarística, la oración central de la Misa. En esta lección su hijo(a) aprenderá que Jesús instituyó el sacramento de la Eucaristía durante la Ultima Cena, la noche antes de morir. En la Misa conmemoramos la vida, la muerte y la resurrección de Jesús y le damos gracias al Padre por su regalo de salvación. Usted puede hablar con su hijo(a) acerca de la importancia de conservar vivos los recuerdos y de manifestarnos nuestra gratitud los unos a los otros y expresársela también a Dios.

La Lección 6, "Danos Hoy," utiliza el Padrenuestro para examinar las diversas clases de oraciones que se reúnen en la Misa. Su hijo(a) aprenderá que la oración es una respuesta natural y amorosa que damos a Dios. Al rezar alabamos a Dios, le damos gracias por los beneficios que de El recibimos, manifestamos arrepentimiento por nuestros pecados y solicitamos la ayuda de Dios para nosotros mismos y para los demás. Usted puede ayudar a construir la vida espiritual de su hijo(a) mediante la oración comunitaria en el hogar, en particular rezando el Padrenuestro y el rosario en familia.

Muchos de estos temas se exploran más profundamente y cobran vida en la revista familiar *La Familia Eucharistia*. Espero que continúen usando éste y otros recursos para enriquecer su participación como familia. Por favor infórmeme si puedo serle de alguna ayuda.

Cordialmente,

____

Catechist Note: Send this letter home with the students upon completion of Lesson 4, "All That We Have."

Dear Family,

Your child has completed Lessons 5 and 6 of *Eucharist*. In Lesson 5, your child was introduced to the Eucharistic Prayer of the Mass, which celebrates the saving actions of Jesus and the institution of the Eucharist. Your child learned the importance of remembering and giving thanks to God. Lesson 6 stressed the Mass as a prayer and introduced your child to the different kinds of prayer that make up our Christian heritage. Of special importance is the Lord's Prayer, in which we pray for the "daily bread" of Holy Communion.

Your child is now moving into the last stages of his or her preparation for First Eucharist. In Lesson 7, "The Bread of Life," your child will learn that Jesus Christ is truly present in the Eucharist. He or she will review the different ways to receive Communion and will learn more about the different objects and vestments used at Mass. You can help your child by making sure that he or she is familiar with the ways to receive Communion and by making it possible for your child to attend all necessary practices for the First Eucharist ceremony. Most importantly, you can give your child a beautiful example by your own participation in the Mass and reception of Holy Communion.

Lesson 8, "Love One Another," will help your child see that the effects of Holy Communion do not end when the Mass is over. We are sent forth to "love and serve the Lord," and the Eucharist strengthens and nourishes us to do God's work in our world. In addition to helping your child plan for the celebration of First Communion, you can lead your child to see that participation in the Eucharist is a lifelong source of grace and joy. The family magazine, *The Eucharistic Family*, contains a number of suggestions for continuing the celebration beyond "the Big Day."

It has been a pleasure for me to work with you and your child during this special time. I look forward to seeing you at the celebration!

Sincerely,

____

Catechist Note: Send this letter home with the students upon completion of Lesson 6, "Give Us This Day." At this time, you might want to attach additional information about the scheduling of practices, family meetings, and the celebration of First Communion itself.

Estimada Familia,

Su hijo(a) ha terminada las Lecciones 5 y 6 de *Eucharistia*. En la Lección 5 su hijo(a) fue instruido acerca de la Oración Eucarística de la Misa, la cual celebra los actos de salvación de Jesús y la institución de la Eucaristía. Aprendió la importancia de recordar a Dios y rendirle gratitud. La Lección 6 enfatizaba el concepto de la Misa como oración e inició a su hijo(a) en las diversas clases de oración que forman nuestra herencia cristiana. Tiene especial importancia el Padrenuestro en el cual rezamos por el "pan nuestro de cada día" que equivale a la Sagrada Comunión.

Su hijo(a) entrará ahora a las últimas etapas de su preparación para la Primera Eucaristía. En la Lección 7, "El Pan de la Vida," su hijo(a) aprenderá que Jesucristo está realmente presente en la Eucaristía. El o ella repasará las diferentes formas de recibir la Comunión y aprenderá más sobre los diferentes objetos y vestiduras que se usan durante la Misa. Usted puede ayudar a su hijo(a) asegurándose de que esté familiarizado con las distintas formas de recibir la Comunión y facilitándole la asistencia a las prácticas necesarias para la ceremonia de la Primera Eucaristía. Lo que es aún más importante, usted puede brindarle a su hijo(a) un bello ejemplo participando personalmente en la Misa y recibiendo la Santa Comunión.

La Lección 8, "Amense los Unos a los Otros," le ayudará a su hijo(a) a ver cómo los efectos de la Sagrada Comunión no terminan cuando finaliza la Misa. Se nos envía a "amar y servir al Señor" y la Eucaristía nos nutre y nos fortalece para cumplir con la labor de Dios en el mundo.

Además de ayudarle a su hijo(a) a planear la ceremonia de su Primera Comunión puede guiarle para que observe su participación en la Eucaristía como una fuente permanente de gracia y de paz a lo largo de toda su vida. La revista familiar, *La Familia Eucharistia*, contiene una serie de sugerencias para continuar la celebración más allá del "Gran Día."

Ha sido un placer para mí trabajar con usted y su hijo(a) durante esta época tan especial. ¡Aguardo con anticipación verle en la ceremonia!

Cordialmente,

____

Catechist Note: Send this letter home with the students upon completion of Lesson 6, "Give Us This Day." At this time, you might want to attach additional information about the scheduling of practices, family meetings, and the celebration of First Communion itself.

PLANNING PRAYER AND LITURGIES

Throughout your teaching of Benziger *Reconciliation*, you will find numerous opportunities for classroom and family prayer and liturgy.

Prayer celebrations and liturgies are not just "icing on the cake" for a sacramental preparation program. They are its core. No matter how limited your teaching time-frame, never give in to the temptation to skimp on prayer and liturgy. Students have a need to feel at home in the worshipping community. You might recall that in the early Church the liturgy itself was the prime source of catechesis for new members, who were initiated into the Sacred Mysteries and then spent a lifetime learning from them. You can give your students or your child this same gift.

In this section you will find a number of helpful suggestions, augmenting those in the lesson plans, for involving middle-grade students in the planning of prayer and liturgy.

THE MIDDLE-GRADE CHILD

Students in the third, fourth, and fifth grades are developing socially. They are aware of the effect that individuals have on a group. They are concerned with order. The students' capacity for expressing themselves is increasing, and caring for others is becoming quite important to them. Middle-grade students enjoy participating in events that they can help plan, such as prayer services and liturgies. They will be fascinated by the order of the service, and will strive to make everything flow smoothly. The students also enjoy seeing their handiwork displayed at prayer services and liturgies.

PRAYER SERVICES

Each lesson in *Reconciliation* and *Eucharist* concludes with an opportunity for the students to pray with their families. The page includes a Family Note with suggestions for doing so.

The prayer is easily adaptable to classroom use. You may be as elaborate or simple as you wish. Be sure the students are involved in as many ways as possible, including the adding of a religious symbol or student handiwork to the prayer area.

You will find that the prayer services grow more complex in the middle-grade *Reconciliation* and *Eucharist* texts, reflecting their own growing abilities.

PREPARATION

Getting ready for prayer and liturgy is an important part of our tradition. Families fuss and prepare for parties: decorating tables, cooking, cleaning, greeting guests. It is also important to invest time in preparing for worship. The more care taken to make sure everything is ready, the better the results will be. With everyone's help all the details can be taken care of carefully and expediently.

ROLES IN LITURGICAL CELEBRATION

In all communal worship, it is important that there be a division of roles. The more the students can participate in the carrying out of the service, the more likely it will hold their attention and take on meaning. As much as possible, during a children's liturgy, the students should have a chance to:

- prepare the materials and the place for celebration
- play musical instruments
- proclaim the Scriptures
- dramatize Gospel stories
- make decorations
- lead responsorial prayers

ATMOSPHERE FOR PRAYER

The parish church is the primary place for communal prayer and worship, but it is not the only place. When prayer and liturgy are celebrated with children, it should be in a place where the students can conduct themselves freely according to the demands of a liturgy that is suited to their age.

It is important that the place chosen be appropriate. The classroom at school and the dining room or family room at home are certainly appropriate for celebrations involving only children or family members. This does not lessen the importance of celebrating in the parish church with the whole parish family.

The use of art, banners, posters, special linens and vestments, attractive Bibles or lectionaries, candles, and flowers are all part of the atmosphere for good worship. The atmosphere that will best suit the students is one in which they have some control. Their creativity in choosing music and art, and their desire to create a pleasant space for celebrations, will contribute to the meaningfulness of the event.

PLANNING TO CELEBRATE THE SACRAMENT OF RECONCILIATION

If you are following most diocesan guidelines, your students or child will be receiving the sacrament of Reconciliation for the first time prior to the celebration of First Eucharist. It is customary to celebrate First Reconciliation with a communal penance service culminating in individual sacramental confession.

Students should be as involved in planning for the celebration of Reconciliation as they are in any other aspect of their sacramental preparation. They might choose music and readings, compose an examination of conscience or penitential litany, design stoles for the priest-celebrants, and so on.

For your convenience, here is the basic format and sample liturgy for a communal celebration of Reconciliation:

Sample Liturgy

1. Introductory Rite

- *Entrance Song*
- *Greeting:* From the beginning, the service should be personalized. The Greeting may include a few words about the sacrament and about the joy that is particular to this celebration of God's love and forgiveness.
- *Prayer:* Before the service, all prayers can be talked about with the priest, and if possible, read aloud to the students to give them a sense of familiarity.

2. Celebration of the Word of God

- *Scripture:* There may be one or more readings. They should be familiar to the students and may be taken from the *Reconciliation* text.
- *Homily:* The presider might gently ask the students about their faith. Or, a brief talk about the significance of Reconciliation may be given.
- *Examination of Conscience:* Be sure the students know the one that will be used. Samples are given in the text; one may also be composed by the students. Whatever form is used, the prayer should be said slowly.

3. Rite of Reconciliation

- *Prayer of Contrition:* If possible, choose this prayer with the priest.
- *Litany or Song:* A litany statement and response written by the students may be read, or a song chosen by them may be sung.
- *The Lord's Prayer:* As a symbol of the peace and unity the Lord offers in Reconciliation, the congregation may join hands during this prayer.
- *Individual Sacramental Confession:* Decide how to structure the time and procedure for confession. Be sure there are enough priests. Musicians may play during this time.
- *Praise of God's Mercy:* A prayer about God's great goodness may be written by the students and read here. Or, an exuberant song may be sung.
- *Common Prayer:* If possible, you may select this prayer with the priest.

4. Concluding Rite

- *Final Blessing and Dismissal:* Before the final blessing, a few words of general rejoicing and an invitation to the families to receive Reconciliation often together, would be appropriate. Reconciliation certificates may be distributed at this time. You may wish to process out the church to a place for a simple cookies and punch celebration.

PLANNING FOR THE FIRST EUCHARIST MASS

Preparation for this special parish celebration should begin as soon as the program is planned. Knowing the date, time, and principal celebrant in advance can make your work with *Eucharist* a gradually unfolding process. It's wise to involve other families and classes preparing for Eucharist, parish staff, and other parishioners from the very beginning.

As part of your ongoing planning, you may wish to involve the students being prepared, their families, and other parishioners in celebrating one or two special Masses before the First Eucharist liturgy takes place. For your convenience, a checklist for planning Eucharistic liturgies follows this section.

As many students as possible should take part in preparing the Mass—for instance, preparing the church or the program booklet with personal drawings, bringing up the gifts, singing, and answering questions posed during the homily.

Customs and practices for celebrating First Eucharist vary widely. The following basic, annotated sample liturgy can be adapted to suit your needs.

SAMPLE LITURGY

This sample liturgy is intended to show a few of the options that can be a part of the First Eucharist Mass. It would be a good idea to use song sheets during this Mass. (A decorated First Eucharist song sheet outlining the Mass would for a nice memento.) Ask the Music Director to practice the songs with the congregation before Mass begins. To help keep the students attentive, large First Eucharist classes can be divided into groups, with each group receiving First Eucharist on a different day or at a different time.

Sample Liturgy

1. Introductory Rite

- *Opening Song:* This should be a lively processional. If those receiving First Eucharist come in together with their families, they might carry banners created with family members.
- *The Greeting:* From the beginning, this Mass should be personalized. Here, it is suggested that the Greeting include a few words before the Mass begins, explaining what is being celebrated, welcoming those visitors who have come especially for the First Eucharist, and offering some words of joy on this happy occasion.
- *Penitential Rite:* "Lord, Have Mercy" may be sung by a leader and the children with the congregation echoing the song.

2. Liturgy of the Word

- *Readings:* The particular readings chosen for this liturgy should be familiar to the students and their families in advance. One or two of the readings might be proclaimed by family members of students receiving First Eucharist.
- *Gospel Acclamation:* Official Church guidelines say that the Gospel Acclamation should always be sung.
- *Gospel and Homily:* We suggest that these be geared to the students and that the homily be given by any adult who is good at communicating with children. If possible, the homily should be no longer than seven minutes.
- *Creed:* The Apostles' Creed, with which the students may be more familiar, may be substituted for the Nicene Creed.
- *Prayer of the Faithful:* It is suggested that students or parents read petitions during this prayer, and that parts of the Prayer of the Faithful relate to the First Eucharist event.

3. Liturgy of the Eucharist

- *Presentation of the Gifts:* First Eucharist families may be invited to bring up the gifts. If your parish allows, the gifts may include the First Communion Reminders which the students have filled out as part of *Eucharist* text activities.
- *The Eucharistic Prayer:* If the group of First Eucharist families is small, the presider may invite them to gather around the altar for the Eucharistic Prayer. In any case, the presider may preface this part of the liturgy with remarks inviting the First Communicants to full participation in the Eucharistic community.
- *Preface Acclamation:* Use a familiar "Holy, Holy, Holy."
- *Memorial Acclamation:* Use a familiar acclamation.
- *The Lord's Prayer:* This may be sung or said, with or without the congregation holding hands.
- *Communion:* The mechanics will vary here, depending on the size of the group. Be sure that practice for the event includes specifics about how Communion will be given (only the Host, or both the Host and the Cup). It is reassuring for family groups to receive Communion together. This initiates a situation that, ideally, will happen again and again in the future.
- *The Final Blessing and Dismissal:* Before the final blessing, a few words of general rejoicing that also invite the families to receive Communion frequently are a good idea. Students also need a reminder about what they have heard and a summing-up giving some practical applications for their own lives. Distribution of First Communion certificates could probably be done at this time. A lively processional hymn is suggested.

WHO IS INVITED?

Families often do not know whether or not to invite those of other faiths to a First Eucharist celebration. Make sure everyone understands that it is a very good idea to invite members of other faiths to a Mass of special celebration such as the First Eucharist event. It is important, however, that family members take the responsibility for explaining to such guests, in advance of the liturgy, that reception of the Eucharist is open only to those in full communion with the Catholic Church.

CELEBRATING AFTER THE MASS

It's an excellent idea for families to meet together for a short celebration after the Mass. This celebration, ideally, is one that has been planned by the families, perhaps of the students who will prepare to receive the sacraments in the following year. The celebration may be open to the entire parish and the friends who have attended the Mass. It might even contain some opportunities for picture-taking, which many feel should not be encouraged during the actual religious ceremony.

Planning Chart for a Eucharistic Liturgy

Theme ______________________________

Location ______________________________ Time ______________________________

Presider ______________________________

Entrance Song ______________________________

1st Reading ______________________________ Reader ______________________________

Psalm Response ______________________________ Response/Leader ______________________________

2nd Reading ______________________________ Reader ______________________________

Gospel Acclamation ______________________________

Gospel ______________________________

Prayer of the Faithful: Petitions ______________________________

Readers of Petitions ______________________________

Offertory Song ______________________________

Preface Acclamation ______________________________

Acclamation of Faith ______________________________

Great Amen ______________________________

Lord's Prayer ______________________________

Communion Song ______________________________

Closing Song ______________________________

Other Roles and Elements ______________________________

Environment ______________________________

Penitential Rite ______________________________

Audiovisual Presentation ______________________________

Offertory Procession ______________________________

Eucharistic Ministers ______________________________

Altar Servers ______________________________

Greeters/Ushers ______________________________

USING MUSIC WITH *RECONCILIATION*

The *Catechism of the Catholic Church* details the importance of music in the Catholic way of worshipping:

> "'The musical tradition of the universal Church is a treasure of inestimable value, greater even than that of any other art. The main reason for this pre-eminence is that, as a combination of sacred music and words, it forms a necessary or integral part of solemn liturgy.' The composition and singing of inspired psalms, often accompanied by musical instruments, were already closely linked to the liturgical celebrations of the Old Covenant. The Church continues and develops this tradition: 'Address one another in psalms and hymns and spiritual songs, singing, and making melody to the Lord with all your heart.' 'He who sings prays twice'" *(#1156).*

Music in Catholic Worship (The Bishops' Committee on the Liturgy, 1972, rev. 1983) defines the place of music in Christian celebration in this way:

> "Music should assist the assembled believers to express and share that gift of faith that is within them and to nourish and strengthen their interior commitment of faith. . . . The quality of joy and enthusiasm which music adds to community worship cannot be gained in any other way. It imparts a sense of unity to the congregation and sets the appropriate tone for the particular celebration. Music can also unveil a dimension of meaning and feeling that is integral to the human personality and to growth in faith" *(#23–#24).*

The bishops' words apply especially to the growth in faith that takes place in students preparing for the sacraments. The music for *Reconciliation* may be found on the Benziger *Come, Follow Me* cassette for Grade 4. Vocals are on one side of the tape, and instrumentals are on the other. Lyrics for the songs are reproduced in the *Reconciliation* student text. For convenience in teaching the songs, lead sheets (words and melody line) appear on the following pages of this catechist edition.

TEACHING THE SONGS

In five of the lessons, a Music Note appears as a wrap feature along the bottom of your Catechist's Edition. It suggests a song to use with the lesson.

You may play the song from the audiocassette several times, and after a time or two, encourage everyone to join in using the lyrics in their texts. If you're a musician, you may wish to play the song yourself. If time allows, reinforce the teaching by incorporating the song into other parts of the lesson as it unfolds.

Eventually, you may wish to incorporate the songs into your planning for the communal Reconciliation service—in which case it should be shared with the parish music director at the earliest opportunity.

We Are a Kingdom People

Words and Music by
CHRISTOPHER WALKER

♩=120

REFRAIN

C D G G D7 G D7

We are a king-dom peo-ple,_ king-dom peo-ple
(an Eas-ter peo-ple)

G D G D G D7 G D7

sent to love and serve our God. We are a king-dom peo-ple,_ king-dom peo-ple

G G/F♯ G/E G/D C D7 G *Fine* G7/B Am/C C (D) G

sent to love and serve our God!

VERSES

C D G 1 Gsus4 G

1. We serve Je-sus ev-'ry time we help our broth-ers and
2. We serve Je-sus ev-'ry time we share the good things God
3. We serve Je-sus ev-'ry time that we are hon-est and

Gsus4 G 2 Gsus4 G C D7 *D.S. al Fine*

sis-ters. broth-ers and sis-ters. We are a
gives us. good things God gives us. We are a
truth-ful. hon-est and truth-ful. We are a

Choices

Words by CATHY RUFF

Music by DAVID PHILLIPS

Country Feel
♩=104
D G A D A
I am learn-ing to make choic-es, and now's the time to start to
lis-ten and o-bey God's rule, the choice is in my heart. I am learn-ing to make choic-es, and
now's the time to start to lis-ten and o-bey God's rule, the choice is in my heart. 1. There's
1,2
al - ways rules to fol - low, at home, at school, at play. God
Gos - sip - ing and ly - ing cause de - struc- tion and des - pair, but
knew I'd need a help - ing hand each and ev - 'ry day. So
hon - es - ty and words of praise show oth - ers that we care. If
God gave us com - mand-ments, rules we must o - bey.
some - how you have hurt some - one, don't think the pain will hide.

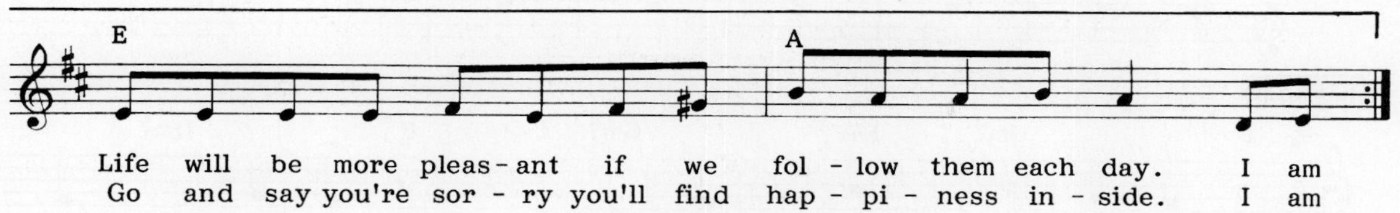
E
A
Life will be more pleas - ant if we fol - low them each day. I am
Go and say you're sor - ry you'll find hap - pi - ness in - side. I am

3
G
D
G
A
D
E
A
Love the Lord your God with all your heart and all your mind. Love your neigh-bor as your-self and

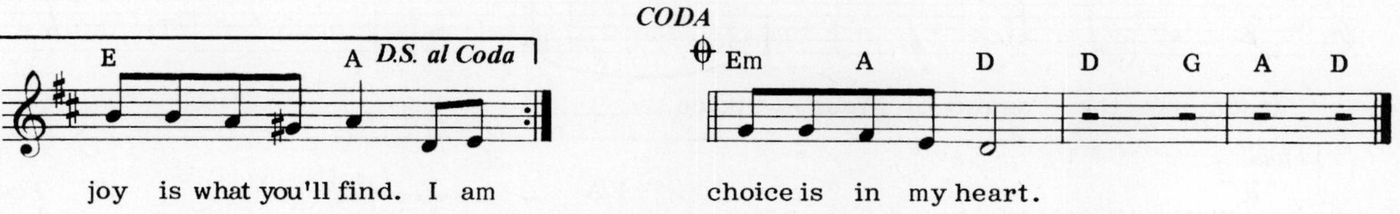
E
A
D.S. al Coda
CODA
Em
A
D
D
G
A
D
joy is what you'll find. I am
choice is in my heart.

Your Way, O God

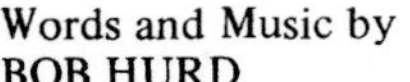

Words and Music by
BOB HURD

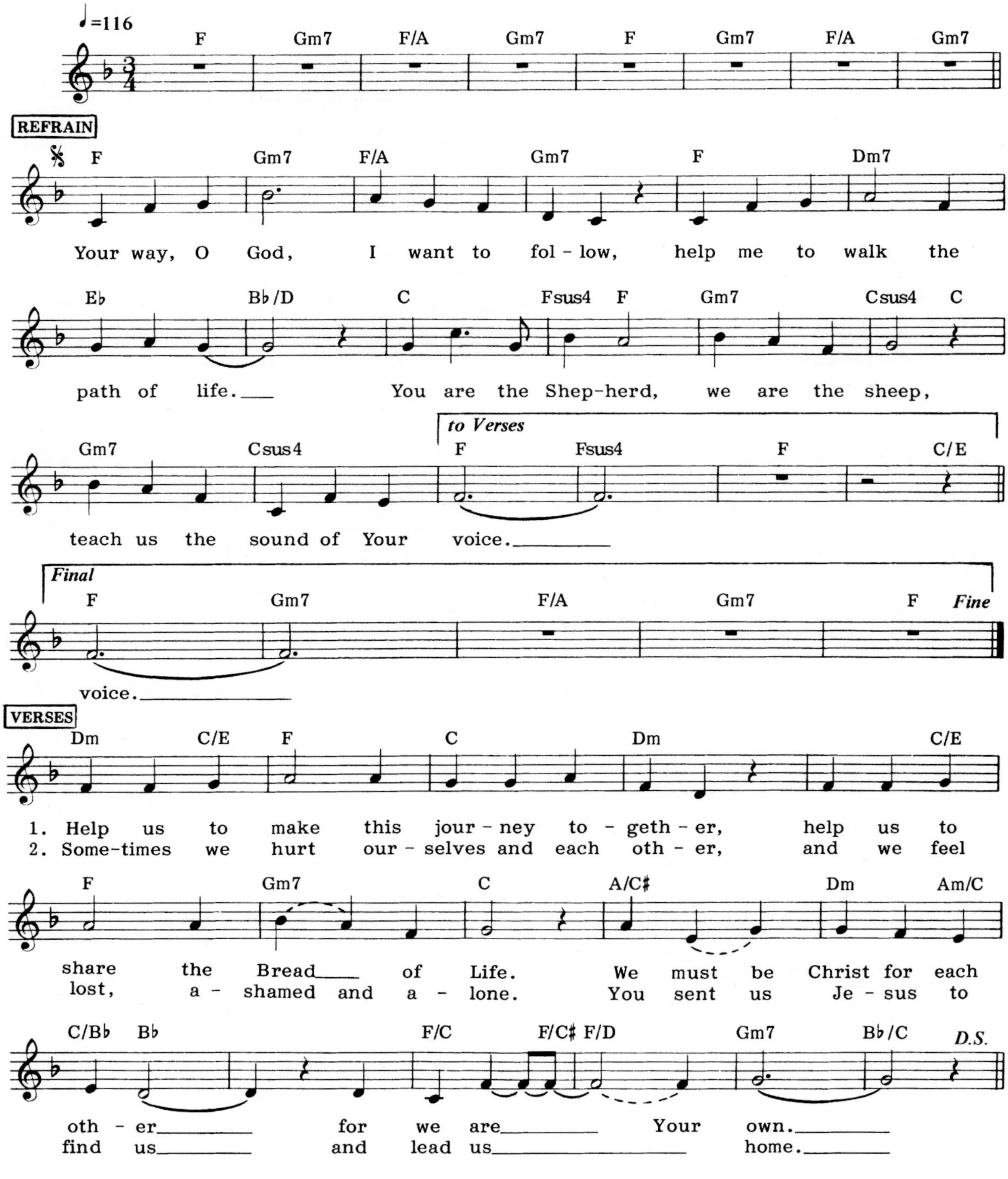

♩=116
F Gm7 F/A Gm7 F Gm7 F/A Gm7
REFRAIN
F Gm7 F/A Gm7 F Dm7
Your way, O God, I want to fol - low, help me to walk the
E♭ B♭/D C Fsus4 F Gm7 Csus4 C
path of life. You are the Shep-herd, we are the sheep,
Gm7 Csus4
teach us the sound of Your
to Verses
F Fsus4 F C/E
voice.
Final
F Gm7 F/A Gm7 F Fine
voice.
VERSES
Dm C/E F C Dm C/E
1. Help us to make this jour - ney to - geth - er, help us to
2. Some-times we hurt our - selves and each oth - er, and we feel
F Gm7 C A/C♯ Dm Am/C
share the Bread of Life. We must be Christ for each
lost, a - shamed and a - lone. You sent us Je - sus to
C/B♭ B♭ F/C F/C♯ F/D Gm7 B♭/C D.S.
oth - er for we are Your own.
find us and lead us home.

More Joy in Heaven

Words and Music by
MARIE JO THUM

VERSE 1 *Brightly*

♩=118
D
There once was a shep - herd who loved_

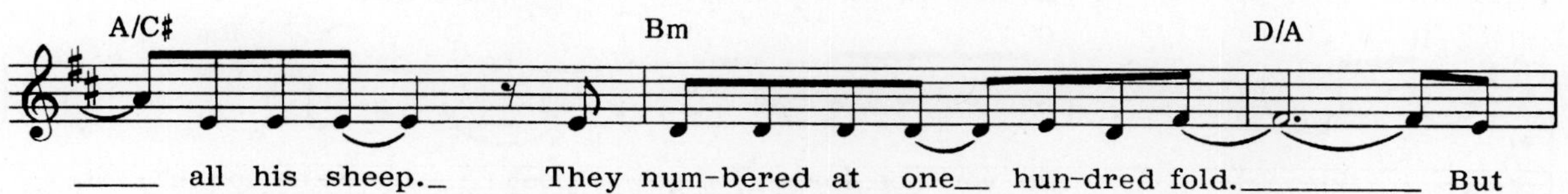
A/C♯
Bm
D/A
_____ all his sheep._ They num-bered at one__ hun-dred fold.__________ But

G
D
Bm
Em

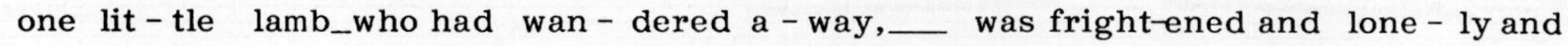
one lit - tle lamb_who had wan - dered a - way,___ was fright-ened and lone - ly and

A
D
F♯m
cold. With nine-ty-nine safe in the field______ the shep - herd set out___

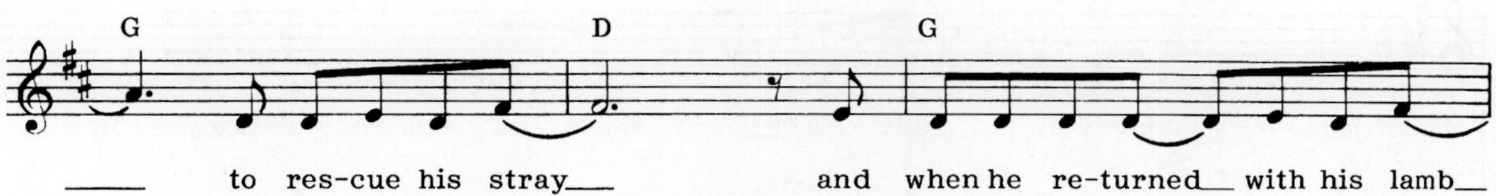
G
D
G
_____ to res-cue his stray___ and when he re-turned__ with his lamb__

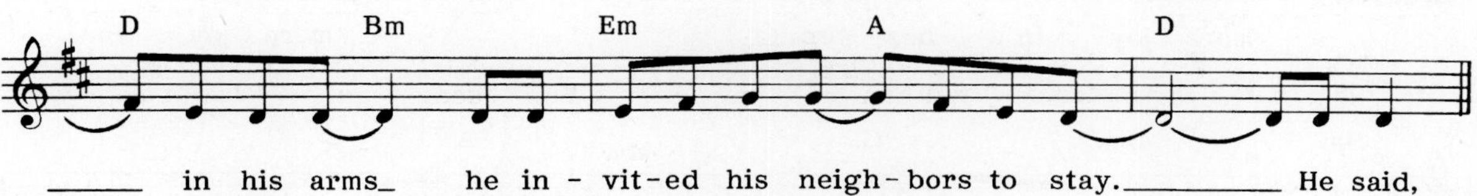
D
Bm
Em
A
D
_____ in his arms_ he in - vit-ed his neigh-bors to stay.__________ He said,

REFRAIN
A
D
G
Come, share my hap - pi-ness, feast at my ta - ble Join me with great_ju - bi - la -
D
G
D
Bm
- tion.__ Do you not know__ what was lost___ has been found? Re -
Em
A
D
joice in my glad__ cel - e - bra - tion!__ And there is
G
A
D
D/C♯
more joy in heav - en,__ there is more joy in
more joy in heav - en,__ more joy in
Bm
Bm/A
G
A
heav - en,__ there is more joy in heav - en__ when the
heav - en,__ more joy in heav - en__ when the

1
2
Em
Asus4
A
D
D
Fine
lost one has re - turned._ And there is (turned.)
lost one has re - turned._ (turned.)
VERSE 2
D
A/C♯
There once was a fa - ther who loved_ both his sons,_ but his
Bm
D/A
G
young-er son want - ed to roam._ He squan-dered their mon - ey and lived_
D
Bm
Em
A
like a fool_ and sad - ly he start - ed for home._
D
F♯m
G
Sor-ry and shame - ful he cried_ to his fa - ther, "Your ser-vant," he said_ "Let me
D
G
D
Bm
be." But his fa-ther em-braced him and said,_ "You're my son,_ and my
Em
A
D
to Refrain
son you al - ways will be."_ He said,

Oh, Happy One

Words and Music by
MARIE JO THUM

♩=126
C Am F C Am F D/F♯ G
C Em F G
REFRAIN
C Am F C Am
Oh, hap-py__ one!__ Come and re-joice!_The king-dom of heav- en be-longs
F D/F♯ G C Am F C Am
_______ to you!_ Oh, hap-py__ one!__ Come and re-joice! The king-dom of heav - en be -
F D/F♯ G C Em F G
Last time only
C
longs to you, oh hap-py one!____
VERSE 1
Dm G C Am F C/E D/F♯ G
1. God is your treas-ure,__ God knows all your needs. Blest are the poor in spir-it.
E Am Am D G G7
D.S.
Look for the good in ev-'ry-thing and ev-'ry-one. Blest are the clean of heart. Oh

Say "yes" to God. Ac-cept God's will with cour-age._ Bless-ed__ are the meek.

Treat oth-er peo-ple as you want them to treat you. Blest are those who hun-ger for jus-tice. Oh

Do the right thing, e-ven when it is not eas-y.__ Blest are those who suf-fer in My name.

Give up pow-er and in-stead bring peace. Bless-ed are those_ who bring peace. Oh

Show God's mer-cy._ Be kind and for-giv-ing.__ Blest are the mer - ci - ful.

Suf- fer with those who hurt and share their tears. Bless - ed are those who mourn. Oh

Commissioning Certificate

❖ ❖ ❖

____

Name

has been commissioned as a _______________________________

Catechist/Assistant

in the name of Jesus Christ
to share God's Word
and to teach the sacramental program
to the children of

_______________________ _______________________

Parish *City*

"We have gifts that differ
according to the favor bestowed on each of us . . .
One who is a teacher should use this gift for teaching."
Romans 12:6–7

_______________________ _______________________

Pastor *Date*

____

Director